Nov. 30, 1929
PAUL V. SPADE

PROTESTANT THOUGHT *Before* KANT

PROTESTANT THOUGHT Before KANT

by
A. C. McGIFFERT

GLOUCESTER, MASS.
PETER SMITH
1971

PROTESTANT THOUGHT BEFORE KANT

*Preface and Bibliography to the
Torchbook edition
Copyright © 1961 by Jaroslav Pelikan*

Printed in the United States of America

*This book was originally published by
Gerald Duckworth & Co., Ltd., London, in 1911,
and is reprinted by arrangement.*

First HARPER TORCHBOOK *edition published 1962*

Reprinted, 1971, by
Peter Smith Publisher, Inc.

TO

ADOLF HARNACK

TEACHER AND FRIEND

IN GRATITUDE AND AFFECTION

PREFACE
TO THE TORCHBOOK EDITION
BY JAROSLAV PELIKAN

Most histories of Christian thought stop just when the story becomes interesting—and complicated. During most of its two centuries as a distinct theological discipline, the history of doctrine has been the history of dogma, *Dogmengeschichte*. It has concerned itself primarily with the origin and evolution of the official dogmas of the Church, especially the dogma of the Trinity and the dogma of the two natures in Christ. Other doctrinal issues and their histories it has tended to treat only as they have affected, or have been affected by, the development of "dogma" in the strict sense of the term. In practice, of course, historians of dogma were not so meticulous as all that in their treatment of problems and movements that did not meet the precise definition of "dogma."

The most serious consequence of this preoccupation with dogma was a chronological rather than a topical mutilation. Because Protestantism has not articulated itself primarily in dogmas, the history of its thought beyond the period of the Reformation did not belong to *Dogmengeschichte*. Harnack did discuss the left wing of the Reformation as the practical dissolution of dogmatic Christianity, and Seeberg certainly gave more attention to the theology of Luther than Luther's place in the history of dogma would warrant. Both of them thus perpetuated the work of Gottfried Thomasius (1802-1875), whose *Dogmengeschichte* Seeberg had once helped to re-edit; for Thomasius believed that in the Reformation, specifically in the Lutheran Reformation and in its confessions, the history of dogma had come to its grand and harmonious climax. The history of Protestant theology became an appendix to the great story of dogma in the making.

Fifty years ago two historians of theology were trying to rehabilitate the history of Protestant thought, and both of them dedicated their books to Adolf Harnack! Otto Ritschl issued the first volume of his *Dogmengeschichte des Protestantismus* in 1908, "in long-standing gratitude" to his old teacher. Three years later A. C. McGiffert, one of Harnack's earliest and most eminent American pupils, published his *Protestant Thought Before Kant,* inscribed "to Adolf Harnack, teacher and friend, in gratitude and affection." These dedications not only provide an insight into the esteem, bordering on reverence, that an entire generation of Protestant scholars bore for *der alte Meister Harnack;* they also suggest the extent to which the issues and methods of Harnack's massive literary output continued to dominate his pupils, even when they ventured into areas which the master had avoided. And where the master had spoken—for example, on the old and the new in Luther's theology—there McGiffert found himself in substantial agreement with Harnack (cf. p. 51 below).

In the fifty years since McGiffert's book first appeared in 1911, every man and movement he discusses has received an impressive amount of study. For German and Scandinavian theology, research into Luther has become virtually a way of life. But even where ecclesiastical and nationalistic loyalties did not conspire to make a man a church father, the historical theologians of the last two generations have been busy reshaping the estimates given here of the chief trends in the theological history of Protestantism between Martin Luther and Immanuel Kant. Puritan theology, for example, looks different now, thanks to the work not chiefly of historians of theology but of historians of literature, political thought, and general culture. The revival of interest in Calvin, while not so overwhelming as the Continental Luther-renaissance, has nevertheless produced a new and exciting picture of the thought of the Genevan Reformer. Protestant Orthodoxy, both Reformed and Lutheran, has begun to come out of the ghetto to which much of the nineteenth century had relegated it. And the Anabaptists, the real *non possidentes* of theological history, have begun to receive an almost embarrassing amount of attention from historians of varying denominational traditions. A study even of the brief English Bibliography appended to this Preface will show how thoroughly many of McGiffert's judgments have been overhauled.

This semi-centennial edition leaves one, nevertheless, deeply impressed with the courage and the competence of McGiffert's work. Bringing to his assignment the erudition and insight of a scholar in ancient church history, an editor and translator of Eusebius, and a historian of Christian thought until the Reformation, McGiffert was inoculated against the major occupational disease of American historians of Protestantism: ignorance, or, at best, mere common-sense knowledge, of the history of the Christian Church preceding and surrounding Protestant Christianity. McGiffert never forgot that the Protestant theologians he was interpreting were not the first to raise these issues; hence he continually placed them into the context of the history of the Church, including the history of ancient dogma. At the same time, he avoided the major occupational hazard of Continental historians of Protestantism: ignorance, or at worst downright snobbery, where British and American Protestantism are concerned. From the handbooks of church history one could multiply instances of this ignorance, which would be humorous if it were not so pathetic. But McGiffert moves back and forth across the English Channel and the Atlantic Ocean with almost unrivaled ease. The contrasts and comparisons that he illumines this way are among the most scintillating paragraphs of this book.

Until a new history of Protestant thought comes along, which will incorporate the results of the research carried on during the past half century, McGiffert's *Protestant Thought Before Kant* will continue to do what he intended it to do: "to make the general course of development plain." This it still does, and better than any other book in English.

The Divinity School
The University of Chicago
October, 1961

ADDITIONAL BIBLIOGRAPHY OF WORKS IN ENGLISH

Cassirer, Ernst. *The Philosophy of the Enlightenment.* Boston: Beacon Press, 1955 (Paperback edition).

Dowey, Edward A. *The Knowledge of God in Calvin's Theology.* New York: Columbia University Press, 1952.

Farner, Oskar. *Zwingli the Reformer: His Life and Work.* London: Lutterworth, 1952.

Littell, Franklin H. *The Anabaptist View of the Church.* Boston: Starr King Press, 1955.

McNeill, John T. *The History and Character of Calvinism.* New York: Oxford University Press, 1954.

Manschreck, Clyde L. *Melanchthon the Quiet Reformer.* New York: Abingdon Press, 1958.

Miller, Perry. *Jonathan Edwards.* New York: W. Sloane Associates, 1949.

——————. *The New England Mind.* New York: Macmillan, 1939.

——————. *Orthodoxy in Massachusetts 1630-1650.* Boston: Beacon Press, 1959 (Paperback edition).

Niesel, Wilhelm. *The Theology of Calvin.* Philadelphia: Westminster Press, 1956.

Pauck, Wilhelm. *The Heritage of the Reformation.* Chicago: The Free Press, 1961 (Revised edition).

Pelikan, Jaroslav. *From Luther to Kierkegaard.* Saint Louis: Concordia, 1950.

Watson, Philip. *Let God Be God.* Philadelphia: Muhlenberg Press, 1949.

Willey, Basil. *The Seventeenth Century Background.* New York: Doubleday, 1953 (Paperback edition).

Williams, Colin W. *John Wesley's Theology Today.* New York: Abingdon Press, 1960.

PREFACE

In accordance with the plan of the series the present volume deals with religious thought alone and not with philosophy, science, or ethics. Even this narrow field is over large for treatment in so small a compass, and in order to avoid making the book a mere encyclopædia of names and opinions it has been found necessary to omit a vast mass of material, some of it perhaps as important, in the judgment of many doubtless more important, than much that is included, but it is hoped that enough has been given to make the general course of development plain, however summary and inadequate the treatment of many topics.

The relatively large space devoted to rationalism is justified by the contrast between it and all that went before. Until the eighteenth century Protestantism moved largely within the confines of an ancient past; only with the spread of rationalism did it enter what was then the modern world of thought. It has therefore seemed imperative for the better understanding both of the older and the newer Protestantism to construct the final chapter on a somewhat different scale from most of the others.

There is an unfortunate lack of works covering the

entire history of Protestant thought; aside from the old one of Dorner there is none of any great value. Particular topics have been treated in numberless books and articles, and a few of the most useful and comprehensive of the former are mentioned in the brief bibliography at the close of this volume.

CONTENTS

PREFACE TO THE TORCHBOOK EDITION BY JAROSLAV PELIKAN vii
BIBLIOGRAPHY TO THE TORCHBOOK EDITION . . xi
PREFACE xiii

CHAPTER I

	PAGE
INTRODUCTION, ...	1
I. MEDIÆVAL CHRISTIANITY, . . .	1
II. THE EVE OF THE REFORMATION, . . .	9

CHAPTER II

MARTIN LUTHER, ...	20
I. THE NEW IN LUTHER'S THOUGHT, . . .	20
II. THE OLD IN LUTHER'S THOUGHT, . . .	46

CHAPTER III

HULDREICH ZWINGLI, ... 61

CHAPTER IV

PHILIP MELANCHTHON, ... 71

CHAPTER V

JOHN CALVIN, ... 81

CHAPTER VI

	PAGE
THE RADICAL SECTS,	100
I. THE ANABAPTISTS,	100
II. THE SOCINIANS,	107

CHAPTER VII

THE ENGLISH REFORMATION,	119

CHAPTER VIII

PROTESTANT SCHOLASTICISM,	141

CHAPTER IX

PIETISM,	155
I. GERMAN PIETISM,	155
II. ENGLISH EVANGELICALISM,	162
III. THE NEW ENGLAND THEOLOGY,	175

CHAPTER X

RATIONALISM,	186
I. IN ENGLAND,	189
II. IN FRANCE,	243
III. IN GERMANY,	247
IV. IN AMERICA,	251
BIBLIOGRAPHY	255
INDEX	263

PROTESTANT THOUGHT BEFORE KANT

CHAPTER I

INTRODUCTION

I. *Mediæval Christianity.*

THE theological system of the Middle Ages was in its controlling principles as old as the Apostle Paul. He was led by his own experience to draw a sharp distinction between the fleshly man, who is essentially corrupt, and the spiritual man, who is essentially holy. The one is natural, the other supernatural. The one is doomed to destruction, the other is an heir of eternal life. The spiritual man does not come from the natural by a process of development and growth, but is a new creature born directly from above. Wherever Paul may have got the suggestion which led him to interpret his experience in this way, his low estimate of man and his contrast between flesh and spirit, revealed the ultimate influence of oriental dualism which was profoundly affecting the Hellenistic world of the day. A sense of moral evil, a conviction of human corruption and helplessness, and a recognition of the worthlessness of the present world, were becoming more and more common, and men everywhere were looking for aid and comfort to supernatural powers of one kind and another. The later Platonism, from which the theological thinking of the great fathers chiefly drew its sustenance, was completely under the sway of this spirit. Justin Martyr, Clement of Alexandria, and some other Fathers felt other influences and emphasised the moral ability of the natural man. But their optimistic view was rare in the early Church, and lasted but a little while. The dominant temper of the age was against it, and in the Epistles of Paul that temper found support. Even where the estimate of human nature was least sombre, it was still such as to make supernatural aid essential to its betterment. No man can enjoy the vision of God and eternal life unless he be born from above, unless he be recreated by divine power. Upon this need the historic Catholic system, both of east and west, was built, and in all its essential features it was complete before Augustine came upon the scene. His extreme doctrine of human bondage and unconditional predestination never found acceptance in the east, and was unpopular even in the west, but the old conviction of man's need still prevailed, and at the second Council of Orange in 529, it was declared in the most unequivocal terms that no one can take even the first step toward the good until he has received divine grace. This remained throughout the Middle Ages not only the official doctrine but also the popular belief of the Catholic Church. Emphasis might be laid upon human merit, and upon man's ability to earn reward by making the right use of grace, but without it he could do nothing at all. Unless regenerated, he was doomed to destruction, and his most strenuous efforts could not avail.

In the canons of the Council of Trent, whose first doctrinal decree had to do with original sin, it is said: 'If any one saith that divine grace is given through Jesus Christ only for this that man may be able more easily to live justly and to merit eternal life, as if by free will without grace he were able to do both, though hardly indeed, and with difficulty; let him be anathema.'

(Session 6, Canon 2.) 'If any one saith that without the prevenient inspiration of the Holy Ghost and without His help man can believe, hope, love, or be penitent as he ought, so that the grace of justification may be bestowed upon him; let him be anathema.' (*Ibid.*, Canon 3.)

The mediæval view involved, not simply the conviction that the natural man is corrupt and depraved, but that he is fallen. Originally created holy, he lapsed from his high estate, and cannot raise himself again without supernatural aid. The idea was the exact opposite of modern evolutionary notions. Man did not begin on a low plane and gradually ascend, but on a high plane, from which he abruptly fell. Having fallen and transgressed the divine law, he is doomed to eternal punishment. God is the great Judge and Avenger, a righteous Being who allows no sin to go unpunished; but He is also merciful, and has provided for guilty men a means of escape from the consequences of their wickedness. The supreme need is salvation from the impending doom, and this God has provided in Christianity. In it is found the promise of divine grace adequate to human wants.

If the mediæval view of man's corruption and inability was due to Paul, the mediæval view of human merit had another root. Paul had denied all merit to man, and made salvation a pure gift of God. But from the second century on, his conception of divine grace, and the common legalism of the early Christians, lay side by side in the thinking of the Church. Without grace no man can be saved; his nature is corrupt and must be transformed by supernatural power. But he must make the right use of the saving grace received through the sacraments. Under its influence, and in the power imparted by it, he must live righteously, overcoming his faults, and growing day by day in virtue. If he does this and secures forgiveness for his sins through the sacrament of penance, he will merit the gift of salvation which

God has in store for him. This form of synergism is technically known as semi-Pelagianism, but it is much older than the semi-Pelagians, being essentially the view of the Church, both east and west, ever since Irenæus.

Upon the conviction of man's need was based the traditional idea of Jesus Christ as a Saviour, and His saving work was so conceived that the belief in His deity necessarily followed. He was thought by Paul to be divine, not because of the perfection of His character, or the completeness of His revelation of God's will and truth, but because by His indwelling the nature of man is transformed. Through Ignatius and Irenæus this idea of Christ's work entered into the thought of the Church, and became the basis of the Nicene doctrine of His deity. From a different point of view Anselm reached the same result when he made the infinite guilt of human transgression require an infinite penance, and hence the death of an infinite Being, the god-man, Jesus Christ. The deity of Christ being the essential element in the historic doctrine of the Trinity, that doctrine, too, rested ultimately upon the belief in human corruption and helplessness, and would not have become a part of the faith of the Church had man been thought of in a different way.

With the traditional view of human nature was correlated the notion of the present world as evil, sharing in the curse of man and doomed to destruction as he is. To escape from it was the one great aim of the serious-minded man. Salvation meant not the salvation of the world itself, its transformation into something better and holier, but release from it in order to enjoy the blessedness of another world altogether. The dominant spirit was that of other-worldliness. To be a Christian meant to belong to another sphere than this, to have one's interest set on higher things, to live in the future, and to eschew the pleasures and enjoyments of the present. Asceticism was the Christian ideal of life. Man stands, as Thomas

Aquinas says, between the goods of this world and those of another. He who would possess the latter must eschew the former. He cannot have both, and he must take his choice. The more he crucifies his worldly desires and affections, and denies himself good things here, the more he may enjoy of future bliss. Christianity promised men blessings in a life beyond the grave at the expense of blessings here. It might, of course, bring happiness in this life, as the Christian contemplated the thought of the eternal felicity to come, but of earthly delight it had none to offer. Rather it demanded the sacrifice of such delight in order to the inheritance of joys belonging to another world. Belief in a future life was fundamental, and immortality an essential article of faith. Given doubt as to its reality, and the whole structure of Christian faith must fall to the ground. The sole significance of the present life lay in the fact that it was a probation for the life to come. It had worth only because of the everlasting issues which were determined by it. The few short years here are as nothing compared with the eternity beyond, and the wise man will think of that eternity, and live for it alone. So far as he may have interest in his fellowmen, and the spirit of love may prompt him to concern himself with their welfare, it will not be their present state which he will chiefly labour to improve. For them, as for himself, earthly conditions are of small account; the one important thing is the salvation of their immortal souls. It was not a mere accident, nor was it due to the immaturity of civilisation and the lack of sensibility to physical comfort, that social service on a large scale was postponed to modern times. Rather, it was because of an altogether different ideal, and an altogether different estimate of the present world.

It was of a piece with the mediæval view of the world that Nature lost independent interest, and was subordinated to the eternal destinies of men. The heavens and the earth were to pass away, and hence it was not important to study them. Only spiritual things were worthy of attention. If Nature was investigated at all, it was for the light it might throw on eternal realities, and the revelation it might give of God and His will. According to Vincent of Beauvais, 'Natural science treats of the invisible causes of visible things,' and 'the knowledge of all wisdom has no value if it remain without the knowledge of God.' The few notable exceptions to this way of looking at things serve only to prove the rule. Under these circumstances, natural science in the modern sense of the term was, of course, impossible. Only supernatural knowledge, which brings a man into touch with eternity and prepares him for life beyond the grave, has real and permanent worth.

Upon man's need of salvation was based the historic view of the Church. Before the end of the second century it had come to be looked upon as the sole ark of salvation, outside of which there was no possibility of life. Cyprian's famous dictum, *nulla salus extra ecclesiam*, and his declaration that he who would have God for his Father must have the Church for his mother, but gave terse expression to a belief common already before his day, and rapidly becoming universal. The necessity of membership in the Church rested upon the theory that saving grace had been entrusted by the apostles to their successors, the bishops, and could be dispensed only by them. Out of communion with the bishop, therefore, meant out of communion with Christ. The clergy who derived their character from the episcopate constituted the sole mediators of saving grace, and upon them the laity were dependent for salvation. In religious things the latter had no rights and privileges of their own; by themselves no access to God or Christ. The Church was composed primarily, not of the laity, but of the hierarchy. Where the bishop is, there is the Church, for there are grace and salvation.

Where he is not, there is no Church, though there be a great multitude of devout believers.

The means of grace, by which salvation is mediated to men, are the sacraments. They have saving efficacy only when administered within the Catholic Church, and by one episcopally ordained, though an exception is made for prudential reasons in the case of baptism. From birth to death the Church accompanies the Christian with its gracious ministrations, supplying him all needed help, sanctifying the most important relationships and experiences of life, and enabling him to atone for his sins, and to secure strength to overcome them. It belongs to her to dictate the terms upon which the reconciliation of the sinning Christian shall be permitted, and to indicate the amount of penance required for his offences. To this was due the great elaboration of rites and ceremonies, sacred days, pilgrimages, hoarding of relics, fastings, and other ascetic practices, which marked the Middle Ages, and were so characteristic a feature of the religious life of the period.

The Christian Church was looked upon, not simply as an ark of salvation, but also as the supreme authority upon earth. The corruptness and inability with which all humanity is beset extends to the intellect as well as the will. Man is blind as well as depraved, and is incapable, not only of doing, but even of knowing the right, unless illuminated by divine revelation. It is true he may possess knowledge sufficient to guide him in the ordinary affairs of life, he may know what common morality requires, and may have the power to perform it, but the conditions of salvation he can learn and the ability to attain it he can gain only from above. And in the one case, as in the other, he owes all he has to the Church. Mediator of grace, she is also mediator of light; by her alone the will and truth of God are infallibly declared. The crisis out of which was born the theory of the Catholic Apostolic Church as the sole ark of salvation, was due to the spread of heretical opinions in the second century, and it was the need of an objective authority that the doctrine of Apostolic Succession was designed by Irenæus to meet. From the beginning, therefore, the Catholic Church was the infallible organ of divine truth as well as the sole mediator of divine grace. The heretic was as much outside of her pale as the schismatic. In his famous work on the city of God, Augustine broadened the traditional notion to include political as well as intellectual and moral authority. In the present millennial age the Catholic Church, which is the kingdom of God on earth, has authority over nations as well as individuals. In Augustine's notion of the *civitas dei* and the *civitas terrena* was rooted the papal theory of the Middle Ages, that the Church has two swords, the spiritual and the temporal, that the Pope, as head of the Church and vice-gerent of Christ, is supreme both in civil and spiritual things, and that all the nations and sovereigns of the earth are subject to him. Thus the Catholic Church of the Middle Ages was at once the sole ark of salvation and the supreme authority upon earth, moral, intellectual, and political, and submission to her was the one indispensable requirement.

The recognition of supernatural authority was carried so far in the Middle Ages that it even controlled men's ideas of the physical universe, and dictated the prevailing world-view of the period. It was commonly believed that in the Bible is contained an inspired account of the origin and structure of the world, and to depart from it is to fall not only into error but also into sin. According to St. Augustine nothing was to be accepted save on the authority of the Scriptures, 'for greater is that authority than all the powers of the human mind.' If any one wished to know more about the world in which he lived, he turned not to the world itself but to the Scriptures. Growth in the knowledge of Nature as well as of spiritual things could come only from a study of divine revelation. The supernaturalism of the Biblical writers was controlling in this sphere as in every other, and the world-view was far more primitive than that of the Greeks, for it was based upon the naïve ideas of the Hebrew Scriptures.

In the Catholicism of the Middle Ages humility, both moral and intellectual, was the supreme virtue, self-confidence the worst of sins. Religion found its highest exercise in magnifying God as the All-holy, Powerful, and Wise Being in contrast with corrupt, helpless, and blind humanity. Pride was the root of all evil. The fall of man, like the fall of Satan, was due to it, and from it sprang sacrilege, schism, and heresy, the most awful crimes; all were the fruits of self-love and self-confidence, the preference of one's own ways and opinions to those prescribed by the Church, God's representative on earth.

II. *The Eve of the Reformation*

The Protestant Reformation was not exclusively nor even chiefly a religious movement. It involved a break with the historical ecclesiastical institution and the organisation of new churches independent of Rome, but the break itself was as much political as religious, both in its causes and in its results. Dissatisfaction with the existing order of things was widespread in Western Europe, and was coming to ever more active expression. It was not confined to one class of society, nor limited to one set of conditions. The period was marked by discontent and unrest, moral, religious, social, economical, and political. The conviction was growing that traditional customs and institutions needed adjustment to the new needs of a new age, and on every hand criticisms of the old were rife and programmes of reform were multiplying. For centuries the Church had been the most imposing institution in Europe, and the most influential factor in its life. Rightly or wrongly it was widely held responsible for current evils in every line, and every project for the betterment of society concerned itself in one or another way with the ecclesiastical establishment. As a rule, however, the criticisms of the existing system affected only superficial details, and were neither radical nor far-reaching. Abuses in ecclesiastical administration, financial exactions on the part of the ecclesiastical authorities, ignorance, immorality, and venality on the part of the clergy—these constituted in most cases the burden of complaint. The fundamental principles on which the mediæval system rested were seldom made the object of criticism or of question. The traditional Catholic dogmas and the beliefs underlying existing religious practices were commonly taken for granted. Criticism confined itself chiefly, either to the over-emphasis of theology and the substitution of barren orthodoxy for practical religion, or to abuses in the application of accepted principles and the displacement of vital piety by formalism and externality.[1]

Notable among the phenomena of the age was the tendency which we know as humanism, the most modern expression of the intellectual life of the period. It is true that its significance has been greatly exaggerated, and the contrast between the intellectual life of the fifteenth and that of the thirteenth century much over-emphasised. At the same time it is abundantly clear that the general temper of those whom we call humanists was unlike that of the leading thinkers of the Middle Ages. The difference was not in the matter of seriousness, as often said, for in spite of the frivolity of many humanists, some of the most notable of them were as earnest in purpose as any of the leaders of the Mediæval Church. It lay rather in a

[1] Cf. what Luther has to say about his predecessors in his 'Table Talk' *Works*, vol. lx. pp. 246, 252; vol. lxii. pp. 118, 124.

INTRODUCTION

difference of attitude toward the present world both of man and of nature, a recognition of its independent value and an interest in it for its own sake. There was widespread rebellion among the humanists against the trammels of mediæval Catholicism, and against the tyranny of the ecclesiastical establishment, and the growing loss of reverence for the existing system which made the spread of Protestantism possible was in no small part due to their influence, as was also the increasing conviction that a reformation of some sort was needed. But with the constructive work of the Protestant Reformation and with the framing of its principles and ideals they had little to do.

Of the humanists who desired to promote a reformation of one kind or another, or at least to improve religious and moral conditions within the Church, Erasmus of Rotterdam may be taken as a representative.[1] To Erasmus Christianity was primarily an ethical system; Christ was its great teacher and exemplar; and to be a Christian meant to conduct one's life in accordance with the principles which governed Him. Jesus appeared in the rôle of a sage, and Christianity under the aspect of a moral philosophy rather than a religion of redemption. In opposition to the schoolmen the elaborate theology of the Middle Ages was pushed to one side and the emphasis laid on practical conduct, and in opposition to the externality and formalism of the prevailing religious life of the day the inner disposition was made alone essential. All the paraphernalia of mediæval Christianity—its sacraments, relics, pilgrimages, rites and ceremonies, ecclesiasticism and asceticism—were looked on as unimportant. Not that they were necessarily bad in themselves, but that they were not of the essence of the Gospel, and became vicious when they obscured the more vital matters. The heart of Christianity, the one all-important thing accord-

[1] See especially his *Enchiridion Militis Christiani* (1503); his *Encomium Moriæ* (1511); and his *Institutio Principis Christiani* (1518).

ing to Erasmus, is love for one's fellows, manifesting itself in charity, sympathy, and forbearance. The governing motive of Jesus' life was brotherly love, and in it the Christian life finds its controlling principle. Erasmus did not break with the Catholic Church, nor did he, in spite of the ridicule he continually heaped upon the follies and vices of priests and monks (as for instance in his *Praise of Folly*), reject the doctrines and principles of the mediæval system. He was an orthodox Catholic, as his work on the Symbol abundantly shows, but his teaching was inevitably disintegrating in its tendency, and Pope Paul IV. was perfectly right in putting his works on the Index. The distinction between essential and non-essential in the existing system, and the reduction of the former to the moral principles taught by Jesus, must accrue to the neglect and disregard of a large part of the traditional theory and practice of the Catholic Church, and though Erasmus might not himself draw the natural conclusion, it was clear enough that others would.

In his endeavour to bring out distinctly the essence of Christianity in contrast with the excrescences which so commonly obscured it, Erasmus, like most of the humanists, was led to lay emphasis upon the supreme authority of the Bible. In the Primitive Church—in the days of Christ Himself and His Apostles—it might be assumed that the Gospel appeared in its purest form, unadulterated by the accretions of the centuries, and so the Bible, particularly the New Testament, became an object of diligent study. Erasmus himself published the first edition of the New Testament in the original Greek in 1516, and followed it with numerous commentaries and editions of the Fathers, who were supposed, after the apostles themselves, to be the most authentic witnesses to Christian truth, and the most competent interpreters of the Scriptures. The recognition of the authority of the Bible was not an innovation; theoretically it had been supreme since an early day. It had been the object of diligent and faithful study on the part of theologians, and the comfort and inspiration of multitudes of devout and pious souls during all the centuries. In the later Middle Ages vernacular translations of it became very common, and in many cases received ecclesiastical approval. But it was not the exclusive authority of Catholic Christians. The Church was believed to be the living and infallible mediator and interpreter of divine truth. To its custody the Bible had been committed, and in the light of its teaching it was read. So long as the Bible and the Church were believed to speak the same language there was no difficulty and no need of defining the authority of the one as distinguished from the other. Only when sectaries and heretics set the Bible against the Church, and employed its teachings as a weapon to break down the existing system, did the ecclesiastical authorities begin to look askance upon it, and to condemn its unauthorised use. The significance of the humanists' attitude in the matter lay just here. Not that they recognised the authority of the Scriptures, but that they saw and emphasised the contrast between Biblical and traditional Christianity, and tried the latter by the former. In the later Middle Ages this was very common even beyond humanistic circles. It became more and more the custom for innovators of all kinds to appeal to the Scriptures against the Church, and to find warrant in the former for every deviation from existing principles and practices in the political and social as well as in the religious sphere. With denunciations of the existing situation were joined representations of the ideal conditions of primitive days to which it was desired to return. Some even went so far as to call the Catholic Church anti-Christian, and the Pope anti-Christ. While most of the humanists, including Erasmus himself, were not as severe and radical as this, the watchword ' back to Christ ' was on the lips of multitudes.

Another influence working in the same general direction, to minimise the importance of external rites and ceremonies, and to magnify the inner and vital essence of religion, was mediæval mysticism. Mysticism has always existed within Christian circles. In the later Middle Ages it was very widespread, and became a disintegrating force on a large scale. The mystics emphasised personal salvation to the exclusion of all else. The contrast between them and the humanists was extreme in this respect. Christianity was regarded not as a moral philosophy but as a religion of redemption. The attention was turned wholly upon the one question of immediate personal concern, How am I to be saved? The mystical interpretations of salvation, widely as they might differ in detail, commonly made it consist in union with God to be brought about by meditation and prayer, carried on largely apart from the ordinary offices of the Church. The result was the growing currency of a non-ecclesiastical piety which might or might not be hostile to the Church and the hierarchy, but was at any rate largely independent of them. By most of the mystics no criticism was passed upon the traditional dogmas or customs of the Church, but they were subordinated to the inner life with God. As is said in the famous *Theologia Germanica*: 'Now what is this union? It is that we should be of a truth purely, simply, and wholly at one with the One Eternal Will of God, or altogether without will, so that the created will should flow out into the Eternal Will, and be swallowed up and lost therein, so that the Eternal Will alone should do and leave undone in us. Now mark what may help or further us towards this end. Behold, neither exercises, nor words, nor works, nor any creature, nor creature's work, can do this. In this wise, therefore, must we renounce and forsake all things, that we must not imagine or suppose that any words, works, or exercises, any skill, or cunning, or any created thing can help or serve us thereto. Therefore we must suffer these things to be what they are, and enter into the union with God.' (Miss Winkworth's translation, chap. xxvii.)

Similarly there was widely current a simple evangelical piety closely akin to that existing in Protestantism from the beginning. Doubtless there had always been a good deal of it, perhaps as much as in the fifteenth and sixteenth centuries, but it is in the literature of that period that we discover the most frequent expressions of it. Its essence was recognition of the love of God revealed in Christ, renunciation of all merit of one's own, dependence upon God and trust in Him. The evangelical theology which Luther later taught came to multitudes of Christians with a very familiar sound. It was in fact little else than a translation into articulate terms of a piety in which they had always lived. This kind of piety also meant as a rule no criticism of or breach with the existing system. Those who were dominated by it commonly remained devout and loyal Catholics, and never thought of questioning the divine character of the Church, but they became inevitably, even if insensibly, less dependent upon external forms, and less subject to an objective authority. They made little stir in the world, but they were quick to respond to such a gospel as Luther proclaimed. The rapid spread of his influence among the German people was in no small part due to the wide prevalence of this kind of piety, and because its existence was hardly suspected by the authorities the success of his preaching remained inexplicable to them.

A characteristic phenomenon of the period was the growth of religious brotherhoods of one kind and another in which both mysticism and the type of piety just described came to concrete expression. To multitudes these brotherhoods, while not hostile to the Church, served in no small degree as substitutes for it, and many Christians found their religious needs largely met and satisfied by them.

The later fifteenth century was a period of religious revival on a large scale in Central and Western Europe. Not only those forms of the religious life which have been referred to but also strictly Catholic piety was everywhere reanimated. It was a time of social and economic chaos. Plague, pestilence, and famine devastated large sections of the continent. New diseases made their appearance as a result of the growing intercourse between Europe and the Orient. The dread of Turkish invasion became more acute, and fear and demoralisation were seizing upon all classes of the community. The feeling of helplessness was common, and men were looking in every direction for the strength and confidence they lacked in themselves. It was widely believed that the end of the world was at hand, and terror was everywhere abroad. Under these circumstances a recrudescence of mediæval piety in its crassest form took place. Pilgrimages, veneration of relics, multiplication of ascetic practices, increase of monasticism, mark the age in a notable degree. Serious-minded men felt themselves driven as seldom before to ward off evil by religious observances. All this was just the opposite of humanism in its effects. If the latter promoted self-confidence and self-reliance, the influences just referred to fostered self-distrust. If the one undermined the traditional superstition and transformed religion into ethics, the other encouraged the most vulgar kinds of religious practice, and strengthened the hold of the most primitive and superstitious rites and customs. To persons of this type humanism must seem barren, insufficient, and irreligious. It might meet the needs of men of modern temper, but it had nothing at all to offer those beset with religious fear and oppressed by their own helplessness. Luther was a typical figure in this respect, and the terror which drove him into the monastery a very common experience. If other forms of piety tended to diminish the influence of the ecclesiastical establishment and of traditional principles and practices, this common religious fear tended to bind them more firmly upon the consciences of the people. At the same time it made them receptive to new religious suggestions from any quarter, and led them to seize blindly upon any help that might be offered. In general the opening of the sixteenth century must be recognised as a time of ferment, excitement, and unrest in religion as in all other lines, a time pregnant of change, equally hospitable to the most radical and to the most reactionary movements. No one could foresee what would come out of it, and even now, looking back upon the period, it seems largely an accident that the current ultimately flowed in the direction it did rather than in some other.

There was in all the tendencies that have been referred to no impulse toward a real reconstruction of the existing system. Things might have gone on much as they always had, and the Catholic Church might have retained its hold upon the minds and hearts of pious people everywhere, had it not been for other and alien influences.

The most radical programme of the age was that of the great English statesman, John Wyclif. Led by political and patriotic considerations to question the authority of the Roman Catholic institution, he set up a theory of the Church which, while not new, was calculated, as he presented it, to undermine completely the authority of the existing establishment.[1] The true Church, he said, following the lead of Augustine, is the totality of the predestinated, and is not identical with the Roman Catholic or any other ecclesiastical body. The elect constitute the true Church of Christ, and only they; and not alone the elect of this age, but of all ages, those already in heaven, both angels and saints, and those not yet born, as well as those now upon the earth. Judas never belonged to the Church, although for a long time an apostle in good

[1] See his *De Ecclesia*.

standing and repute, and Paul always belonged to it, even before he became a Christian, and while he was still a persecutor. Of course, on this theory membership in the visible Catholic Church has nothing to do with membership in the true Church of Christ or with participation in the sacraments. To the elect the sacraments are unnecessary, to the non-elect vain. To be within the visible Church is no help, to be without it no hindrance. The predestinated who constitute the true Church of Christ are known to nobody but God. They are not even sure that they are themselves elect, much less can they tell whether their fellows are, and so no social bond holds them together. Here on earth they do not form a community in any sense, and the word Church loses all meaning in its application to them. It signifies no more than the sum of the scattered and mutually unrelated individuals who will one day be gathered in heaven, and there for the first time compose a real community. What we have in this is really not a new idea of the Church substituted for the old, but the idea of the Church destroyed altogether. For whatever it may be called, a totality of segregated and independent units, unknown both to themselves and to others, certainly has no attributes which entitle it to bear the name of Church.

It is clear that Wyclif's theory, carried out as it was in a thoroughgoing fashion, and with explicit denial of the traditional claims of the Catholic Church to be the true kingdom of God, was completely destructive of the existing ecclesiastical system, and if taken up by Christians in general and given practical application, would have split the Church in pieces. It is not surprising that Wyclif was regarded by the Roman authorities as the worst of heretics. Only his political prominence and his influence with the English government saved him from condemnation and death. His followers, the Lollards, though proscribed and persecuted, kept his principles alive for some generations, but his theory of the Church found no general acceptance in England. It was taken up, however, by his younger contemporary, John Huss of Bohemia, who added nothing essential to it, and did not modify it in any important way, but set it out so clearly, and so divorced from the many other matters in which Wyclif was interested, that it made a much greater impression than it had in Wyclif's writings, and was speedily known far and wide. It cost Huss his life. In 1415 he paid the penalty at Constance for Wyclif's attack upon the time-honoured system. Catholic theology had no dogma concerning the Church, but the authorities were quick to crush anything that threatened the time-honoured theory upon which the whole ecclesiastical structure was reared.

The Protestant Reformation was not the result of the work of Wyclif and Huss and of the many other Christians of the period who were criticising and attacking the existing system on one and another ground. But they assisted to prepare the way for it, and the widespread questioning as to the nature and identity of the Church, which resulted from their attacks upon the traditional theory, made the work of Luther and his fellow reformers easier.

CHAPTER II

MARTIN LUTHER

I. *The New in Luther's Thought*

THOUGH educated in the University of Erfurt, the centre of humanistic culture in Germany, Luther was singularly untouched by the intellectual currents of his day. The impulses which controlled him were never those of the scholar, the scientist, or the philosopher. He cared little for clearness and consistency of thought. A satisfactory and adequate world-view was none of his concern. Of intellectual curiosity he had scarcely any; of interest in truth for truth's sake none at all. He had a marvellous command of the German language, and was a writer of great force and vigour, but he was no litterateur, and his works are strikingly devoid of the literary artifice and self-consciousness of his day. He was far and away the most commanding personality of the age, and he had mental gifts of a very high order, but his genius was wholly practical. He was pre-eminently a religious character, and his great work was accomplished in the religious sphere; but even there he was not controlled by intellectual motives. At a time when the spirit of the modern age was beginning to make itself felt in the religious thinking of his contemporaries, and questions as to the truth of traditional doctrines were widespread, he remained entirely without intellectual difficulties, finding no trouble with the most extreme supernaturalism and the crassest superstitions of the current faith. His confidence in the Catholic system was absolute, and his acceptance of its tenets complete, until he was shaken out of it by practical considerations which had nothing to do with theology, and were not in the least of an intellectual order. Under these circumstances it is a mistake to think of him as a theologian and of his work as a reformation of theology. It is equally a mistake to think of him as a reformer in the institutional sphere. Existing institutions, like traditional theology, might be changed to a greater or less degree as a result of his labours, but the effect was incidental in the one case as in the other. His interest was wholly in the practical religious life, and all the differences between him and his Catholic contemporaries were simply the consequence of a radical divergence in this sphere.

His own conception of the Christian life was the fruit of a personal experience too familiar to need recounting here. Driven into a monastery by fear of the wrath of God and by the desire to earn divine forgiveness and approval by meritorious works, he discovered that it was impossible to secure peace of mind by such a method, and was finally led to believe that the only road to peace lay in repudiating all righteousness of his own, and depending wholly upon the free grace of God in Christ. The conviction was not original with him. Not only Paul and Augustine, but many another pious soul had trodden a similar road and had reached the same goal. To suppose that Luther's gospel of the free, forgiving love of God in Christ was unknown in the ancient and mediæval Church is a great mistake. Particularly in the Middle Ages it found frequent expression. But not before had the conviction meant so complete a revolution in a Christian's religious life, and never had it borne so radical fruit. This was due in part to Luther's temperament, which made compromise either with himself or with others impossible, in part to the uncommon zeal with which he had thrown himself into the task of winning the favour of God

—a zeal which brought him the reputation of extraordinary sanctity far beyond the confines of his monastery and his order, and gave the contrast between the old and the new way an exaggerated sharpness; in part to the fact that he had grown up under the influence of the common popular notions of religion, and without any early theological training. His youthful ideas of God, of Christ, of the future life and of the unseen world were very crass. Widely current as they were among the common people, they were for the most part but caricatures of Catholic doctrine. Had he been brought up in theological circles his experience would never have meant such a break with his own past as it did. Catholic theology always laid emphasis upon the forgiving love of God, and upon the vanity of independent human merit, but the popular interpretation of it was very different. Luther's own study of some of the great mediæval mystics, and of Augustine and Paul, which had assisted him to his new way of looking at things, led him at first to suppose that that way was genuinely Catholic, and for some years he was entirely at peace within the Catholic Church. But ultimately, as a result of the controversy over indulgences, the conviction was forced upon him that the Roman Church was irrevocably committed to the vicious notions which he had for ever abandoned. The break for such a man as he was inevitable. Thenceforth it was impossible for him to be just to the old system. He interpreted Catholic theology, or rather the scholastic theology of the Middle Ages, which he held responsible for all the errors of the day, in the light of his own early misconceptions, and never ceased to denounce the schoolmen as corrupters of the true Gospel of Christ and as genuine pagans like their master Aristotle. His hostility to them, similar as it was to that of the humanists, though for a very different reason, brought him for a time into an artificial and unnatural alliance with the latter, who thought him one of themselves, and were the more incensed when they discovered their error, as they soon did, for he and they were of an entirely different spirit, and their religious programmes totally unlike.

Luther's interpretation of scholastic theology had another and more important effect. It led him to draw an unwarranted contrast between the Ancient and the Mediæval Church, and to treat the latter as an apostate from the principles of the former. In this, too, he resembled the humanists, but as in the other case the ground of offence was dissimilar. During the Middle Ages the penitential system underwent large development, and the schoolmen felt obliged to devote themselves to its elucidation and defence. The controlling principles of the system existed as early as the second century, and all that followed was a natural and legitimate evolution, but the necessities of the situation made Christology the principal subject of dispute and official pronouncement in the ancient Church, and the theological emphasis of that age was thus very different. Because of this the oneness of principle between the Ancient and Mediæval Church was overlooked by Luther, and the purity of the former was extolled at the expense of the latter. This explains, at least in part, the devotion which he always showed to the dogmas of the Ancient Church, and in which he was followed by the whole Protestant communion. But as a matter of fact the difference between Luther and the early Fathers was at bottom as great as between him and the schoolmen. It did not lie in the sphere of theology —there was much in common among them all—but in their respective conceptions of the nature of the Christian life. Here, in part, but only in part, under the guidance of Paul, Luther went his own way independent of all predecessors.

His religious experience, I have said, though exceptional, was by no means unique. But some of the conclusions which he drew from it were entirely new, newer, indeed, than he himself realised. The significant thing was that his experience led him to believe himself already a saved man, not a mere candidate for salvation, and hence to interpret the Christian life as the effect rather than the condition of salvation. How he reached this conclusion it is not difficult to discover. Had he been either a speculative theologian or an ethical philosopher, it would probably have been impossible to him. But influenced by the common popular way of looking at God, he conceived Him so exclusively under the aspect of an angry judge that the one thing needful seemed escape from the divine wrath. His sin troubled him, not on its own account, but solely on account of the wrath of God which it entailed. 'As wrath is a greater evil than the corruption of sin, so grace is a greater good than the perfect righteousness which we have said comes from faith. For there is no one who would not prefer (if this could be) to be without perfect righteousness than without the grace of God.'[1] It was a religious not an ethical motive which controlled him; not to attain moral purity, but to be on good terms with God was the supreme need of his being. To claim that the Protestant Reformation was due primarily to ethical considerations, and was the result of dissatisfaction with the moral state of the world, and of the desire to raise the moral tone of society, is nothing less than a travesty upon the facts.

Dominated as Luther was by the sense of the divine wrath, and the supreme need of escape from it, the peace which resulted from throwing himself upon the free grace of God, and repudiating all merit of his own, could hardly be interpreted as anything less than the escape which he coveted, or in other words as salvation itself. If salvation had meant freedom from sin he could not have thought

[1] *Against Latomus*; Erlangen edition of the *Opera Latina Varii Argumenti*, vol. v. p. 489.

of it as a present possession, for he knew well enough he was still a sinner. But if it meant release from God's wrath and the enjoyment of His favour, then it was his already. The significance of Luther's position at this point lies in the fact that he claimed to be already saved, not because already pure and righteous, but on other grounds altogether, and while still continuing to be impure and unrighteous. This constitutes the great difference between him and the Apostle Paul. Paul, too, thought of salvation as a present possession and of the Christian as already saved, but the ground of his salvation was moral transformation, not divine forgiveness. By the indwelling of the Spirit the Christian is not merely in process of sanctification, but is actually changed already into a holy being, or, in other words, is already saved. Paul was moved primarily by moral considerations, as Luther was not. To Paul the one dreadful thing was the corruption of the flesh to which the natural man is subject. To be freed from it by the agency of divine power—this and this alone meant salvation. The influence of Paul, or the influence of the same forces which he felt, continued to dominate Christian thought, and salvation was always interpreted by Catholic theology, if not always by the Catholic populace, as salvation from sin. But the consciousness of sin was too general, and the sense of the divine presence and power too feeble to permit the heroic faith of Paul to continue, and salvation was inevitably pushed into the future, and the transformation of human nature was thought of as a gradual process completed only in another world. Luther broke with the Catholic theory, not by going back to Paul and asserting a present and instantaneous sanctification, but by repudiating altogether the Pauline and Catholic notion of salvation, and making it wholly a matter of divine forgiveness rather than of human character. Divine forgiveness had, of course, always been regarded as an element in salvation.

Luther, for the first time, made it the whole of salvation. That he was able to do it shows clearly enough where his controlling interest lay. Peace with God in the assurance of his forgiving love was the one thing he coveted, and the one thing that always seemed most precious to him.

The divine forgiveness which, according to Luther, is the whole of salvation, is a complete and perfect thing. It does not have to do with particular sins, some of which may be forgiven and others not. The sinner is either wholly forgiven or not forgiven at all, or, in other words, he is either wholly under God's favour or wholly under His wrath. 'Now it follows that those two, anger and grace, are so constituted when they are without us that they act as one whole, so that he who is under anger is wholly under anger, and he who is under grace is wholly under grace, because both anger and grace have to do with persons. For whom God receives into grace He receives wholly, and whom He favours He favours wholly. On the other hand, with whom He is angry He is wholly angry, for He does not divide His favour or grace as gifts are divided, neither does He love the head and hate the feet, or favour the soul and hate the body. . . . Grace must be sharply distinguished from gifts, for grace alone is life eternal, and anger alone is death eternal.'[1] This makes it clear enough where Luther's interest lay, and how little he was controlled by ethical considerations.

Closely connected with the Catholic notion of salvation as only a future reality, consisting in complete release from sin, was the belief that it was in some sense at least a reward of human merit. It is true that it was taught that no man can save himself or even take the first step toward salvation without the assistance of divine grace; in other words, there is no such thing as independent human merit. But salvation was thought of as depending upon the use a man makes of the divine grace given him

[1] *Against Latomus*, ibid., p. 490.

in the sacraments. It was represented as a product, not of divine grace and the effort of the natural man, but of divine grace and the effort of the regenerated man, whose nature had been made capable of co-operation in the attainment of holiness. The teaching of Paul shows that this notion of human co-operation is not a necessary, but it is certainly a natural consequence of interpreting salvation in ethical terms. It must always be difficult to disconnect human effort from human character, and to regard the latter as the unaided work of divine power, particularly so if the process of transformation be looked upon as gradual. Augustine essayed the task, but his failure to secure a following, to say nothing of his own inconsistencies in carrying out his principle, serves only to illustrate the fact. To Luther the step was made easy by his reinterpretation of salvation. If it be nothing else than the divine favour, and not identical with the transformation of human character, it may also be independent of all human effort. The truth is, he was moving in a different sphere from his predecessors, and was actuated by an altogether different interest. To look at him therefore from their point of view is utterly to misunderstand him.

The contrast between Luther's notion of salvation and the traditional Catholic conception is illustrated by the difference between their respective ideas of grace. To Catholic theology the word signifies a divine substance bestowed upon man. As a contemporary of Luther put it : ' That which truly justifies the heart is grace, which is daily created and poured into our hearts.'[1] To Luther, on the other hand, grace is simply the favour of God, and to be saved by grace means not to receive some substance, or thing from above, or to be transformed by divine activity, but simply to be forgiven and restored to the

[1] Quoted by Planck (*Geschichte der protestantischen Theologie*, vol. i. p. 32) from Bishop Fischer's *Refutation of Luther*, published in 1528.

divine favour. As he says in his work, *Against Latomus*: 'Grace I understand here properly as the favour of God as it should be understood, and not as a quality of soul' (p. 489). In other words, by divine grace Luther meant nothing else than graciousness, and if the latter word were always used instead of the former in reproducing his teaching, much confusion would be avoided.

Though Luther believed, as I have already said, that salvation is of God alone, independent of all human effort, he yet taught that it is conditioned upon faith. Following Paul, who became here the interpreter of the reformer's own experience, he maintained constantly that man is saved by faith and not by works. His position at this point is the most familiar part of his teaching. But is not salvation thus made dependent after all upon human activity? Is not the substitution of 'faith alone' for the traditional formula 'faith and works' simply the substitution of one form of human merit for another? This would be so if faith were man's own work, but, according to Luther, it is the work of God. He produces it, and so it is not in any sense a form of human merit. God reveals Himself in Jesus Christ as a gracious and forgiving Father, and in the man who is conscious of his sin and of his consequent need of forgiveness the revelation arouses an instinctive response. Feeling his need, which has been brought home to him by the revelation of the divine law, he finds in the vision of God in Christ the answer to his need and faith is inevitable. That he believes is no merit of his. It is because God has shown Himself a gracious God in whom he cannot help believing. The revelation is entirely in God's hands. He discloses Himself to whom He pleases, and thus faith, which is man's response, is wholly God's work. The revelation of which Luther speaks is not the general revelation contained in the Scriptures and recounted continually from the pulpit, which everybody knows who happens to read the Bible or enter a church. It is rather the inner disclosure of God's gracious love to the heart of one and another man to whom He chooses to reveal Himself. The disclosure is made only through the written and spoken word, but not to everybody is the vision vouchsafed.

Luther was thus a thoroughgoing predestinarian; but his predestinarianism was not a theological or metaphysical affair. It is true that in his desire to do away with all human merit, and show the sole activity of God in the salvation of man, he was led to present his predestinarian convictions in theological form, to give them theoretical support in a doctrine of the absolute and unconditioned will of God, taken directly from scholasticism, and to draw from them deterministic conclusions of a very extreme type. But none of this is of the essence of the matter, and it should not be made the starting-point in interpreting his thought. His belief in predestination was the fruit of experience, not of speculation. This is made abundantly clear, for instance, by the fact that while he frequently asserts, in the most categorical fashion, the absolute bondage of the human will, and declares that all our deeds, evil as well as good, are directly caused by God, he yet recognises man's freedom in matters which do not concern his salvation. Evidently his controlling interest was not to safeguard the divine omnipotence, but to give expression to his own experience of God's controlling power in saving him. Peace came to him, after his long struggle to appease the wrath of God by meritorious works, solely because of his vision of the forgiving love of God in Christ. The peace was God's work, not his own. God had disclosed Himself, and his salvation consisted, not in anything that he did in consequence of the disclosure or under its influence, but in the disclosure itself. He found God gracious, he did not make Him so. The very essence of the experience lay in the fact that God had given it. To resolve it into its divine and human constituents, to mark off the agency of God and the co-operation of man, one from the other, in traditional theological fashion, would have been to take all meaning out of it. Not two separable and distinguishable acts, that of God and that of man, but the one act of God disclosing Himself as a gracious and forgiving Father, this meant faith, this meant trust, this meant peace and salvation.

Luther's notion of salvation as a present reality led him to look upon the Christian life, as Paul did, as a life of perfect liberty. The man who trusts in God revealed as a gracious Father is already saved and has nothing to fear in life or in death. His salvation does not depend upon the success with which he may meet temptation and fulfil the divine law; it is already complete. He is now as truly as he will ever be a child of God, under His fatherly care and protection, and enjoying His gracious favour and forgiving love. Thus he is set free from the necessity of working out his own salvation. The bondage of the law is removed. It has done its complete and perfect work in bringing him to a consciousness of sin and of the need of divine forgiveness. Henceforth he is released from its control and becomes a free man in Christ Jesus. The principle of Christian liberty was fundamental with Luther. The most beautiful of all his works, and the one which contains the finest statement of his Christian faith is entitled *The Liberty of the Christian Man*. Through faith in Christ, he says, the believer becomes a 'most free lord of all and subject to no one,' and what he means by this appears clearly enough in such passages as the following: 'It is clear then that to a Christian man his faith suffices for everything, and that he has no need of works for justification. But if he has no need of works, neither has he need of the law; and if he has no need of the law, he is certainly free from the law.'[1] 'This is a spiritual power, which rules in the midst of enemies, and

[1] Wace and Buchheim's edition of *Luther's Primary Works*, p. 262.

is powerful in the midst of distresses. And this is nothing else than that strength is made perfect in my weakness, and that I can turn all things to the profit of my salvation, so that even the cross and death are compelled to serve me and to work together for my salvation. This is a lofty and eminent dignity, a true and almighty dominion, a spiritual empire, in which there is nothing so good, nothing so bad, as not to work together for my good, if only I believe. And yet there is nothing of which I have need—for faith alone suffices for my salvation—unless that in it faith may exercise the power and empire of its liberty. This is the inestimable power and liberty of Christians.'[1]

'A Christian man needs no work, no law, for his salvation; for by faith he is free from all law, and in perfect freedom does gratuitously all that he does, seeking nothing either of profit or of salvation, since by the grace of God he is already saved and rich in all things through his faith.'[2]

His idea of Christian liberty was the most modern element in Luther's teaching, and did more than anything else to undermine the authority of the Catholic Church. One of the watchwords of the dawning modern age was liberty; escape from the trammels of traditional authority, and the assertion of the independence of the individual. Already this had voiced itself in various ways, but for the religious man there was apparently no escape from the dominance of the ecclesiastical system. It seemed that one could be completely free only by becoming irreligious, could throw off the thraldom of the Church only by repudiating all for which it stood, and giving up religious faith and aspiration altogether. The Church had gained its power because it was believed to be the only ark of salvation, and so the only means of escape from eternal punishment. A man might free himself from bondage to the Church by giving up his belief in a future life, and

[1] *Luther's Primary Works*, p. 268.   [2] *Ibid*. p. 276.

thus denying the need of salvation, as many did, or he might free himself from its bondage, as Luther did, by throwing himself in faith upon the gracious favour of God revealed through Jesus Christ. Meritorious works done under the direction of the Church, participation in the sacraments administered by her, and submission to her dictates in things moral and intellectual—all become unnecessary to the man who has this saving faith. Thus without becoming sceptical or irreligious, while still believing in the divine punishment due for sin, and in God's supernatural salvation, Luther was set free from dependence upon the authority of the historic ecclesiastical institution, one of the great foes of the dawning spirit of liberty.

Freedom from the necessity of earning one's salvation by engaging in particular religious practices and performing works of special merit meant also the recognition of the sacredness of all callings, even the most secular and the most humble, and the possibility of serving God in worldly profession, business, and trade as truly as in monastery and priesthood. For many centuries it had been supposed that the most truly religious life was that of the monk or nun who lived apart from the distractions and pleasures of the world in religious devotion, and in the practice of rigorous self-discipline. To be in the midst of society, to engage in trade, to indulge in the pleasures of friendship, to marry and enjoy the delights of home, all this was legitimate, but distinctly less honourable than the life of celibacy and seclusion. Other-worldliness was the dominant note of traditional Christian piety. Not to make a man a good citizen of this world, but to prepare him for citizenship in another and altogether different world beyond the grave, where there is neither buying nor selling, eating nor drinking, marrying nor giving in marriage, and where life is a continuous and uninterrupted round of devotional exercises—to prepare him for such a world was thought to be the supreme aim of Christianity. And so the more unworldly this life could be made, the more completely detached from the ordinary interests and concerns of earth, the more Christian it seemed. In opposition to this Luther taught with the greatest possible emphasis the sacredness of this life and the holiness of ordinary human callings and relationships. The Christian is already a saved man, and his life here on earth is as sacred as his life in heaven will be, and in it he may express as truly as there his Christian character as a son of God, not by detaching himself from employment and family and friends and giving himself to ascetic and religious practices, but by doing the daily task faithfully and joyfully, with trust in God and with devotion to His will.

Luther's writings, particularly his sermons, are full of this message. Thus he says:—

'What you do in your house is worth as much as if you did it up in heaven for our Lord God. For what we do in our calling here on earth in accordance with His word and command He counts as if it were done in heaven for Him.'[1] 'Therefore we should accustom ourselves to think of our position and work as sacred and well-pleasing to God, not on account of the position and the work, but on account of the word and the faith from which the obedience and the work flow. No Christian should despise his position and life if he is living in accordance with the word of God, but should say, "I believe in Jesus Christ, and do as the ten commandments teach, and pray that our dear Lord God may help me thus to do." That is a right holy life, and cannot be made holier even if one fast himself to death.'[2] 'It looks like a great thing when a monk renounces everything and goes into a cloister, carries on a life of asceticism, fasts, watches, prays, etc. . . . On the other hand, it looks like a small thing when a maid cooks and cleans and does other housework. But because

---

[1] *Works*, vol. v. p. 102. [2] *Ibid.* vol. iv. p. 341.

God's command is there, even such a small work must be praised as a service of God far surpassing the holiness and asceticism of all monks and nuns. For here there is no command of God. But there God's command is fulfilled, that one should honour father and mother and help in the care of the home.'[1]

An important corollary of this estimate of the common life of man was the breaking down of the old distinction between the clergy and the laity. The life of the clergyman is no more sacred than that of the layman. Faith in God and devotion to His will make him as good as the faithful and believing merchant or shoemaker, but no better. The virtue of a calling is measured, not by its relation to the future life, but to this life. Religion becomes a thing of the people, not merely of the priest. Upon them rest its responsibilities, and to them belong its privileges as truly as to him. It was, therefore, no mere dictate of expediency which led Luther in his famous Address to the German Nobility to call upon them to take up the work of religious and ecclesiastical reformation. The clergy are only the representatives of the people, and their ministers or servants in religious things; let the people, not the hierarchy, rule. In his distrust of popular wisdom Luther himself might draw back from democracy, whether in affairs civil or religious, and might substitute for the traditional ecclesiastical authority a secular authority scarcely less despotic, but liberty for the soul of man lies in his recognition of the sacredness of man's common life, and of the independence of the people in religious things, and that recognition, in spite of all obscuration and misinterpretation, has borne rich fruit in Protestant lands.

But was not such liberty as Luther taught subversive of all morality? To set a man free from the obligation to work out his own salvation, and to give him the assurance

[1] *Works*, vol. v. p. 100.

that he is already completely saved—is it not to take away all incentive to holy living and to promote carelessness and vice ? The answer is found in Luther's conception of the nature of virtue and in his interpretation of the Christian life. True virtue, he says, is disinterested. 'Whoever turns good works to his own advantage does no good work.'[1] 'If you ask a chaste man why he is chaste, he should say, not on account of heaven or hell, and not on account of honour and disgrace, but solely because it would seem good to me and please me well even though it were not commanded.'[2] And so the Christian life which is the highest of all must be wholly disinterested. It consists, in fact, of self-forgetful service. 'The highest art, the noblest life and holiest conduct is the practice of love for God and one's neighbour.'[3] And what Luther means by loving God and one's neighbour is made abundantly clear by the words, 'What is it to serve God and to do His will ? Nothing else than to show mercy to our neighbour. For it is our neighbour who needs our service, God in heaven needs it not.'[4] Over and over again Luther sums up the Christian life in this way. It is most beautiful and inspiring to see how in sermon after sermon he shows what service of one's fellows means, and how rich and manifold a thing it is as it expresses itself in the various relationships and conditions of life : between husband and wife, parent and child, tradesman and customer, master and servant, prince and people, towards friends, strangers, and enemies, on the part of rich and poor, learned and ignorant, high and low alike. He was so deeply concerned in the practical application of the principle that he even ventured in his preaching and writing into the sphere of finance, and undertook to show how love may find play in the world of business as

---

[1] *Works*, vol. vii. p. 168.   [2] *Ibid.* vol. x. p. 88.
[3] *Ibid.* vol. v. p. 163.
[4] *Ibid.* vol. vi. p. 395 ; cf. also *Christian Liberty*, pp. 279, 280.

well as everywhere else.[1] Never, indeed, has love for others, expressing itself in social service, been more persistently emphasised, and never has it been raised to a higher plane and given a more controlling place.

But to be a Christian means also, according to Luther, to live a life of purity and righteousness. In emphasising disinterested love, he did not undervalue or lose sight of the other moral virtues. To overcome sin, to grow daily in temperance and sobriety and honesty and patience and meekness, to fulfil the will of God in all its parts, is as truly the duty of the Christian man as to serve his neighbour. But it is significant that Luther brought all the moral virtues into subordination to the controlling principle of loving service. As he says in his *Christian Liberty*, 'For man does not live for himself alone in this mortal body, in order to work on its account, but also for all men on earth, nay, he lives only for others, and not for himself. For it is to this end that he brings his own body into subjection, that he may be able to serve others more sincerely and more freely. . . . Thus it is impossible that he should take his ease in this life, and not work for the good of his neighbours, since he must needs speak, act, and converse among men, just as Christ was made in the likeness of men and found in fashion as a man, and had His conversation among men. Yet a Christian has need of none of these things for justification and salvation, but in all his works he ought to entertain this view and look only to this object—that he may serve and be useful to others in all that he does, having nothing before his eyes but the necessities and the advantage of his neighbour. . . . It is the part of a Christian to take care of his own body for the very purpose that by its soundness and well-being he may be enabled to labour, and to acquire and preserve property, for the aid of those who are in want,

[1] See his striking tract on *Trade and Usury*, published in 1524 (*ibid.* vol. xxii. pp. 199 *sq.*).

that thus the stronger member may serve the weaker member, and we may be children of God, thoughtful and busy for one another, bearing one another's burdens, and so fulfilling the law of Christ. Here is the truly Christian life, here is faith really working by love, when a man applies himself with joy and love to the works of that freest servitude in which he serves others voluntarily and for nought, himself abundantly satisfied in the fulness and riches of his own faith' (p. 279). Whether it be personal purity or love for one's fellows, in any case the Christian life must be a life of unselfish devotion, lived not for one's own gain, and not to win one's own salvation, but in utter self-forgetfulness.

But as the essential quality of the Christian life is its disinterestedness, it can be truly lived according to Luther only where there is moral freedom. The principle of liberty involved in the belief that the Christian man is already saved, so far from interfering with Christian living, alone makes it possible in any genuine sense. No one can give himself in self-forgetful love to the service of his neighbour so long as he is anxious and troubled about his own fate. Only when he has gained the assurance of salvation through faith in Christ is he set free from the shadow of fear, and enabled to devote himself unreservedly to his brother's good. So long as he feels himself unsaved, he cannot do otherwise, as a serious-minded and religious man, than give thought and time to his own state. Whether he shall pass Eternity with God or with Satan must be a question of paramount concern not to the selfish man merely, but to the man of noblest religious aspirations. And hence to be set free from anxiety about one's own eternal destiny is the first step toward singleness of devotion to the service of one's fellows. In the tract on Christian liberty, Luther undertakes to show that just because the Christian man is 'the most free lord of all, and subject to none,' he is, and can be, 'the most dutiful servant of all and subject to every one.' As he says in one of his sermons, ' You must have heaven and be already saved before you can do good works.' And again, ' When you know that you have, through Christ, a good and gracious God who will forgive your sins and remember them no more, and are now a child of eternal blessedness, a lord over heaven and earth with Christ, then you have nothing more to do than to go about your business and serve your neighbour.'

It is true that liberty from anxiety about one's own eternal destiny, which Luther regards as essential to disinterested service, may be the fruit of scepticism as well as of faith. The loss of belief in immortality and consequent indifference as to the future may have the same result as the assurance of salvation. But Luther's trust in God as a loving and gracious Father meant, not only escape from fear of the future, but release as well from the fear of the present. Trusting in God, man rises superior to all the ills of life. The world in which he lives is his Father's world, and no evil can befall him. He learns to receive all that comes in confidence and peace, to accept life's blessings with joy and its trials with cheerful submission, seeing in everything the hand of a loving Father. He becomes a victor over the world, not by crushing it underfoot, but by being at home in it and unafraid as a child in his Father's house. He has acquired a new point of view and a new estimate of values. Life as well as death has lost its terrors for him, and he can give himself to Christian service with a singleness of devotion otherwise impossible.

And not simply has his faith brought him freedom, it has brought him motive power as well. He is not only set at liberty to live Christianly, he is impelled and inspired to do so. As Luther says in the Schwabacher Articles : ' Such faith, because it is not a mere fancy or darkness of heart, but a powerful, new, living notion, bears much fruit, doing good continually toward God in praise, thanksgiving, prayer, preaching, and teaching, toward the neighbour in loving, serving, helping, advising, giving, and suffering all sorts of evil even unto death.'[1] And in the Introduction to the Epistle to the Romans: 'Oh, faith is a living, busy, active, mighty thing. It is impossible that it should not always be doing good. It asks not whether good works should be done, but before one asks it does them, and is always doing them.'[2] This could not be otherwise, according to Luther, for faith which alone makes the Christian man is nothing else than trust in the forgiving love of God in Christ. Such faith is impossible to a man who has not had a consciousness of sin and has not felt himself to be under the wrath of God because of it. Unless he has felt a need of the divine forgiveness, forgiveness can mean nothing to him. It is inconceivable that he should have saving faith and be without the desire and the impulse to overcome sin. Moreover, the joy which one knows who has experienced the divine forgiveness, freeing him from death and bringing him life and peace, must make him eager to do all he can in return for God's undeserved kindness. It is God's will that he shall devote himself to his brother's good, and shall live purely and soberly and uprightly for his sake; and out of gratitude to God and through the pressure of His love revealed in Christ, and under the inspiration of Jesus' life of service he cannot do otherwise than give himself in glad surrender to God's work. Thus a present salvation by the free grace of God alone, through faith and not through works, meant to Luther, not sloth and carelessness in Christian living, but new aspiration and power. Confidence instead of fear, liberty instead of bondage, gratitude instead of the desire for reward, love for others instead of thought of self—the ethical quality of such teaching as this, and the psychological insight

[1] *Works*, vol. xxiv. p. 325. [2] *Ibid.* vol. lxiii. p. 125.

displayed in it are worthy of profound admiration. It was in his conception of the Christian life, indeed, that Luther broke most completely with Catholic tradition.

I have said that salvation according to Luther is by faith in the forgiving love of God. But such faith can exist only as God reveals Himself as a forgiving God, and this He does in Jesus Christ alone. Without a knowledge of Christ, faith and salvation are impossible. The proclamation of His gospel is an indispensable condition of salvation. This gospel Luther called the 'Word of God.' The word is, therefore, to use the traditional phrase, a means of grace, and the one and only necessary means. Wherever it is heard there may be faith and salvation, but only there. The word of God may be read in the Bible, it may be communicated orally, particularly by preaching, or it may be set forth by visible signs. These signs are the sacraments of baptism and the Lord's Supper, with which, for a time, Luther associated the sacrament of penance. By them the forgiving love of God is proclaimed in vivid and impressive fashion. They have significance only as they declare the word, and consequently are without effect unless their message is understood and believed. It is not the signs themselves that have value, but only the word of which they are the signs. Without it no man can be saved, but without the sacraments he may be, provided he hear the word in some other way, and understand and believe.[1] Strictly speaking there is thus, according to Luther, only one means of grace, the gospel of God's forgiving love in Christ, of which the sacraments are a visible expression. This does not mean that Luther thought lightly of the sacraments; on the contrary, he laid great emphasis upon them. He who has been baptized has always with him a convincing

[1] Cf. *Works*, vol. xxxi. p. 351. 'The sacraments without the word are not able to do anything, but the word without the sacraments is. If necessary one can be saved without the sacraments, but not without the word.'

testimony that God has forgiven and continues to forgive his sins, and he who partakes of the Eucharist finds in the broken body and shed blood of Christ tangible evidence of God's gracious love for the sinner.

It is in the light of his notion of the word and the sacraments that Luther's theory of the Church is to be understood. It is often said that he repudiated altogether the traditional doctrine of the Church as a means of salvation. This is true in part, but only in part. With his idea of salvation as a present reality conditioned by faith alone, the Church lost its significance as a sacramental institution dispensing saving grace. Its members, if possessed of faith, did not depend upon its ministrations for salvation, and if without faith its ministrations had no value to them. With the traditional idea of the Church as a sacramental institution went also the traditional notion of the hierarchy. The priestly offices of the clergy ceased to be necessary to the laity, and thus a fatal blow was struck at the ecclesiastical domination of the Middle Ages. Having rejected the doctrine of the Church as a saving institution, external to the laity, and composed in reality of the clergy alone, Luther at first substituted for it the theory of Wyclif and Huss, that the true Church is the totality of the predestinated, and includes all the elect, born and unborn, living and dead, believers and unbelievers, angels as well as men. But this idea represented an alien point of view, and took all meaning out of the word church, and Luther soon abandoned it for a notion more in harmony with his controlling interest and nearer to the historic use of the term. The true Church, he said, is a community of all true believers, and since believers are already saved, it may be called a community of saints— the *communio sanctorum* of the Apostles' Creed.[1] It is

---

[1] Luther always liked the word *Gemeine* (community) better than *Gemeinschaft* (communion), for the latter seemed to convey no clear meaning. See his *Larger Catechism*, part ii. art. 3.

spiritual and invisible, for it is composed only of true believers and is not identical with the Church of Rome, or with any other ecclesiastical organisation. On this account Luther's idea is often confounded with that of Wyclif and Huss, but it is in reality very different. It makes the constitutive element of the Church faith instead of election; it confines the Church to living believers, and in particular it emphasises its social character. According to Luther the Church is a real community, not a mere totality of unrelated units. He was continually reverting to this feature of it. Christianity meant, not isolation, but association and fellowship; not the mere relation of the individual soul to God, but a binding together of many men in common service of God and their neighbours, and in mutual service of each other. In his Exposition of the Ten Commandments, the Creed, and the Lord's Prayer, he says: ' I believe that there is on earth, wide as the world is, not more than one holy general Christian Church, which is nothing else than the community or assembly of the saints. . . . I believe that in this community, or Christendom, all things are common, and each one shares the goods of the others, and none calls anything his own. Therefore all the prayers and good works of the entire community help me and every believer, and support and strengthen us at every time in life and death. So every one bears his brother's burden as St. Paul teaches.'[1] For such a community as this the word Church is a proper designation, as it is not for the mere totality of segregated and unrelated units of which Wyclif and Huss thought.

But Luther differed still more radically with Wyclif and Huss in making the Church an indispensable means of salvation. In his *Larger Catechism* he says that the Holy Spirit ' has a special community in the world, which is the mother that conceives and bears every Christian by the word of God.'[2] And in his *Kirchenpostille*: 'Who-

[1] *Works*, vol. xxii. p. 20.   [2] Part ii. art. 3.

ever would find Christ must first find the Church. How should one know where Christ and His faith are, so long as one does not know where His believers are? He who would know something about Christ must not trust himself, or build bridges into heaven by his own reason, but must go to the Church, visit and make inquiry of it. The Church is not wood and stone, but the mass of people who believe in Christ. To them one must turn and must see how they believe, live and teach, who certainly have Christ with them. For outside of the Christian Church is no truth, no Christ, no salvation.'[1] This does not mean that there is no salvation outside a particular institution, but simply that God saves men only through the word, and the word is known and proclaimed only where there are Christian believers, or, in other words, only where there is the Christian Church. The Church is the agent by which alone the revelation of the forgiving love of God in Christ is made known to men. It is therefore primary, not secondary, a means of salvation, not merely a company of saved men. It is a means of salvation indeed as truly as to the Catholics, though for a very different reason—because it teaches the gospel, not because it conveys grace.

But if the word is proclaimed only where there are Christian believers, then one may know from the preaching of the word that the true Church is present. Where the word is, there the Church exists, and where the word is not, there is no Church. 'It is impossible,' Luther says, 'that there should not be Christians where the gospel goes, however few they may be, and however sinful and imperfect, just as it is impossible that there should be Christians and not mere heathen where the gospel does not go, and where human doctrine reigns, however many they may be, and however holy and fine their conduct.'[2] The word is thus a mark of the true Church, and as the sacraments are simply visible signs of the word, they, too,

[1] *Works*, vol. x. p. 162. [2] *Ibid.* vol. xxii. p. 142.

if rightly administered, that is with an understanding of their meaning as testimonies to the forgiving love of God in Christ, are marks of the Church. Where they are thus administered the true Church is certainly present, where they are lacking or wrongly used the true Church is ordinarily absent. As Luther says in his work on the Papacy: 'The signs by which one may know where the Church is are baptism, the sacrament [*i.e.* the Lord's Supper], and the gospel, and not Rome or this or that place. For where there are baptism and the gospel no one should doubt that there are saints.'[1] Thus arose the traditional Protestant formula that the notes of the true Church are the word and the sacraments. But it must be remembered that, according to Luther, the word alone is necessary, and the sacraments have significance only because they are testimonies to it.

The Church, as has been said, was an indispensable agent of salvation, without which no one can be saved. But how far Luther was from identifying the Church, which is the mother of believers, with any ecclesiastical organisation is clear enough from such a passage as the following: 'Now Christ says that not alone in the Church is there forgiveness of sins, but that where two or three are gathered together in His name they shall have the right and the liberty to proclaim and promise to each other comfort and the forgiveness of sins. . . . So that not alone in the congregation may they find forgiveness of sins, but also at home in the house, in the field, in the garden; wherever one meets another there he may find comfort and rescue. . . . When I lay my troubles before my neighbour and ask him for comfort, whatever comfort he gives and promises me, that will God in heaven ratify.'[2] It is in harmony with this that Luther lays frequent emphasis upon the fact that all Christians are priests, and have direct access to God, both for themselves and for

[1] *Works*, vol. xxvii. p. 108.   [2] *Ibid.* vol. xliv. p. 108.

others. There is no special priest class in the Church, upon which other Christians must depend, and whose intercession alone prevails with God. 'We are not only kings and the freest of all men, but also priests for ever, a dignity far higher than kingship, because by that priesthood we are worthy to appear before God, to pray for others, and to teach one another mutually the things which are of God.'[1] It is clear enough from such passages as these that it was not a hierarchical interest which led Luther to put the Church before the individual, but rather a recognition of the social nature of Christianity, of the fact that the gospel has for its end not merely the salvation of individual and separate souls, but the establishment of the kingdom of God, a kingdom within which men live together in mutual love and service.

This naturally suggests the question as to Luther's idea of the relation between the Church and the kingdom. The primitive Christians commonly thought of the kingdom of God as a future reality only, and of the Church as an agency for gathering and preparing men to enjoy its blessings. Augustine, on the other hand, identified the kingdom of God with the visible Catholic Church, and this identification remained controlling in mediæval thought. But Luther took a position different from both of these. The kingdom of God consists of the reign of God or of Christ in the hearts and lives of men. It is established by the preaching of the gospel, and exists wherever there is faith in Christ and forgiveness through Him. In its present form it is identical with the true Christian Church, but it belongs also to the heavenly world. There, too, God reigns in the hearts and lives of his children.

The kingdom of God was a favourite conception with Luther, and its conflict with the kingdom of Satan here on earth a favourite theme.[2] In it Christ rules, and the Christian believer, put by his faith within the kingdom of

[1] *Christian Liberty*, p. 268.   [2] Cf. *e.g. Works*, vol. viii. p. 218.

his Lord, reigns with Him, and becomes a victor over all opposing powers. 'As regards kingship, every Christian is by faith so exalted above all things that in spiritual power he is completely lord of all, so that nothing whatever can do him any hurt. Yea, all things are subject to him and are compelled to be subservient to his salvation.' 'Who then can comprehend the loftiness of that Christian dignity which by its royal power rules over all things, even over death, life, and sin ?'[1] But the victory is not for the Christian's sake alone. As always, Luther keeps the idea of serving and sharing to the front. 'Who then can comprehend the riches and the glory of the Christian life ? It can do all things, has all things, and is in want of nothing ; is lord over sin, death, and hell, and at the same time is obedient and useful servant of all. But, alas, it is at this day unknown throughout the world. It is neither preached nor sought after, so that we are quite ignorant about our own name, why we are and are called Christians. We are certainly called so from Christ, who is not absent, but dwells among us, provided that is we believe in Him, and are reciprocally and mutually one the Christ of the other, doing to our neighbours as Christ does to us.'[2]

II. *The Old in Luther's Thought*

I have been dealing hitherto with the new in Luther's religious thought, with those ideas which were at variance with traditional theory, and to which Protestant theology owed its inception and separate existence. But there was much in which he agreed with his Catholic contemporaries, and which he took over from the old system almost, or quite, unchanged. This was not due, as is often said, to his conservatism, or to his indifference in matters which did not directly affect his central doctrine of salvation.

[1] *Christian Liberty*, p. 267 *sq.*   [2] *Ibid.* p. 283.

He retained the old because it was congenial to him—no small part of it because his experience made it necessary to him. Instead of regarding it as an inconsistency in his system—a mere traditional excrescence upon his thought—we must recognise it as of the very essence of the matter. Unless we do this we shall fail to understand Luther himself, and the development of Protestant thought which followed.

Fundamental in all his thinking was the doctrine of the depravity and helplessness of the natural man. This was not a mere accidental survival of the traditional way of looking at things, it was confirmed by his own experience, and remained permanently an essential part of his system. The peace which he finally attained in the monastery at Erfurt was not the result of a recognition of the moral ability and independence of man. On the contrary, he reached it only when he became convinced of the utter vanity of human effort, and renounced all merit whatsoever. It was the fruit, not of a new estimate of the nature of man, in line with the modern spirit, but of the old estimate made more extreme, and carried out in a more thoroughgoing fashion than ever. The old, in spite of its sombre interpretation of man's character, had left at least some place for human merit. Luther gave it no place whatever; everything he put into God's hands. Nothing of good, either in the unbeliever or in the Christian, is of himself, all is of God alone. Luther's remarkable work on the *Bondage of the Will* (*De Servo Arbitrio*) was not an exceptional utterance, due only to the heat of controversy. On the contrary, it represented his controlling thought, and to the end of his life he regarded it as his best, as it was certainly his most careful and studied, production. To throw any doubt on human depravity, to lighten in any way the picture of human guilt, and to suggest the existence of any virtue or merit in man—this was to belittle divine grace, and was the worst and most dangerous of errors. Luther regarded it indeed as the root of all the heretical opinions and vicious practices of his Catholic contemporaries. It is evident that at this point he was totally out of sympathy with the tendencies of the dawning modern age. Compared with Erasmus and with the humanists in general, he was a reactionary, and the effect of his teaching could only be to bind the traditional supernaturalism more firmly than ever upon the minds of men. Its effect was also to confirm, and in many cases, to rehabilitate the greater part of the historic system of theology.

One of the notable elements in Luther's religious thought was his conception of God as a loving Father, who graciously and freely forgives sin, and saves men without any merit on their part. But this did not mean that he broke away from the idea of God as a stern and angry Judge—the avenger of sin who will let no guilty man escape. On the contrary, it was his vivid sense of God's wrath that drove him to despair, and God's wrath constituted, not simply the precondition, but the permanent background of his doctrine of divine forgiveness. It is only in Christ, and only to the Christian believer, that God discloses himself as a gracious Father; outside of Christ there is only wrath and vengeance. The explanation Luther found in the atoning work of Christ. It is true that in his impatience with the Catholic theory of penance, and with the interpretation of Christ's work in its light, he used words on one occasion which have been taken to mean the rejection of the doctrine of the atonement. 'Therefore this word satisfaction ought to be used no longer in our churches and theology, but should be commended to the judges and lawyers, to whom it belongs, and from whom it was taken by the Papists.'[1] But quite apart from the isolated character of this utterance, to interpret it thus is to misunderstand Luther. The doctrine of the atonement

[1] *Works*, vol. xi. p. 280.

was absolutely fundamental with him. That God was gracious to the Christian and forgave his sins freely was due to the fact that Christ had suffered the penalty of human sin, and had moreover lived a life of perfect obedience, so that His merit could be imputed to the believer. 'In the first place, do not doubt that you have a gracious God and Father who has forgiven all your sins, and saved you in baptism. In the second place, know, in addition, that all this has happened not for nothing, or without the satisfaction of His righteousness. For there is no room for mercy and grace to work over us and in us, or to help us to eternal blessings, and to salvation, unless enough has been done to satisfy righteousness perfectly; as Christ says: "Not one jot or tittle of the law shall pass away."'[1] The traditional scheme of redemption thus retained its place in Luther's thinking, and the Anselmic theory of the atonement, modified and supplemented in ways that need not be further indicated here, acquired a prominence hitherto unknown. Had Luther's experience been of another type—the fruit of a more modern estimate of man—he might have repudiated altogether the mediæval notion of God as an avenger of sin, and with it the doctrine of the atoning work of Christ. As it was, only that doctrine made it possible for him to justify his faith in the forgiving love of God, and hence it became more central and important then ever.

With the doctrine of the atonement is connected the dogma of the Deity of Christ. Unless He possesses the divine nature, the work which He does has finite value only, and cannot avail to atone for human sin. And so the Deity of Christ also constituted an essential element in Luther's faith. It was retained, not out of mere conservatism, or respect for the traditional system, but because it was necessary to his fundamental belief in God's forgiving love. An added emphasis was given to the

[1] *Works*, vol. vii. p. 175.

Deity of Christ by the fact that only in Him is God apprehended as a gracious Father. Were it not for His revelation God would be known only as a God of wrath. It is significant that the contrast which Luther drew between the Christian God and the God of natural theology was not the traditional contrast between a personal father and the abstract absolute, but between a gracious and an angry God. The latter alone is known apart from Christ, and as the former is the object of the Christian's faith, the Deity of Christ is made more vitally essential than ever.

The belief in the Deity of Christ is the central element in the historic doctrine of the Trinity; and so again it is no accident and no mere sign of conservatism that Luther retained that doctrine. It is true that in his insistence upon the fact that all knowledge of God outside of Christ is 'empty fancy and mere idolatry,' he was led at times to oppose all speculation about the divine nature. It is therefore not surprising that all Trinitarian formulæ are entirely wanting in his *Little Catechism*, and that on more than one occasion he criticised the doctrine of the Trinity, declaring that 'the words Trinity and Unity are mathematical words,' [1] and that ' the expression Trinity is not in the Scriptures, and sounds cold, and we shall do much better to speak of God, and not of Trinity.' [2]

But, on the other hand, although his interest, like that of Athanasius himself, was always more in the Deity of Christ than in the distinction of persons within the Godhead, he yet commonly emphasised the doctrine of the Trinity, and gave it a prominent place in his preaching and writing.[3] Moreover the doctrine was not merely a traditional form of words to him. He knew how to make it practically

---

[1] *Works*, vol. iv. p. 168.
[2] *Ibid*. vol. xii. p. 378. Cf. vol. vi. p. 230 *sq*.
[3] Cf. *e.g. ibid*. vol. ix.

useful, and to give it a vital place in the experience of the Christian.[1]

Christ's Deity meant to Luther, as to the Catholic theologians, the possession of a dual nature, the divine and the human. He thought in terms of the traditional ontology, and drew the same distinction between the nature of God and the nature of man that the Fathers and schoolmen had drawn. As a consequence, though in his interest in Christ's redemptive work he always laid emphasis rather upon the unity than upon the distinction of His natures, he yet found the historic Christological formulæ entirely congenial, and his faith expressed itself naturally through them. It is therefore not surprising that the Nicene and Athanasian Creeds, as well as the Apostles', which was interpreted as a Trinitarian formula, were accepted by him and handed down to his followers as expressions of the truth which every Christian must accept. In the dogmas of the Trinity and the Person of Christ he found his gospel of the forgiving love of God confirmed and guaranteed. Where they are believed and properly interpreted there exists ample assurance that God is a gracious Father through Jesus Christ; where they are doubted or denied all ground of assurance is gone. He thus read into them a significance which they had not before possessed, and gave them a reality and vitality lacking since the days that gave them birth. During the Middle Ages they had been largely matter of tradition. Now they became again in Luther's hands expressions of practical Christian faith. It may thus be fairly said, with Harnack, that they were not simply preserved, but rehabilitated.

While Luther denied that salvation depends in any way upon a man's own efforts, and so destroyed the traditional

[1] Not infrequently Luther indulged in speculations as abstract and as disconnected with the practical religious life as those of any schoolman. But all this must be recognised as secondary not primary with him.

incentive to virtue, his conception of faith, as has already been said, was such as to guarantee the Christ-like character of the believer's life. But unfortunately he was not always true to his own convictions in this matter. Sure as he was that the Christian believer cannot do otherwise than live as Christ would have him live, the influence of Catholic tradition was so strong, and his distrust of men so ingrained, that it proved impossible for him to maintain his belief that faith alone is sufficient for holiness, and he was obliged to add the sanctifying influence of the Holy Spirit. In spite of what he says about the ethical power of faith, he yet frequently declares that even the Christian man is weak and frail, and cannot live as he ought without the presence and power of the Spirit.[1] This mystical idea was evidently due largely to the influence of the Apostle Paul. But while Paul made the presence of the Spirit, transforming man from a corrupt to a holy being, the ground of salvation, Luther conceived salvation in an entirely different way, in such a way as to make the Spirit quite unnecessary. The two points of view were wholly distinct, and only ambiguity and inconsistency resulted from their combination.

Intimately bound up with the Pauline idea of the presence of the Spirit was the mystical conception of faith as uniting the believer to Christ in such a way that he ceases to be himself, and becomes one person with Christ.[2] This idea also, inconsistent as it was with his controlling way of looking at things, and with his general view of faith, Luther took over from Paul. His doctrine of salvation was not in the least mystical; it moved wholly in the sphere of personal relationships. The adoption of mystical conceptions and forms of speech, whether due to the influence of Paul or of Catholic tradition, worked

[1] Cf. *e.g. Works*, vol. iv. p. 68 *sq.*; and the *Disputatio de justificatione et de muliere peccatrice*, § 8 (in Drews's *Disputationen Dr. Martin Luthers*, p. 50).
[2] Cf. *Christian Liberty*, p. 264.

only confusion, and prevented his gospel from being fully understood and appreciated by those who came after him.

Similar difficulty arose in connection with the sacraments. Consistently with his notion of salvation by faith in the forgiving love of God in Christ, Luther held that the sacraments are nothing else than signs. They have no efficacy in themselves. Only as the word is believed to which they bear testimony have they any value or influence. But he was led in part by the comforting nature of the rite, as a pledge of God's forgiving love received at the very beginning of life, and constituting an assurance of His favour through all the years to come, in part by hostility to the radicals of the day, who commonly rejected it, to retain the time-honoured practice of infant baptism. The consequence was a serious inconsistency in his sacramental theory. Believing that a sacrament could have efficacy only where there was faith in its message, he was led to adopt the curious notion that faith is directly bestowed upon the infant in the act of baptism. Baptism thus became a channel of faith as it had been to the Catholics a channel of grace. It is not surprising in view of this interpretation of infant baptism that Luther should have accepted the traditional doctrine of baptismal regeneration. The whole notion of regeneration is out of line with his idea of salvation, and represents another point of view altogether. Where salvation means transformation of man's nature, as it meant to Paul and to the Catholics in general, the idea of regeneration is, of course, entirely in place. But where it means simply the divine forgiveness, to talk about regeneration is to introduce an alien notion which is bound to work confusion. Luther's retention of the idea was due in part to the necessity of giving some significance to the rite of infant baptism, in part to the influence of theological tradition, in still greater part to his inherent distrust of human nature, and his conviction that it needed radical transformation by supernatural power. It was thus of a piece with his emphasis upon other parts of the traditional system, and had ultimately the same root. The entrance of the doctrine into Reformation theology worked permanent confusion, and did perhaps more than anything else to prevent his followers from understanding his gospel, and making it actually controlling in Protestant thought.

Equally disturbing in its influence upon Luther's thought was his belief in the real presence of the body and blood of Christ in the Eucharist. It was a strange belief for one who held that the sacraments were nothing but signs, but Luther's acceptance of it is easy to explain. His tremendous interest in the gospel of God's forgiving love in Christ led him to seize eagerly upon the doctrine of the real presence. If the participant finds the body and blood of Christ in the Eucharist, he has an irrefragable proof of Christ's death for the sinner, and hence of the truth of the gospel. To have denied the real presence would have been to lose a testimony whose convincing power could not be overestimated. It was therefore natural enough that he should retain the traditional belief, and interpret Christ's words: 'This is my body,' in a literal sense. The fact that the symbolic view of the Eucharist was accepted and emphasised at an early day by various leaders of the radical wing of the Protestant movement served only to confirm him in his own view, and to make him more rigidly insistent upon it.

The belief in the real presence is not necessarily inconsistent with the notion that the Sacrament is a sign or pledge; the presence may be simply for the sake of making the testimony more sure. But, of course, the natural tendency of it was to promote the idea that in partaking of the Lord's Supper one feeds upon the body and blood of Christ, and so to give the sacraments another significance altogether. To this tendency Luther not infrequently yielded, speaking of the Eucharist in traditional fashion as the 'Medicine of immortality,' and as food for the spiritual nature of the redeemed man.[1] This is genuinely Catholic, like the idea of baptismal regeneration. It is true that Luther's doctrine of salvation found consistent application when he rejected the notion of the Eucharist as a sacrifice and good work, and with it the dogma of transubstantiation. He did much at this point to liberate Christians from the domination of Church and hierarchy. But the other element in the traditional view of the Eucharist, the recognition of it as a realistic vehicle of supernatural grace, transforming human nature and making it immortal, inconsistent as it was with his controlling thought, found as massive expression in his doctrine as in the theory of transubstantiation. The result was again to obscure his gospel and limit its influence.

Another inconsistency in Luther's thought was his notion of Biblical authority. The basis of his Christian faith was not the authority of the Scriptures. He needed no external guarantee whatever. He believed the revelation of God's forgiving love in Christ primarily, not because he found it in the Bible, but because his own experience testified to its truth.[2] But in controversy with his Catholic opponents the need of some external authority to set over against ecclesiastical tradition and enactment made itself vividly felt. It was natural under these circumstances that he should turn to the Scriptures, whose character as a divinely inspired and infallible book had been everywhere recognised since the second century, and to which particularly in his day it had become common to appeal when any one had fault to find with current religious opinions and practices. Luther was only following the example of others in appealing at the famous Leipsic colloquy of 1519 from the Church to the Scriptures.

[1] Cf. *Works*, vol. xxx. p. 93 *sq.*
[2] Cf. *ibid.* vol. xxviii. p. 340; vol. xlvii. p. 353.

But his attitude toward the Bible, first clearly announced at that time and maintained permanently, was not the mere result of controversial necessity. It was the controversy which first brought him to a clear consciousness of the contrast between Biblical and ecclesiastical teaching, but quite independently of the respect in which the Scriptures were held by others, their divine character had vindicated itself in his own experience, and when an objective authority was needed it was to them that he instinctively turned. It was in his study of the Bible, particularly of the epistles of Paul, that he discovered the gospel of God's forgiving love in Christ, and more and more as time passed he found it taught everywhere, in Old Testament as well as New. It was this gospel that gave the Scriptures their value; apart from it they had no real worth. It thus became a criterion by which to test the various parts of the Bible. Some books, he recognised, gave clearer and more faithful expression to it than others, and they were to be most highly prized and most diligently read. The New Testament, taken as a whole, is superior to the Old, and the Gospel of John, certain epistles of Paul, and 1 Peter, are superior to the rest of the New Testament. In comparison with them such a book as James is only an epistle of straw, and the Apocalypse is altogether worthless.[1]

Luther's distinction between the Bible and the word of God gave him an uncommon independence and freedom in dealing with the Scriptures. He did not hesitate to question the authenticity of a Biblical book, to pronounce one more trustworthy than another, and to recognise mistakes and inaccuracies in both Testaments.[2] The primary value of the Bible lay in the fact that it was a means of grace—a revelation of the gospel, and hence such defects in it did not disturb him. Nor did they prevent

---

[1] *Works*, vol. lxiii. pp. 115, 170.
[2] Cf. *ibid.* vol. viii. p. 23; vol. xlvi. p. 174.

him from calling it in traditional fashion the 'word of God.' Commonly he meant by that phrase only the gospel of God's forgiving love in Christ, but finding this gospel, as he believed, set forth in most parts of the Scriptures, and finding his religious life and that of his associates fed upon them more and more abundantly, it was easy for him to fall into the common custom, and to give the name 'word of God' to the whole. This he frequently did without taking pains to distinguish between the gospel and the Scriptures in which it was found. Among his followers the distinction was almost wholly lost, and the consequence was that his insistence upon the word of God as the primary means of grace, and as absolutely necessary to faith and salvation, resulted in the elevation of the Bible to a place which it had never before had, and gave it a religious influence hitherto unknown.

Moreover, Luther's appeal to its authority against that of the Church gave it a new significance in the ethical and theological realm, which was emphasised still more when controversy with Protestant radicals succeeded the original controversy with the Catholics. Its authority was no mere form of words; on the contrary, it was taken very seriously by Luther himself as well as by his followers. He rejected wholly the allegorical method of exegesis, and insisted upon a literal interpretation of the text, and Biblical teaching increasingly crowded out the experience of God's forgiving love in Christ as the ground of faith and the source of Christian doctrine. The result was a growing failure on his part to bring his religious thinking under the dominance of one great controlling principle, and therefore increasing inconsistency and confusion.

Luther's controversy with Protestant radicals of various types, and particularly with the Swiss reformer, Zwingli, ultimately drove him even further in his emphasis on external authority in matters of doctrine. In his

Bekenntniss vom Abendmahl Christi of 1528, he says, 'I confess for myself that I regard Zwingli as no Christian, with all his doctrine, for he holds and teaches no article of the Christian faith rightly.'[1] And in the Schwabacher Articles of 1529, referring to the true Church, he says: 'Such church is nothing else than the believers in Christ who believe the above stated articles' (Article XII.). As the Articles referred to are not mere expressions of the gospel of God's forgiving love in Christ, but comprise many other matters quite unrelated thereto, Luther's declaration meant a complete departure from his principle that faith in the Gospel is the whole of salvation, and involved a repudiation of his own doctrine of Christian liberty. In his work, *Dass eine christliche Versammlung oder eine Gemeinde Recht und Macht habe alle Lehre zu urtheilen*, etc., he had declared that every Christian has a right to test every doctrine for himself, and to believe in all matters as his experience of God's forgiving love suggests.[2] But this broad platform, consistent as it was with his own fundamental principles, he soon abandoned, and maintained thenceforth a doctrinal position as narrow in effect as that of the Catholics themselves.

Moreover he carried matters so far as even to insist that force should be used by the civil government in order to maintain sound teaching in the churches. All preachers who opposed the Reformation were to be displaced by the civil government, and only supporters of it accorded freedom of speech. 'Not that one should kill the preachers,' he says, ' this is unnecessary. But they should be forbidden to do anything apart from and against the gospel, and should be prevented from doing it by force.'[3] 'If any teach against a public article of faith which is clearly founded upon the Scriptures, and is believed by all Christendom . . . for instance if any one teach that

---

[1] *Works*, vol. xxx. p. 225. [2] *Ibid.* vol. xxii. pp. 146 *sq.*
[3] *Ibid.* vol. xxii. p. 49.

Christ is not God, but a mere man, and like any other prophet, as the Turks and the Anabaptists hold, such a person is not to be tolerated, but is to be punished for profanity, for he is not merely a heretic, but an open blasphemer.'[1] Other errors which Luther would see suppressed by the civil authorities were the denial of Jesus' death for our sins, of the resurrection of the dead, and of heaven and hell. This means as extreme intolerance as under Catholicism. The difference is that in this case, not the Church, but the civil government is to decide what is orthodox and what heretical. In the work just quoted Luther says that if in any town Catholics and Lutherans are teaching diverse doctrines and attacking each other, the municipal government is to interfere, to take the matter under consideration, and to stop the mouths of those who are not preaching in accordance with the Scriptures. This involves a connection between Church and State, and a subjection of the former to the latter not recognised under Catholicism. The influence upon the religious life of Germany, ever since the Reformation, has been very marked, but of that I cannot speak here. It is to be noticed that according to Luther, while the determination of the teaching to be tolerated is to be left to the civil authorities, their decision must be governed by the Bible. Not what they may happen to like, but only what agrees with the Scriptures is to be permitted. It is thus the principle of Biblical as over against ecclesiastical authority which he is still insisting on. But even so tradition is given a large place. Not every interpretation of the Bible is to be approved. It is assumed that there exists among Christians a consensus of opinion as to the true teaching of the Scriptures, and with this the individual must agree.[2] Here belong, for example, the three ecumenical creeds, whose acceptance

[1] *Works*, vol. xxxix. p. 250.
[2] Cf. *ibid.* vol. liv. p. 288; vol. lv. pp. 74 *sq.*

is required of every Christian. The principle of Biblical authority as used by Luther was thus after all not so completely opposed to the principle of ecclesiastical authority as it might seem. Corporate rather than individual opinion was still made supreme.

It should be noticed still further that Luther's insistence upon faith as distinguished from works gave to orthodox belief a much more prominent and important place in Protestantism than in Catholicism. Luther himself never identified saving faith and orthodox theology. The latter was rather, like Christian conduct, a necessary fruit of the former. But the distinction between the two was not always observed by his followers, and it was inevitable that as the word of God tended more and more generally to be identified with the Bible, faith in it should be identified with the acceptance of the teachings of the Scriptures. The result was that orthodoxy increasingly overshadowed everything else, and instead of enjoying greater freedom in religious thought, Protestants were more completely in bondage than their fathers had been.

It is clear that Luther was far from being a modern man in his interests and sympathies. With all his emphasis on the liberty of the Christian man, he failed to set him completely free. The old ecclesiastical fetters were broken, but the theological bondage of the past still continued, and it remained for a much later period to complete the work he had only begun.

CHAPTER III

HULDREICH ZWINGLI

To the great Swiss reformer, Zwingli, is due a type of Protestant thought very different from Luther's. His figure has been unduly obscured by the fame of his younger contemporary, Calvin. His place in the history of thought is really more important than Calvin's, for he was an originator where the latter was only a follower. At an early day he came under the influence of humanism, and gave himself with enthusiasm to the pursuit of the new learning. He became a parish priest at the age of twenty-two, but a year after Luther found his way into the monastery at Erfurt. His motive in entering the priesthood was not at all like that which drove Luther into monasticism. An uncle and other relatives were clergymen, and he was early destined by his parents for the same profession. He had himself no objection to it, for he saw in it, as many of his contemporaries did, opportunity and leisure to carry on his classical studies and, through the instruction of the young, to spread the influence of humanistic principles. Of such a religious crisis as Luther passed through he knew nothing. Entered upon his parish work at Glarus, he soon found his interest enlisted in the religious and moral welfare of his flock, and in spite of his scholarly pursuits, he gave himself with uncommon zeal and devotion to his pastoral labours. In 1516 he removed to Einsiedeln, where there was a famous shrine to which pilgrims resorted in large numbers. There he found religious conditions even worse than at Glarus, and he became aroused to the need of a reformation in the country at large. He belonged to the humanistic circle of which Erasmus was the great ornament, and it was natural that he should share the ideals of the more serious and earnest-minded humanists, and should make their programme of reform his own. He differed from most of them, however, in two respects. They were, as a rule, intellectual aristocrats, and looked down upon the uneducated multitude; he had gained in his parish work a profound interest in the common people. They were cosmopolitan in their sympathies, and delighted in calling themselves citizens of the world; he was a devoted patriot, not the least of whose concerns was the welfare of his native land. Both of these traits fitted him to understand Luther.

He became active in the cause of reform, and entered upon a campaign against current religious abuses before he knew anything of the older reformer. He remained for some years a faithful son of the Church, and continued to enjoy a papal pension, as many of his fellow humanists were doing, but he found himself as time passed more and more critical of the existing ecclesiastical system, and in Zurich, where he became pastor of the principal church in 1519, he preached such doctrines, and advocated such practical innovations as to bring himself into open conflict with the Roman authorities. The result was a permanent break with the Catholic Church, not only for himself, but for the municipal government as well, and the establishment in the city of a new religious régime. The example of Zurich was speedily followed by other cities, and the Reformation movement was soon making rapid strides throughout the country.

Before he left Einsiedeln, Zwingli had heard of Luther, and had begun to read his writings. As a consequence his religious views underwent a change. He had long shared the common humanistic recognition of the supreme authority of the Bible, and had appealed to it in support of his reforming efforts. He had learned to emphasise, as many humanists were doing, salvation by the grace of God alone, and the futility of pinning one's faith to the elaborate penitential discipline which had grown up during the Middle Ages. He had read Huss on the Church, and had been led to radical views upon that important subject. When Luther's teaching came to his notice he was fully prepared for it. It was a more definite and complete formulation of ideas which he himself already held, and at the same time in its over-mastering emphasis upon salvation by grace alone, through faith, and not through works, it supplied an organising and dominating principle hitherto lacking. He was speedily convinced of the Biblical character of Luther's teachings, and of their perfect adaptation to the situation which he was facing. The crying need was liberation from dependence upon human authority as represented in the great mass of traditional religious practices. Luther's gospel met the need in the completest and most thoroughgoing fashion. Thenceforth it was Zwingli's own, and upon its basis he instituted a campaign far more radical than he had hitherto intended.

It is not surprising under the circumstances that Zwingli should deny, as he frequently did, his dependence upon Luther, and should insist that he had gained his principles for himself. He was independent in no small degree, and yet he certainly felt the influence of the Wittenberg reformer, and accepted his gospel without reserve. At the famous Zurich disputation of 1523, which resulted in the open break with the Catholic Church, that gospel found clear and unequivocal expression, and the growth of the new movement in Switzerland meant the spread of Luther's principles. Thus both reformers taught the depravity of the natural man and his inability to save himself; the vanity of all human effort and the impossibility of meritorious works on man's part; the gospel of God's forgiving love in Christ, and of present salvation through His free grace, by faith and not by works; the sole activity of God in the work of salvation and the predestination of some to life and others to death; the liberty of the Christian man and his assurance of salvation; the universal priesthood of believers and the true Church a community of saints. They also maintained much of the traditional system of theology, including the doctrines of the person and work of Christ and the Trinity. They were one in rejecting the authority of the Roman Church and papacy, the hierarchical principles of Catholicism, the doctrines of the mass and of purgatory, five of the seven sacraments, including the whole penitential system, the ascetic interpretation of the Christian life, monasticism and the celibacy of the clergy, and the great mass of ecclesiastical rites and ceremonies, feasts, fasts, pilgrimages, and the like. They introduced radical changes in traditional forms of worship, Zwingli going much further at this point than Luther, and they gave the civil government a larger measure of control in ecclesiastical affairs than it had hitherto enjoyed. There was thus a considerable area of agreement between the two reformers, and their common thought was inherited by all the Protestant churches.

But there were also divergences. Zwingli's training and experience had been very unlike Luther's, and it was inevitable that the gospel which he learned from him should occupy a different place in his thinking, and should be interpreted in other ways. Under the circumstances it is surprising that the two men differed as little as they did. But differences there were, and some of them are historically important, for they represent permanent differences between the Lutheran and Reformed wings of Protestantism.

Zwingli's departures from Luther had a common root

and were all of a piece. Humanist as he was, he had a wider horizon than the Wittenberg reformer, and was unable to look at matters so exclusively in the light of the work of Jesus Christ. Religion he defined as the worship of God and the doing of His will.[1] He recognised that many besides Christians, and quite independently of the Christian revelation, had been religious in this sense, for instance Hercules, Theseus, and Socrates, and he maintained that they were saved as truly as Christian believers.[2] Under Luther's influence he frequently asserted that salvation was through Christ alone, but the broader view was truer to his own way of thinking, and was never abandoned by him. God, he taught, has revealed Himself, not only through Christ, but in many other ways. From the beginning He has been making His will known to men, and has had His true worshippers and obedient children.

Christianity is God's supreme revelation, and is therefore the highest and best of all religions. This revelation is set forth in the Bible, which is the word of God, not because it contains the gospel of God's forgiving love in Christ, but because it reveals God's will. From it one can learn as from no other source what God would have men believe and do. It is not a means of grace in Luther's sense, but a guide for Christian faith and life. His distinction between the gospel and the Bible as a whole is lost sight of, and the latter is treated as equally authoritative in all its parts.

The work of Christ consisted chiefly in the revelation which He brought of the divine will. Because of it He is the Saviour of men. The contrast between God's disclosure of Himself in Jesus Christ and His general activity as Ruler and Governor of the world largely disappears. The same is true of the contrast between law and gospel, of which Luther made so much. The gospel is

[1] *Works*, vol. iii. p. 175 *sq*.   [2] Cf. *ibid*. vol. iv. p. 65.

God's total revelation and includes the law. The two are in principle one. 'The gospel is itself a new law.'[1] Both of them are declarations of God's will, and the one supplements and perfects the other. The ceremonial law is done away by Christ, but not the moral law, which is written upon the hearts of men as well as upon the tables of stone. Christian liberty means release, not from all law, but only from subjection to human enactments in religious affairs, that is from the enactments of the Church. The Christian is still bound to obey God, but not man.

Of a piece with his wider view of Christianity was Zwingli's conception of faith. Faith is not only trust in God's forgiving love in Christ, but also the acceptance of His truth and confidence in His providential love revealed in all His works. Much is made of the goodness of God which controls all His activities, and manifests itself, not simply in the salvation of sinners, but in the entire government of the world. Heathen have believed in God as well as Christians, though they have known nothing about Christ, and the faith which the Christian has in God is of the same general nature, though more intelligent and better grounded.

It is consonant with this general way of looking at things that Zwingli laid less stress than Luther upon the word and the sacraments as means of grace. While ordinarily faith and salvation follow the preaching of the gospel, they may be independent of it; and still less are the sacraments indispensable. For some time Zwingli repudiated altogether the idea that the latter are means of grace, and asserted that they constitute only pledges which the Christian gives of his faith and discipleship.[2] Later, however, he recognised that they might have value as testimonies to God's forgiving love,[3] but he never made as much of this aspect of them as Luther did, and so it was easy for him to give up altogether the traditional notion

[1] *Works*, vol. i. p. 211. [2] Cf. *ibid.* vol. iii. p. 231. [3] Cf. *e.g. ibid.* vol. iv. p. 57.

of the real presence in the Eucharist, and to adopt the symbolical interpretation of the rite first suggested to him by the writings of Erasmus.[1] The current idea seemed to carry with it the crass superstitions of the Catholic faith in regard to the nature of salvation, and he denounced it with increasing vigour. The result was a serious controversy with Luther and a permanent and disastrous division in the ranks of Protestantism. It may seem that the controversy concerned only a minor matter, and that the difference between the two reformers was of no such importance as to justify a break, but in reality the two men, as Luther himself clearly recognised, were of an altogether different spirit, and the disagreement touching the Eucharist was only the symptom of a far deeper disagreement concerning the nature of Christianity and the way of salvation. Zwingli's humanistic sympathies were alien to Luther, and his wider interpretation of the gospel was contradictory of all he held most dear. From Zwingli's point of view the difference was of relatively little importance. It was easy for him to be tolerant in his treatment of Luther. But for Luther to tolerate Zwingli would have been to betray the very heart of his gospel.

Consistent with his general attitude was Zwingli's rehabilitation of natural theology which Luther's teaching had threatened with destruction. He had no such contempt for the natural reason as Luther had. On the contrary, he treated it with the greatest respect and accorded it a large place in the discovery of religious truth. The Wittenberg reformer regarded all knowledge of God apart from Christ as vain and worthless. Zwingli laid great emphasis upon it, declaring that the ' knowledge of God in His own nature precedes the knowledge of Christ.' [2] Accordingly, we find him elaborating a philosophical

---

[1] See letter of Melanchthon to Aquila in *Corpus Reformatorum*, vol. iv. col. 970.   [2] *Works*, vol. iii. p. 180.

theory of God on a large scale. He thought of the Deity in much more abstract terms than Luther. God was less a personal Father than the Creator and Ruler of the world, and the attributes which Zwingli ascribed to Him were those of traditional theology, omnipotence and omniscience occupying a chief place.[1] This is particularly manifest in connection with his doctrine of predestination, which finds its most elaborate and systematic expression in his *De Providentia Dei*. His acceptance of the doctrine was due primarily to his desire to undermine all dependence upon human merit in connection with salvation, but having accepted it, he worked over his doctrine of God in its light, and reached a metaphysical determinism of the most extreme type, which became controlling in all his theological teaching. Luther went as far as he in his assertion of the inability of man and the absolute control of God, but he did not make God's omnipotence the centre of his system as Zwingli did. According to the latter it belongs to the nature of God to be eternally active. In reality he is the only active Being in the universe. He is not merely the first cause, but the only cause.[2] All activity is His activity; evil as well as good is His work.[3] If this be not admitted His power is limited, and He is made less than infinite. He is above all law, and consequently, though all the actions of men are His, He cannot do wrong. What is sin to them who are under law is no sin to Him.[4] Not only the deeds of all men, but their destinies as well are determined by God. He predestines some to eternal life and others to eternal death, that He may display His mercy in the case of the former, and His justice in the case of the latter.[5] Zwingli's doctrine of predestination was more than a mere matter of abstract speculation. It acquired practical importance by being

---

[1] 'We call God Father,' Zwingli says, 'because He can do what He pleases with us'
[2] *Works*, vol. iv. p. 96.
[3] *Ibid.* pp. 108, 112   [4] *Ibid.* p. 112.   [5] *Ibid.* p. 115.

given a fundamental place in his interpretation of the conditions of salvation. The ground of salvation is not faith or anything else in man, but the divine election.[1] 'The elect are children of God,' he says, ' even before they believe.' [2] 'Election precedes faith, and so it comes to pass that those who are elect, and do not come to a knowledge of the faith, as *e.g.* children, nevertheless attain eternal blessedness, for it is election which makes blessed.' [3] This gives justification and consistency to his contention that even heathen who have never heard of Christ may be among the number of the saved; they may be subjects of election even though they do not attain to Christian faith. Thus his philosophical theory of divine omnipotence fell in with his humanistic tendency to broaden the range of God's saving activity and to make Him independent of the ordinary means of grace. It was in election that Zwingli found the ground of assurance, which he was one with Luther in emphasising as absolutely essential to Christian liberty, and so to genuinely Christian living. The Christian is assured of salvation, not because he believes in the forgiving love of God revealed in Christ, but because he is conscious of his election. His faith is a sure sign of election; for faith is given only to the predestinated.[4] But faith is an uncertain and variable thing, and only the eternal and unchanging predestination of God is an adequate basis of assurance.

It was in accordance with his emphasis upon predestination that Zwingli supplemented his earlier notion of the Church as a community of saints with Wyclif's idea of it as the *numerus electorum*, or totality of the elect.[5] As such it includes heathen as well as Christians, unbelievers as well as believers, infants as well as adults, and the dead

---

[1] Cf. *Works*, vol. vi. part i. p. 340; part ii. p. 106.
[2] *Ibid.* vol. iii. p. 426.
[3] *Ibid.* vol. iv. p. 123. Zwingli taught the salvation of all infants dying in infancy; cf. p. 125 *sq.*
[4] *Ibid.* vol. iv. p. 122; vol. vi. part ii. p. 156.
[5] Cf. *ibid.* vol. iv. p. 8.

as well as the living. Between this invisible company and the visible church made up of professing Christians, there is no necessary connection.[1] The tendency of the notion was thus to take all real significance out of the latter, and to give it a much less important place than Luther assigned to it. At this point, as at many others, Zwingli was influenced by hostility to the Anabaptists, who were strong in Switzerland, and whose radical views had sufficient kinship with Zwingli's teaching to make him particularly sensitive in his attitude toward them.

It is evident that though Zwingli accepted the gospel of Luther, and became one of the fathers of Protestantism, the differences between him and the Wittenberg reformer were many and far reaching. Though he came to his death at an early day (1531), and though the influence of other men soon became prominent among the Protestants of Western Europe, his thinking gave permanent direction to their theology. Instead of giving the controlling place in Christian thought to a personal religious experience— the consciousness of divine forgiveness—he gave it to a theoretical doctrine—the absolute and unconditioned will of God. Instead of viewing the Christian life as the free and spontaneous expression of gratitude to God, he conceived it as obedience to the divine will revealed in the Scriptures. Instead of finding the significance of the Bible in the proclamation of the gospel of God's forgiving love in Christ, he found it in its revelation of the divine will, and made it an authoritative code for the government of Christian life and thought, rather than a means of grace. In all these matters the reformed wing of Protestantism followed him rather than Luther; in all of them the distinctive character of its theology is clearly revealed. From the beginning it has been more external, objective, and legalistic, and in so far more Catholic than Lutheran theology.

[1] Cf. *Works*, vol. iv. p. 10.

CHAPTER IV

PHILIP MELANCHTHON

The creative work of Luther and Zwingli was naturally followed by the effort to formulate and systematise their teachings. In the Lutheran camp this work was done chiefly by Melanchthon, in the Reformed by Calvin. Philip Melanchthon was born in South-western Germany in 1497, was educated at Heidelberg and Tübingen, and became Professor of Greek in the University of Wittenberg at the age of twenty-one. He was a nephew of the famous humanist, Reuchlin, and from the beginning was thoroughly committed to the cause of humanism. He was a precocious genius, and when he came to Wittenberg was already recognised as one of the rising scholars of the day. His interests were not simply philological and literary, but ethical as well. Like many another humanist, he was attracted particularly by the great classical moralists, and found in their ethical teaching inspiration and instruction of permanent worth. The practical interest was always controlling with him, and he conceived all study vain which did not improve the character as well as the mind. He also had a very marked pedagogical instinct. The title of Preceptor of Germany, by which he ultimately came to be known everywhere, was richly deserved. He was the greatest teacher of his day, and did more than any one else to improve the educational methods of Germany.

He did not go to Wittenberg because of any interest he

had in Luther or his cause. He had apparently given no special thought to religious matters. His studies had lain in other lines, and he was a total stranger to the needs and impulses which dominated the Augustinian monk. But he soon came under the influence of Luther's robust personality, and was won over completely to his support. He recognised the Biblical character of his teaching and the great advance it marked upon current ethical and religious principles, and he threw himself with youthful enthusiasm into the cause of reform which Luther was championing. He remained permanently a layman, but at Luther's suggestion took the degree of Bachelor of Divinity in 1519, and thereafter gave courses in theology, particularly Biblical exegesis, as well as in the classics and kindred subjects.

Of permanent importance for Protestant thought was the combination in Melanchthon, the first great Protestant theologian, of the humanist and the Lutheran. In his devotion to the new cause, he turned his back for a time upon some of his humanistic studies, notably Aristotle, and spoke in contempt, as Luther was fond of doing, of human wisdom and the pursuit of secular learning. But his earlier interests soon reasserted themselves and he made it thenceforth one of the aims of his life to combine and reconcile the gospel of Luther with the conclusions of natural reason. Had he not come under Luther's influence, he would doubtless have remained a mere humanist. As it was, he put his humanistic training and acquisitions completely at the service of Luther's gospel, placing the latter in a large setting, and bringing it so far as he could into harmony with the best thought and learning of the day.

In 1521 he published the first edition of his famous *Loci Communes*. In later editions the work became an elaborate system of theology, but in its original form it was simply a concise statement of the fundamental principles of Luther's gospel, with a discussion of certain practical matters affected by it. Doctrines which had no direct bearing upon life were omitted altogether. 'This is Christian knowledge,' he says, 'to know what the law demands, where you may find power for doing the law, and grace for sin, how you may strengthen the feeble mind against the devil, the flesh, and the world, how you may console an afflicted conscience. . . . In his epistle to the Romans, when he wrote a compendium of Christian doctrine, did Paul philosophise concerning the mysteries of the Trinity, the mode of the Incarnation, creation, active, and passive ? What did he deal with ? Truly with the law, sin, and grace, upon which subjects alone the knowledge of Christ depends. . . . So we will delineate the reason of those matters which commend Christ to thee, which confirm the conscience, which strengthen the mind against Satan.'[1]

The work is true to the teaching of Luther from beginning to end, and contains a great many beautiful statements of one and another feature of his gospel. Some of the definitions are unsurpassed for conciseness and clearness in all theological literature. 'Grace is nothing else than the forgiveness or remission of sins' (p. 170). 'Faith is nothing else than trust in the divine mercy promised in Christ' (p. 175). 'The gospel is the promise of grace or the forgiveness of sins through Christ' (p. 210). 'We are justified, therefore, when, having been mortified through the law, we are raised by the word of grace, which is promised in Christ, or the gospel of the forgiveness of sins, and cleave to it in faith, doubting not at all that the righteousness of Christ is our righteousness, the satisfaction of Christ our expiation, the resurrection of Christ our resurrection. In short, doubting not at all that our sins are forgiven, and God now favours us and wishes us well. Not our works, therefore, however good they

[1] Plitt-Kolde's edition of the *Loci*, p. 64 *sq.*

may seem to be, constitute righteousness, but only faith in the mercy and grace of God in Jesus Christ' (p. 170). 'Whatever is done by the powers of nature is carnal; the constancy of Socrates, the moderation of Zeno are nothing but carnal affections' (p. 112). 'The law demands impossible things, the love of God and one's neighbour. . . . Therefore it is not the work of the law to justify, but it is its proper work to reveal sin and confound the conscience' (p. 208 ff.). 'So far as we believe we are free, so far as we disbelieve we are under law' (p. 217). Such brief and pregnant sentences show clearly enough that Melanchthon had made his own the very heart of Luther's gospel.

And yet there are significant differences even in this early work. Melanchthon's pedagogic concern reveals itself frequently in his care in guarding against possible misunderstandings of Luther which may lead to practical abuses of one kind and another. His controlling ethical interest also appears over and over again, particularly in his discussion of the place and province of law, where he is very careful to insist upon the holiness of the Christian life, and to repudiate libertinism of every sort.

There is also a complete lack of reference to Luther's distinction between the Word of God and the Scriptures. No doctrine of the Bible is given, but it is quoted as if all its parts were of equal authority, and it is evident that Melanchthon so conceived the matter. This was entirely natural under the circumstances. His lack of a religious experience like Luther's, and his pedagogic concern for the moral welfare of his readers made some external authority necessary. That it should be the Scriptures was inevitable, both for the humanist and for the follower of Luther. The supreme authority of the Bible was thus a fundamental postulate with him from the beginning.

If we would rightly estimate Melanchthon's influence

upon Protestant theology, we must not confine our attention to the first edition of his *Loci*. The later revisions, which appeared in 1535 and following years, were of much greater historical significance. While the original edition was not intended to be a work on dogmatic theology, the second and following were avowedly such. The doctrines of God, the divine Unity and Trinity, the two natures in Christ, and the mode of the incarnation, omitted in the original work because without direct bearing on the practical life, are all discussed at length in the later editions. The gospel of Luther, which stood out so prominently and beautifully in the former was thus obscured, and the way opened to the scholastic notion that the importance of a doctrine depends on its place in the system rather than on its practical value. Though his ethical interest kept Melanchthon from becoming purely scholastic, and giving himself wholly to barren speculation, there was a great deal of scholasticism in his later *Loci*, both in spirit and in method, and the work grew less vital and attractive with each successive revision.

Again, the influence of his humanistic training had an increasing effect on Melanchthon's religious thinking. When he wrote his original *Loci* he was largely under the control of Luther's anti-humanistic spirit. He shared his contempt for the natural reason, and made the Bible the sole source of theology. But as time went on his humanism reasserted itself, and he repudiated Luther's sharp dualism between reason and revelation, and undertook to commend the truths of revelation to the natural reason, and to show their harmony with it as the mediæval schoolmen had done. He did not go as far as they, but the tendency was similar. The result was the modification of some of Luther's extreme views, notably his doctrine of predestination and of the real presence in the Eucharist, but more important than this, the placing of reason and revelation beside one another as the two sources for a knowledge of religious truth and the recognition of natural and revealed theology as together making up the sum of Christian faith. The natural theology which he accepted was the common traditional thing, involving a purely mechanical view of the universe. The revealed theology was that of the three ecumenical creeds, with the fuller and clearer exposition of Scripture found in the teaching of Luther, and particularly in the Augsburg Confession.

Melanchthon's recognition of reason and revelation as co-ordinate sources of theology gave the scheme for all subsequent Protestant dogmatics. Natural theology prepares the way for revealed, and hence the study of the sciences precedes the study of the Bible and promotes the true faith. Reason and revelation cannot be out of harmony. Revelation does not contradict natural theology, it supplements it. The full knowledge adequate for salvation, that is, the knowledge of the gospel, comes only with revelation, but it presupposes an acquaintance with God and His works open to all. The tendency was thus to view Christianity as a purely intellectual matter, as a supernatural communication of divine knowledge. Melanchthon did not lose the sense of the vital and experimental character of the Christian faith; it meant to him, as to Luther, the conviction of sins forgiven and personal trust in a loving Father. But the effect of his teaching was to obscure this conception and promote the idea that the gospel is simply a system of truths which it is our duty to accept. Accordingly the later editions of the *Loci* contain a formal apologetic for Christianity as a divinely revealed philosophy. The antiquity of the Christian revelation, which includes the Old Testament, the excellence of its doctrine, the continued existence of the Church, in spite of the hostility of the world, the flesh, and the devil, the attestation by miracles—all these are cited in support of the gospel in good traditional fashion.

In accordance with his intellectual notion of Christianity, Melanchthon widened the idea of saving faith to cover the acceptance of all the truths of divine revelation. Not simply the gospel of God's forgiving love in Christ is the object of the Christian's faith, but the whole Bible as interpreted by the three ecumenical creeds, and by the teaching of Luther. Accordingly sound doctrine is made one of the notes of the true Church. The Church is composed 'of those who hold pure doctrine and agree in it.'[1] Upon the orthodoxy of the evangelical church he laid the very greatest stress; it is truly Catholic because it accepts the prophetic and apostolic teaching according to the opinion of the true Church. 'Thus in our confession we profess that we embrace the whole teaching of the word of God, to which the Church gives testimony, and, indeed, in that sense which the symbols show.'[2] He meant here the ecumenical symbols, that is, the Apostles', the Nicene, and the Athanasian Creeds, and the agreement with the tradition of the Church which he claimed for Protestant doctrine was agreement with the ancient, undivided Church. He was always conservative, sometimes timidly so, and his conservatism expressed itself particularly in emphasis upon the traditional character of the evangelical faith. 'In the true faith,' he says, 'I include the whole doctrine handed down in the books of the prophets and apostles, and comprehended in the Apostles', Nicene, and Athanasian creeds.' 'We have brought into the Church no new dogma, but we renew and illustrate the doctrine of the Catholic Church.'[3] The reactionary and Catholic character of all this is abundantly evident. It is not that Melanchthon took positions wholly foreign to Luther's, but that what with Luther was exceptional, and due principally to controversy, with Melanchthon was habitual and controlling.

[1] *Corpus Reformatorum*, vol. xi. p. 273. [2] *Ibid.* vol. xxiv. p. 398.
[3] *Ibid.* vol. iii. p. 222.

Closely connected with the rehabilitation of natural theology, referred to above, was Melanchthon's loss of the distinction between law and gospel which meant so much to Luther, and which was brought out so clearly and admirably in the first edition of the *Loci*. In the later editions reason is associated with law and revelation with gospel. By natural reason we gain a knowledge of law, by revelation a knowledge of the gospel. As natural reason is not superseded but supplemented by revelation, the law is not superseded but supplemented by the gospel, and is therefore permanently binding upon believers as well as unbelievers. Melanchthon did not return to the Roman Catholic position and make the observance of the law a condition of salvation in the same sense as faith, but he introduced a view of the law which tended to do away altogether with Luther's principle of Christian liberty. He avoided the difficulty involved in asserting the Christian's bondage to the law, and at the same time denying that it has saving value, by drawing a scholastic distinction between justification and regeneration. The Christian is justified on the ground of faith alone, but justification must be followed by regeneration through the indwelling of the Spirit. Only as the Spirit takes possession of the justified man and enables him to keep the law of God is he truly saved.[1] This means, in fact if not in form, a return to the Catholic conception of salvation as a transformation of character. The ethical interest becomes again predominant, and though Luther's position is nominally maintained, it is really abandoned. The Christian life is once more made to all intents and purposes a probation for the life to come, and the magnificent liberty of the Christian man is little better than an empty phrase.

I have spoken of Melanchthon as a formulator of Lutheran theology. His character in this regard appears

[1] Cf. *Corpus Reformatorum*, vol. xxi. p. 428 *sq.*

not only in the successive editions of his *Loci* but also in the Augsburg Confession and in the *Apology* for it, both of which were prepared by him. The former was the earliest confessional statement of Protestant doctrine. It was drawn up in 1530 and presented to the Emperor at the Diet of Augsburg of that year as a vindication and defence of the Protestant position. It was not intended as a symbol for the use of the Protestants themselves, but as a statement of their faith which should induce the Emperor to think better of them than he did. Under these circumstances the Confession was naturally framed in such a way as to magnify the agreements and minimise the disagreements between Protestants and Catholics. It is claimed that the Protestants hold the faith of the ancient Fathers, and that the differences between them and the Catholics are due to mediæval corruptions, which they repudiate. The effort is made, of course, to show that those for whom Melanchthon is speaking are not guilty of the innumerable heresies that have been charged upon them by the Catholics, and to this end the views of the radical Protestants, such as the Zwinglians and Anabaptists, are emphatically denounced at every possible point.

The Confession, so far as it went, was a true statement of Lutheran doctrine. Though prepared by Melanchthon it did not show the departure from Luther's teaching which marked the later editions of the *Loci*. It was brief and to the point, and was free from the scholasticism found there. But it was not such a confession as Luther would have written. He would have expressed himself in a more outspoken and polemic fashion, and would have emphasised the differences rather than the agreements between himself and the Catholics, as he did, for instance, in the 'Smalcald Articles,' composed half a dozen years later.

The Confession dealt with doctrine in twenty-one brief articles, and then with practical abuses needing reformation in seven longer ones, which made up two-thirds of the whole document. The doctrinal part closed with the statement that the chief differences between Protestants and Catholics were not theological—here there was general agreement—but practical. 'This is about the sum of doctrine among us, in which can be seen that there is nothing which is discrepant with the Scriptures, or with the Church Catholic, or even with the Roman Church, so far as that Church is known from writers. This being the case, they judge us harshly who insist that we be regarded as heretics. But the dissension is concerning certain traditions and abuses, which without any sure authority have crept into the churches.'[1] 'Those things only have been enumerated which it seemed necessary to say, that it might be understood that in doctrine and ceremonials among us there is nothing received contrary to Scriptures or to the Catholic Church, inasmuch as it is manifest that we have diligently taken heed that no new and godless doctrines should creep into our churches.'[2]

Before turning from Melanchthon, it may be well to call attention to the resemblance at many points between him and Zwingli. Both had the same conception of the authority of the Bible, of the relation of natural and revealed theology, of the oneness of law and gospel, and of the nature of faith. Zwingli was not as scholastic as Melanchthon; he was more of an originator and less of a formulator. But, except in the matter of predestination, where Melanchthon's later views were very different, their general tendency was strikingly similar. This was apparently due, not to the influence of the one over the other, but to the fact that they came to evangelical Christianity, not through a profound religious experience like Luther's, but through the conviction that his gospel was Biblical and therefore true. In this they anticipated the course very commonly taken since their day.

[1] Part i. art. 22. [2] Part ii., conclusion.

CHAPTER V

JOHN CALVIN [1]

Although Zwingli was the founder of what may be called the reformed type of theology, and Calvin its great formulator, the relation between the two men was very different from that between Luther and Melanchthon, the founder and the formulator of Lutheran theology. In the case of the German reformers, the younger was the devoted disciple of the older, and even when in course of time he deviated at some points from the teaching of his master, he remained a reverent follower. Calvin, on the other hand, was never consciously a disciple of Zwingli. His conversion to Protestantism occurred after Zwingli's death, and independently of his influence. He regarded Zwingli with respect,[2] but he spoke rather slightingly of him on more than one occasion,[3] as he did for that matter of most of his contemporaries, and in a letter to Farel,[4] written in 1540, he declared Luther to be a much greater man. In fact, he always regarded Luther as his spiritual father, and recognised him as the greatest of the reformers.

At the same time Calvin's theology was in no small measure identical with Zwingli's and the identity was not a mere accident. It was due, in part, to similarity of circumstances and situation, but in part also to the influence of Zwingli's thinking. That influence was

---
[1] Calvin's 'Works' are published in the *Corpus Reformatorum*, vol. xxix. *sq.* The volumes are also numbered independently (vols. i.-lix.), and are so referred to in this chapter.
[2] Cf. e.g. *Opera*, vol. viii. p. 182; vol. xii. p. 11.
[3] *Ibid.* vol. xi. pp. 36, 438.   [4] *Ibid.* vol. xi. p. 44.

apparently not direct, but it was none the less potent. The Zurich reformer had a large following, both in Switzerland and in South-western Germany. His notion of the Eucharist, even where not itself accepted, had led to a considerable modification of the Lutheran doctrine as held by the Protestants of that region, and his predestinarian views had become common property among them. In his theory of predestination, as already seen, he was moved, not only by Luther's practical interest, but also by a theological motive which the Wittenberg reformer did not share, and he carried the theory further than Luther did, and gave it a more controlling place in his thinking. But there was no inconsistency at this point between his teaching and Luther's, and it was natural that his more logical and thoroughgoing treatment of the matter should commend itself to that part of the world where he was known and revered. His *De Providentia*, in which his doctrine received its most extreme statement, was warmly praised by Bucer, Myconius, Judas, and others, and the doctrine itself was recognised as an essential part of the Protestant faith.

The most prominent theologian in South-western Germany, who had more than any one else to do with the spread of a modified form of Zwinglianism in that part of the country, was Martin Bucer, the celebrated Strassburg reformer.[1] It was Luther's work and teaching that won him to Protestantism, but he early came into communication with Zwingli, and felt the influence of his thought. He was a man of unionistic tendencies, and made it one of his chief concerns to overcome differences, and to promote harmony between the divergent factions of Protestantism. To this end he formulated a Eucharistic doctrine which he thought conserved all that Luther was really interested

[1] See Lang's *Der Evangelien-Kommentar Martin Butzers und die Grundzüge seiner Theologie* (*Studien zur Geschichte der Theologie und der Kirche*, ii. 2), 1900.

in, while avoiding the materialistic notion so repugnant to Zwingli. He emphasised the significance of the Lord's Supper as a testimony to God's forgiving love in Christ, and while denying the material presence, he taught a spiritual presence which guaranteed participation in the body and blood of the Lord by the believing participant. His efforts to bring about a permanent union between the two parties were unsuccessful, but his compromise view of the Lord's Supper was widely accepted and ultimately became predominant throughout the Reformed wing of Protestantism.

In his predestinarian ideas, Bucer agreed with Zwingli, but he made more of the conception of the glory of God which is found in Zwingli's writings, but is not prominent there. God's glory appears chiefly in His omnipotence, by which He rules and governs all things, and it is the ultimate ground of predestination both to salvation and to condemnation. Zwingli commonly made the good of the creature the controlling motive in all divine activity, but in his work, *On Providence*, in the passage already referred to, he spoke of election as a manifestation of divine mercy and of reprobation as a manifestation of divine justice.[1] By Bucer this idea was made controlling, and the motive of predestination was represented, not as the good of the creature, but as the exhibition of the glory of God. To this end God decreed the Fall, and to the same end He determined to save some out of the mass of perdition and to condemn the rest to eternal punishment for their sins.

The principal importance of Bucer in the history of Protestant thought is due to the fact that he influenced the great Genevan reformer, John Calvin, and through him affected permanently the theology of the reformed churches.

Calvin was born at Noyon in North-eastern France in 1509. His father at first intended him for a clerical

[1] *Opera*, vol. iv. p. 115.

career, but afterwards changed his plan and set him to studying law. He completed his legal studies, but found the pursuit of classical literature more to his taste, and in 1532 published a commentary on Seneca's *De Clementia*, which gave striking proof, both of his extraordinary scholarship and of his profound ethical interest. He had a naturally religious disposition, but there is no sign that he was particularly concerned about religious matters until 1533, when we find him one of a little group of reforming spirits in Paris. He had already, like many others in France, begun to feel the influence of Luther's teaching, but it was apparently some time before he recognised himself as a Protestant. The circumstances of his conversion to the new faith are quite unknown. There is no reason to suppose that he passed through a spiritual struggle like Luther's. It would seem rather that he was drawn naturally, perhaps almost insensibly, by his associations into sympathy with the humanistic reforming ideas which were abroad in France as elsewhere, and which made much of the authority of the Scriptures and a return to the greater simplicity and spirituality of primitive days. From this position he was carried over into Protestantism by his conviction that Luther and his followers had the Bible on their side, and that the visible Roman Catholic institution in which he had been brought up was not identical with the true Church.

In 1534 he gave up his ecclesiastical benefices, which he had held since boyhood, and thenceforth had no connection with the Church of Rome. France being unsafe, or at any rate uncomfortable territory for a Protestant, he made his way to Basel in 1535, and there, in 1536, published the first edition of his famous *Institutes of the Christian Religion*, with a dedicatory letter to King Francis I. in which he defended evangelical Christianity in a masterly fashion.[1] The book and the letter ac-

[1] Published in Calvin's *Opera*, vol. i.

companying it at once brought him into prominence and marked him as a rising leader in the Protestant cause.

The work was intended as an introduction to the study of the Bible for the use of theological students, and particularly as an apology for Protestantism in the form of a brief and popular presentation of its teachings, especially upon practical matters. It followed rather closely the order of Luther's *Catechism*, and while much more elaborate and doctrinal in character, contained little theology in the strict sense. It was divided into six chapters: the first on the law, with an exposition of the Decalogue; the second on faith, with an exposition of the Apostles' Creed; the third on prayer, with an exposition of the Lord's Prayer; the fourth on the sacraments of Baptism and the Lord's Supper; the fifth, the most polemic of all, on the other so-called sacraments; and the sixth on Christian liberty, ecclesiastical power, and civil administration.

In this little book the doctrine of predestination is referred to in passing, but though it appears in its double form, as election and reprobation, it is evident that Calvin was interested only in the former, not the latter, and that it was important to him because it guaranteed the sole activity of God in the work of redemption, and also because it gave an adequate basis for the assurance of salvation. There is nothing peculiar in the doctrine as expressed in this work. It was a common reformation belief, and seemed to Calvin, as to most Protestants, a necessary accompaniment of the doctrine of salvation by faith alone, and the only adequate safeguard against the Catholic theory of human merit with all that it involved.

In a second and greatly enlarged edition of the *Institutes*,[1] which appeared in 1539, while Calvin was residing in Strassburg, a special chapter was given to the subject

[1] Published in *Opera*, vol. i. A French translation of this edition was made by Calvin himself in 1541.

of predestination (chapter xiv.), and the doctrine assumed the character which it permanently bore in his teaching. In the first edition it was denied that God is the author of sin, but in the second His agency in effecting the Fall and all the actions of men of whatever sort is explicitly asserted. Moreover, His own glory is represented as the controlling motive in the predestinating activity of God. The explanation of this change is to be found in the influence of Bucer, whose *Commentary on Romans*, in which his doctrine of predestination received its fullest statement, appeared in 1536. Calvin, who was already an admirer of the Strassburg reformer, was greatly impressed by it, and was led to put his emphasis where Bucer did. The likeness between his own discussion and Bucer's is very striking.[1] There is the same assertion that God's will is the cause of all things, and that there is nothing back of it or above it controlling or determining it; the same repudiation of the notion of a permissive decree in connection with the Fall; the same emphasis on the Biblical basis of the doctrine, and the same caution against being wise beyond what is written. There are also the same answers to objections: Who is man that he should call God to account? He is quite incompetent to fathom the will of God or to pass judgment on His acts. Whatever the Ruler of the world does is just and right, whether it squares with our notions or not.

Calvin's temperament and religious experience were both such as to make Bucer's doctrine congenial. Even before he became a Protestant he recognised the nothingness of man and the overmastering power of God. The thought of divine sovereignty was always dear, and his religious devotion instinctively expressed itself in magnifying the divine omnipotence. In his dedicatory letter to the king, accompanying the first edition of his *Institutes*, he had a great deal to say about the glory of God, which

[1] See Lang, *ibid.* p. 339 *sq.*

was evidently already a favourite idea. It is not surprising that he made Bucer's doctrine his own, and followed him in connecting divine predestination directly with the divine glory, and in emphasising God's activity in bringing about the Fall.

The significance of Calvin's presentation of the doctrine is not that he added anything to Bucer's teaching or differed with him at any point, nor even that with his logical mind he stated it more clearly and consistently, but that he made it an integral part of a complete system of theology, and inserted it in his *Institutes*, which was to become the theological text-book of all western Protestantism. The importance of this fact should not be underestimated. Standing by itself, the doctrine of absolute and unconditioned predestination would probably not long have found general acceptance, and would unquestionably have been crowded into the background by other interests, as in Lutheranism. But Calvin gave it an essential place in a system whose controlling principle was the majesty and might of God. As a result to reject or even to minimise it seemed to limit God and throw contempt upon Him. The imposing character of the system as formulated by Calvin gave it compelling power, and that he was not the creator of the doctrine of predestination, and that he added nothing to it, does not in any way detract from his credit for its almost universal acceptance and dominating influence in western Protestantism.

Calvin's doctrine of God occupied the same central place in his system as in Zwingli's. But while it resembled closely the earlier reformer's doctrine, it was less profound and was worked out with less consistency. To the Genevan reformer God is a strictly personal Being whose will controls the universe; to Zwingli He is the only real Being, the all-pervading energy and the immanent cause of all things. The practical effects are the same, but the philosophical basis is different, or rather it should be said that while Zwingli's is a philosophical theory, Calvin's is theological only. The younger reformer had apparently no philosophical interest, and Zwingli's ontological speculations did not appeal to him in the least. He blamed the older man for them, and claimed that he himself followed Scripture only, and allowed human reason no place in the formation of his views. He was mistaken in this. His ideas touching God's character and activities were in no small part the result of logical deduction from a preconceived theory of deity. Scripture, though continually appealed to and ostensibly made the sole source, really did no more than supply some of the data upon which a logical theory was constructed. These data harmonised with his own temperament and experience, and so were made use of to the exclusion of all others.

Calvin's appeal to the Bible rather than to philosophy in support of his teaching did much to establish the doctrine of absolute predestination in the reformed church. The philosophical considerations of Zwingli carried little weight except among philosophers. The Biblical argument, which both Zwingli and Bucer had employed, but which Calvin presented with new emphasis and in greater fulness, was much more convincing.

Calvin's claim that the Scriptures alone were to be followed, and that no one was to go beyond what was written, made it possible for him frequently to avoid drawing the obvious conclusions of his own theory. He contrasts his moderation in this respect with Zwingli's greater consistency, and criticises the latter for his extreme statements.[1] As a matter of fact, Calvin's theory led exactly where Zwingli's did, and his customary reticence was less creditable than the outspokenness of the older reformer.[2] But it undoubtedly served to obscure

[1] See his letter to Bullinger, *Opera*, vol. xiv. p. 253; on the other side his response in the *Process of Bolsec*, viii. 182.
[2] In his *Institutes*, edition of 1559, bk. I. chap. xviii., Calvin declares in full agreement with Zwingli that God is Himself the cause of men's evil deeds.

some of the most obnoxious features of the doctrine, and thus made it more acceptable to the church.

Correlative with his conception of God was Calvin's idea of man and his duty. No one can understand and estimate himself aright unless he knows God. 'For such is the inborn pride of us all that we invariably esteem ourselves righteous, innocent, wise, and holy, until we are convinced by clear proofs of our unrighteousness, turpitude, folly, and impurity. But we are never thus convinced while we confine our attention to ourselves and regard not the Lord who is the only standard by which judgment ought to be formed.'[1] 'Man is utterly corrupt and depraved, and humility alone becomes him in the presence of God, who is all that he is not. To know God is to be struck with horror and amazement, for then and only then does one realise his own character.'[2] Man exists for the sake of God's glory, and his supreme duty is to promote it. There is no true virtue where concern for God's glory is not present, and the worst of all sins is giving to oneself the glory due to God.[3] Man can best promote the divine glory by reverencing, fearing, and worshipping God, and by rendering perfect obedience to His will. Pure and genuine religion consists 'in faith united with a serious fear of God—such a fear as comprehends willing reverence and results in legitimate worship agreeable to the injunctions of the law.'[4] It is all-important, therefore, that man shall know God and His will. This knowledge is written upon the pages of nature and the tables of the heart, but man has been blinded by sin, and so a clearer revelation is given in the Bible, which is God's highest and final communication of His will. Like Zwingli, Calvin recognised God's general revelation of Himself, and he even declared that the knowledge of God in Himself precedes the knowledge of Christ, but he

---

[1] *Institutes*, edition of 1559, bk. I. chap. i. § 2. [2] *Ibid.* § 3.
[3] *Ibid.* bk. II. chap. iii. § 4. [4] *Ibid.* bk. I. chap. ii. § 2.

denied its efficacy and sufficiency. The only adequate and trustworthy declaration of God's will is found in the Scriptures. The Bible is conceived, as by Zwingli, not primarily as a means of grace, but as a revelation of the divine will. From beginning to end it is the word of God, and is equally authoritative in all its parts.

Man needs, not only a revelation of God's will, but also power to obey it, and forgiveness for disobedience. This he gets through Christ, whose work is pictured in the same traditional way as by the other reformers. Faith in Christ justifies man and frees him from the divine condemnation; salvation is by faith alone. But this is not enough, for he is utterly corrupt, and can do nothing good unless regenerated by the power of the Spirit. He is predestinated, not simply to salvation, but to holiness. He is called to do God's will, and for this end he was created. The Christian life consists simply in keeping God's commands, and that not because they are good, but because they are commanded. It is not the free and spontaneous expression of the character of the child of God, but faithful obedience to the divine will laid down in the Scriptures. As is said in Book IV. chap. x. § 7 : 'Everything pertaining to the perfect rule of a good life the Lord has so comprehended in His law that there remains nothing for man to add to that summary. And He has done this, first, that since all rectitude of life consists in the conformity of all our actions to His will as their standard, we might consider Him as the sole master and director of our life ; and secondly, to show that He requires of us nothing more than obedience.'[1] Calvin has a section on Christian Liberty in all the editions of his *Institutes*, but it is a very different kind of liberty from that which Luther taught. Not liberty, but bondage was dear to Calvin. He dis-

[1] This is a genuinely Catholic position. With it might be compared the definition of the essence of Christianity in the new *Catholic Encyclopædia*: 'Obedience of the mind and will to the Supreme Power, *i.e.* faith and works' (vol. vi. p. 529).

trusted, not only the natural man, but the Christian man as well, and believed that he must be held strictly to the observance of the divine law, or he would go astray and fall into sin. By Christian liberty he meant freedom from dependence upon the works of the law for justification—how could any man justify himself in the sight of God?—and also freedom from the obligation to obey the commandments of men, particularly the oppressive regulations of the ecclesiastical authorities.

Calvin's ideal of the Christian life was rigorous in the extreme. Other-worldliness was its principal characteristic, abstinence from the pleasures and frivolities and luxuries of this world, as well as from its sins. As he says in his *Institutes* (Book III. chap. ix.): 'With whatever kind of tribulation we may be afflicted, we should always keep this end in view, to habituate ourselves to a contempt of the present life that we may thereby be excited to meditation on that which is to come' (§ 1). 'There is no medium between these two extremes, either the earth must become vile in our estimation, or it must retain our immoderate love. Wherefore if we have any concern about eternity, we must use our most diligent efforts to extricate ourselves from these fetters' (§ 2). 'It should be the object of believers, therefore, in judging of this mortal life that, understanding it to be of itself nothing but misery, they may apply themselves wholly with increasing cheerfulness and readiness to meditate on the future and eternal life. When we come to this comparison, then indeed the former will be not only securely neglected, but in competition with the latter altogether despised and abhorred. For if heaven is our country, what is the earth but a place of exile? If the departure out of the world is an entrance into life, what is the world but a sepulchre? What is a continuance in it but an absorption in death? If deliverance from the body is an introduction into genuine liberty, what is the body but a prison? If to enjoy the presence of God is the summit of felicity, is it not misery to be destitute of it ? But ' until we escape out of the world we are absent from the Lord. Therefore, if the terrestrial life be compared with the celestial, it should undoubtedly be despised and accounted of no value ' (§ 4). ' Therefore, though the liberty of believers in external things cannot be reduced to a certain rule, yet it is evidently subject to this law that they should indulge themselves as little as possible ; that on the contrary they should perpetually and resolutely exert themselves to retrench all superfluities and to restrain luxury ; and that they should diligently beware lest they pervert into impediments things which were given for their assistance ' (chap. x. § 4). In his effort to stamp this ideal upon the city of Geneva, Calvin was simply following the example set by Bucer, whose principles were of the same sort, but he carried matters much further and succeeded much better than the Strassburg reformer.

In his conception of God and of man's relation to Him, Calvin agreed with Zwingli, but he was ethically more rigorous, and conceived the Christian life in a much more Puritanic fashion. Zwingli was engaged chiefly in breaking the control of Rome, and in securing a foothold for the new faith. Calvin devoted himself very largely to strengthening, consolidating, and purifying a Protestantism already established before he began his work. We call Calvin one of the Reformers, but he belonged to the second generation, and his task was to conserve rather than to create. This is illustrated both in his theology and in his practical work.

It was a mark of Calvin's greater conservatism that he made more than Zwingli did of the means of grace. He saw, as Luther did, in Zwingli's liberal attitude toward the non-Christian world a dangerous error. No one has ever been saved or can possibly be saved except through Christ. It is true that God elects whom He pleases, and that His election is the ultimate ground of salvation, but

He saves no one apart from Christ. Although Calvin recognised the possibility that the Spirit of God might act independently of the ordinary means of grace in certain special cases, as, for instance, in the case of infants and idiots, he yet made much more of those means than Zwingli, and attached salvation, as Luther did, to the word and the sacraments. His view of the Lord's Supper he took from Bucer, teaching the spiritual presence of Christ in the elements and the nourishment of the regenerated life by Him. The idea is more Catholic than the controlling idea of Luther, even though it substitutes a spiritual for a material presence, for Luther laid emphasis on the testimony borne by the sacrament, while with Calvin the important thing was feeding upon Christ. Calvin's adoption of the doctrine gave it a permanent and indisputable place in reformed theology. In 1549, by the Consensus Tigurinensis, even Zurich accepted it, and thenceforth it was the only recognised doctrine in the reformed wing of Protestantism.

The sacrament of baptism Calvin brought into connection with regeneration, as Bucer, and before him, even Luther himself had done, and thus both sacraments found their significance rather in the fact that they imparted grace to the recipient than that they were signs or testimonies to the gospel. In other words, the Catholic prevailed over the genuinely Protestant conception of their meaning and value.

In his doctrine of the Church Calvin was also more conservative than Zwingli, and stood nearer to Luther than he. He defined the Church in agreement with Zwingli and Bucer as the totality of the elect, and he made predestination its constitutive factor. But the Church is visible as well as invisible, and its marks are the word and the sacraments. Where the word is truly taught and the sacraments rightly administered there is the Church, and outside of its pale there is ordinarily no salvation. Calvin was very insistent upon this point. 'What God has joined together,' he says, 'it is wrong to put asunder; for to those to whom God is a Father the Church also is a mother.'[1] And again: 'As our present design is to treat of the visible Church, we may learn even from the title of mother how useful and even necessary it is for us to know her, since there is no other way of entrance into life unless we are conceived by her, born of her, nourished at her breast, and continually preserved under her care and government till we are divested of this mortal flesh and become like the angels. For our infirmity will not admit of our dismission from school until we have been disciples to the end of our lives. It is also to be remarked that out of her bosom there can be no hope of remission of sins nor any salvation.'[2]

This was not in consequence of any necessity due to the nature of the case—because one could not believe without hearing the gospel of God's forgiving love in Christ, and could not hear it apart from the Church, as Luther said, but because it was God's will that it should be so. He could have fixed other conditions, but He has actually fixed these, and that is all we need to know. God might, Calvin said, have made his people perfect in a moment, but it was not His will that they should grow to mature age save under the education of the Church.[3] The test of every system, institution, and means of grace is not its fitness to the work in hand, but its conformity to the will of God. What He has ordained is necessary and right because He has ordained it. This principle gave to the life, the polity, and the worship of the Calvinistic churches a very different cast from the Lutheran. God's will as expressed in the Bible must be followed in everything, and for every part of the ecclesiastical system directions must be found there. Of the freedom of the Spirit there remained very little. The control of the letter was minute and far reaching.

[1] *Institutes*, bk. IV. chap. i. § 1.   [2] *Ibid.* § 4.   [3] *Ibid.* § 5.

By the word of God, which is one of the marks of the Church, Calvin understood, not the gospel of God's forgiving love, but the Bible as a whole, or rather the Bible properly interpreted—in other words, sound doctrine. Where such doctrine is faithfully taught, there is the true Church; where error is substituted for it, the Church is destroyed.[1] It was upon the basis of this principle that Calvin justified Protestant secession from the Church of Rome.

Attention has already been called to Calvin's rigorous interpretation of the duties of the Christian life, and to his distrust even of the Christian man. This led him to lay great stress on ecclesiastical discipline. The Christian Church is a people predestinated to holiness. Their supreme duty is not to serve their fellows and to establish the reign of the spirit of love in all the institutions and relationships of this earth, but to walk humbly with God, to obey Him in all things, and to keep themselves unspotted from the world. The Church is a body apart, a community of holy people, pure both in doctrine and in conduct, because governed wholly by the word of God. Ecclesiastical discipline, therefore, must be very strict. 'As the saving doctrine of Christ is the soul of the Church, so discipline forms the ligaments by which the members of the body are joined together and kept each in its proper place.'[2] In the exercise of its disciplinary authority, the Church must admonish or visit with its censures all sorts of offenders, and must altogether exclude from its communion those guilty of gross and flagrant sins.

Moreover, the exercise of its disciplinary functions Calvin lodged in the officers of the Church. They are charged with the responsibility of keeping the Church pure, and the members must submit to their authority. Here is revealed, what appears in many other connections, Calvin's deep-rooted aversion to democracy. He did not trust the ordinary man, even though a Christian. He

[1] Cf. *Institutes*, bk. IV. chap. i. § 12.   [2] *Ibid.* chap. xii. § 1.

was instinctively an aristocrat in religious as well as in civil matters, and he believed that the Church could be properly governed, and its character preserved, only when a large measure of control was lodged in the hands of its ministers. Their authority did not rest upon the fact that they were successors of the Apostles, and had received from them a deposit of saving grace which they might dispense or withhold, in other words it was not sacerdotal, but upon the fact that they were ministers of the word. Because called and commissioned by God to preach the word, they were also intrusted with the responsibility of exercising discipline in accordance therewith. Calvin's influence in promoting civil liberty and democracy is often spoken of and counted to his credit. As a matter of fact, it was far from his intention to promote either, for he was opposed to both. He did much to break the power of the Pope in Western Europe, and so to prepare the way for the growth of a larger liberty in later days, but he was at best only indirectly responsible for a development which he would have been entirely out of sympathy with had he lived to witness it.

One more matter in which Calvin differed both with Zwingli and with Luther was the relation of Church and State. He agreed with them in laying upon the civil government the responsibility to cherish and support the external worship of God, to preserve the pure doctrine of religion, to defend the constitution of the Church, and to suppress idolatry, sacrilege, blasphemy, and other offences against God.[1] But while the older reformers gave civil governors the power of determining what is true religion according to the word of God, and expected them to support the true and prohibit the false thus determined, Calvin, though distinguishing the functions of Church and State, and recognising the difference between their spheres, yet followed the Catholics

[1] *Institutes*, bk. IV. chap. XX. § 23.

of the Middle Ages in regarding the civil government as only the handmaid of the Church in carrying out its behests. It lies with the Church, and particularly with the clergy, as ministers of the word, to determine God's will and truth, and upon the civil government is laid the obligation of acting accordingly. The power of the sword is lodged only in the State, but it is to be exercised for the support of the true Church, and for the overthrow of its enemies, who are the enemies of God.

In Geneva Calvin's principles were put into striking practice, and the influence of his work there, Catholic as were the underlying principles on which it was based, constituted Western Europe's greatest bulwark against the encroachments of a newly awakened papacy and a regenerated Catholicism. His historical significance is far greater in the sphere of government than in that of theology. It was as an ecclesiastical statesman that he did his greatest work. In his theology there was nothing new, but in his career as an organiser and dictator of the forces of western Protestantism, there was displayed a genius for leadership and a power of initiative and of control unsurpassed in the period of the Reformation.

It is evident in the light of all that has been said that between Calvin and Zwingli, the two great fathers of the Reformed Church, there were both resemblances and differences of considerable importance. It is often claimed that Calvin was more at one with Luther than with Zwingli, and undoubtedly he did in most respects stand nearer Wittenberg than Zwingli did. But it must not be forgotten that he remained in the Reformed wing of the Church of which Zwingli was the earliest leader. That he did so was not due to the mere accident of geography, but to the fact that he was really, in spite of his greater respect for Luther, far more profoundly one with Zwingli and the Reformed type of piety. This was of greater importance than all oneness in theology. Zwingli, Bucer, Calvin, and the Reformed churches in general represent a type of piety strikingly different, at least in its controlling tendency, from that of Luther and his followers. To the Wittenberg reformer the experience of God's forgiving love in Christ was fundamental. To the Reformed theologians, though they recognised this, and even emphasised it, the dominating element in experience was the consciousness of the power and ordaining will of God. Zwingli was nearer Luther than Calvin was in his greater emphasis on the goodness of God, but to both of them, and particularly to Calvin, God as Sovereign loomed larger than God as Saviour. God in Christ was the God of Luther's experience, God the Creator and Ruler of the world the God of Zwingli and of Calvin. This difference made itself seen in all their religious feeling, thinking, worship, and service, and the difference has been marked ever since in the two divisions of Protestantism. If justification by faith is the fundamental doctrine in Lutheranism, the controlling will of God is fundamental in the Protestantism of the Reformed churches.

Our study of the different reformers has made it clear enough that they all lived in the mediæval world. Of modern views in philosophy, science, history, or politics, there is scarcely a trace in any of them. They all believed in the depravity and helplessness of man, and in his need of a miraculous redemption. They all looked upon Christianity as a supernatural system in the fullest sense. They were all more or less consistent authoritarians, Calvin the most so of all, and while Luther had a magnificent conception of Christian liberty, which was thoroughly in harmony with the best spirit of the modern age, he held as firmly as the others to the bondage of the natural man, with the result that his higher view was obscured and generally lost sight of.

In certain ways, nevertheless, the Reformation did promote the spirit of liberty in the modern world. It broke the hold of the Roman Church, the greatest foe of liberty, and by its own inner dissensions and divisions prevented any new church from gaining the control which the old institution had exercised. In the conflict of the sects freedom had room to grow. Moreover, the assertion of the right of private judgment in the interpretation of the Scriptures, though so limited by the reformers themselves and by their followers, that it promoted the existence of sects, but long meant nothing at all for individual liberty, did ultimately make possible the gradual growth of a real freedom within Protestantism. Other influences than the Reformation had to do with the rise and spread of liberty in the modern world, but the divisions among Protestants and their theory of private judgment gave it a chance to penetrate the Protestant churches much more easily and rapidly than the Catholic church. Protestantism throughout most of its history has been fully as narrow and as conservative as Roman Catholicism, but it is not an accident that liberalism has had a larger and longer development within it than within the older communion.

CHAPTER VI

THE RADICAL SECTS

I. *The Anabaptists*

THE sixteenth century was marked by the rise of many radical sects. Some of them were the fruit of the Protestant Reformation, and were due to the more consistent application of principles, explicit or implicit, in the teaching of the great reformers; others were of independent origin. Their radicalism was of various kinds and degrees; sometimes religious only, often social and political as well. Generally they were quiet and harmless folk, but not infrequently revolutionists and even anarchists. They were regarded with peculiar bitterness by the Protestant leaders, because their radicalism brought disrepute upon the whole Protestant movement, which was commonly held accountable for them, and the result was that they received as severe, or even severer treatment from their hands than from the hands of the Catholics.

There was little discrimination in their opponents' judgment of them. They were all charged with the excesses of the few and were visited with like condemnation whatever their personal character and individual aims. As the Catholics held the Protestants responsible for all the radicalism and fanaticism of the age, the Protestant leaders held all who were more radical than themselves responsible for the worst excesses of the revolutionists. Because many of the sects were one in insisting upon the baptism of believers only, and in repudiating infant baptism, they were known by their opponents as Anabaptists, or rebaptisers, and the name came to be a common appellation for religious radicals of the day, whatever their attitude on this particular point. It was everywhere used as a term of reproach, and to call a man an Anabaptist was to condemn him to general obloquy. In view of the loose and indiscriminate use of the term it is quite impossible, and indeed unimportant in a book of this kind, to take account of all those known as Anabaptists. Some of the positions, however, which were common to many of them, had considerable influence upon the development of Protestant thought and life, and they demand at least brief attention.

At two points the Anabaptists differed widely with the great Protestant reformers—in their theory of the Christian Church, and in their view of the Christian life. They took their stand upon the authority of the Bible, particularly the New Testament, which they believed Protestants in general were not following as they ought, and in accordance with what they understood to be its teachings they regarded the Church as a community of saints composed of true believers alone—and by this they meant, not the invisible Church, of which the reformers were talking, but the visible Christian community. Following the primitive Christians, who knew no such artificial distinction as that between the visible and invisible Church, they undertook to make the Christian community actually a community of saints. It is, they maintained, the visible embodiment of the kingdom of God, and contains only those who are truly citizens of that kingdom. Holding this theory of the Church, they withdrew from the ecclesiastical bodies to which they had belonged, believing it impossible to transform them into genuine churches of Christ, and formed conventicles or churches of their own, to which only those were admitted who gave evidence in character and conduct of having been truly regenerated, and of being in possession of saving faith. These churches they regarded as alone genuine churches of Christ, and they commonly refused altogether to commune with those who were not members of them.

Of a general ecclesiastical body controlling the individual communities they would hear nothing. Not only of individualism in religion, but also of the independence of each group of true Christians and their freedom from outside domination, they made much. The greatest emphasis was laid upon the moral character of the regenerated, and the strictest discipline was exercised, the effort being to exclude from the Church all whose lives did not bear constant witness to the new birth and the sanctifying influence of the Holy Spirit. The following quotation from the *Twelve Articles of Christian Belief*, by Balthasar Hübmaier, one of the earliest and most influential of their leaders, indicates clearly enough the conception of the Church shared by most of them. 'I believe also and confess a holy Catholic Christian Church, which is the communion of saints, and a brotherhood of many pious and believing men, who unitedly confess one Lord, one God, one faith, and one baptism; assembled, maintained, and ruled on earth by the only living and divine Word, altogether beautiful and without any spot, unerring, pure, without wrinkle, and blameless.' 'I believe and confess also the remission of sins, so that this Christian Church has received keys, command and power from Thee, O Christ, to open the gates of Heaven for the sinner as often as he repenteth and is sorry for his sin, and receive him again into the holy assembly of believers in Christ, like the lost son and the repentant Corinthian. But when he, after the three-fold brotherly reproof, will not abstain from sin, I firmly believe that this Church also has power to exclude him and to hold him as a publican and heathen. Here I believe and confess openly, my Lord Jesus Christ, that whomsoever the Christian Church on earth thus looseth, he is certainly loosed and released in heaven. Again, whomsoever the Church bindeth and casteth out of her assembly on earth, he is bound before God in heaven and excluded from the Catholic Christian Church (out of which there is no salvation).'[1]

Emphasis was laid also upon the contrast between the Church and the world, and the effort was to withdraw as far as possible from contact with all outsiders, who were condemned as worldly whether they were within the existing ecclesiastical establishment or not. The separateness and aloofness of the Christian Church from all the rest of the world was in fact a fundamental tenet; ' Come ye out from among them and be ye separate' a favourite text. Unworldliness and other-worldliness were constant watchwords, and tendencies toward a more or less extreme asceticism were very common.

The true Church, according to the Anabaptists, was composed only of the regenerated, and moreover not necessarily of all the regenerated, who were known only to God. It was a visible, not an invisible Church, and in it were only those who accepted Christian baptism, and so publicly declared themselves followers of Christ, and testified to their own experience of regeneration. In other words, entrance into the Church was by the voluntary act of those already regenerated. To be regenerated was not the same as to enter the Christian Church. The latter was a step by itself but a necessary step. If one refused to accept baptism and to enter into public covenant with God, one could not be saved, for to do so was to disobey the express command of God; but there was no saving virtue in baptism as such. In fact the sacramental view of both baptism and the Lord's Supper was commonly rejected by them, though they continued to practise both, the one as a sign of regeneration and pledge of Christian

[1] Quoted from Vedder, *Balthasar Hübmaier* (*Heroes of the Reformation Series*), p. 134 *sq.*

living, the other as a common meal memorialising the death of Christ, and symbolising communion with Him and with each other.

Their notion of the voluntary character of the Christian Church, as a body constituted by the free act of Christian men, is of the very essence of the Anabaptist theory of the Church. As a result of this action infants were not regarded as members of the Church, and hence infant baptism was rejected, not only as unnecessary, but as sacrilegious. Baptism was looked upon, not as a means of regeneration in the traditional Catholic way, but as a sign that it had been accomplished. Only those already regenerated were to be baptized, and a pre-condition of regeneration was conscious faith. It is evident that there is here only the more consistent carrying out of Luther's fundamental principle of salvation by faith alone, a principle which he was himself untrue to, when he retained infant baptism while continuing to look upon it as a sacrament. If it be a sacrament then it is inconsistent with Protestant principles to administer it to those who have no faith.

A farther consequence of the Anabaptists' conception of the Church as composed only of true believers and distinguished sharply, not only from the world, but also from all existing ecclesiastical establishments, was their common insistence upon the separation of Church and State. A Church composed only of the regenerate could not exist under the control of the civil government, bound by laws of its making, and subject to its authority. Nor was it proper for members of the true Church to give themselves to the service of the world in positions of civil responsibility. In Seven Articles, agreed upon in 1527, by the Anabaptists of Switzerland and South-western Germany,[1] it is declared among other things that while civil government and the exercise of civil authority are of

[1] See Moeller's *Kirchengeschichte*, vol. iii. p. 402 *sq.*

divine appointment, the Church has nothing to do therewith. In it only spiritual discipline is to be exercised, and Christians are not to take part in affairs of State, or hold official positions of any kind. The separation, in other words, between civil and spiritual affairs is to be complete.

The severance of Church and State upon which the Anabaptists insisted, carried with it the rejection of the age-long notion that physical compulsion may rightly be exercised in matters of faith. The Church, the Anabaptists claimed, may excommunicate the heretical as well as the unholy, but its authority is spiritual only, and the civil power has no rights in the premises. They were thus in advance of all the great reformers in insisting upon freedom of conscience, and condemning religious persecution of every kind, and their influence along this line was ultimately very great.

Equally important with the Anabaptist theory of the Church, and still more at variance with common Reformation doctrine, was their notion of salvation and the Christian life. Luther's idea of salvation by the grace of God alone through faith, and not through works, found little acceptance among them. On the contrary, they were in sympathy with traditional Catholicism in emphasising the free will of man, and the necessity of earning future blessedness as a reward. Their doctrine was legal to the last degree. Not, to be sure, by ecclesiastical rites and ceremonies, and not by works of penance—all these they repudiated, but by the faithful observance of the law of God, and particularly by brotherly love and holiness, the Christian man must win the guerdon of eternal life. No one can earn salvation by himself; regeneration by divine grace is always necessary. But the regenerated man must make the proper use of his opportunities or he will infallibly perish. Of divine predestination they would hear nothing, of individual responsibility and capacity they made much. It is evident that men who held such positions can hardly have learned their Christianity from Luther or Zwingli. As a matter of fact their ideas were for the most part formed independently of the great reformers. They belonged, as is now generally recognised, to circles which had already largely broken with the Roman Catholic establishment, at least in spirit, before Luther came upon the scene. When he began his reforming work, he attracted multitudes of them, for he seemed to promise the liberation from the old system for which they had long been praying; and his theory of the Church as a community of saints doubtless had its influence. But they soon discovered their differences. Some of Luther's principles were utterly opposed to theirs; and some of the principles which they held in common he applied much less consistently, or in altogether different fashion. As a result, they broke with him and went their independent way. They broke also with Zwingli on the same general ground, and they were denounced by both reformers alike, and, in reaction against them, both became more conservative than would otherwise have been the case.

It is evident, in the light of what has been said, that it is only partially correct to call the Anabaptists the radicals of the Reformation period. In many respects they were more radical than the great reformers and their followers, but in some ways they were more conservative, and retained mediæval conceptions which the reformers rejected. Both in their radicalism and in their conservatism they resembled Calvin more than Luther. In their emphasis upon the absolute authority of the Bible and the necessity of regulating all things by its teachings; in their insistence upon strict discipline in order to keep the Church pure; and in their legalism, their other-worldliness and their asceticism, they were far nearer the younger than the older reformer. It is, therefore, no accident that in spite of their rejection of the doctrine of predestination, and their emphasis upon human freedom, they had much larger and more lasting influence within the Reformed wing of Protestantism than within the Lutheran. They got a permanent foothold at an early day in Holland, where they took the name of Mennonites, from Menno Simons, one of the leading Anabaptists of the sixteenth century; and the Independents, who have played so important a part in the life of England, and particularly of New England, since the seventeenth century, owed their inception to them.

II. *The Socinians*

Like Anabaptism, Socinianism was in part, but only in part, the fruit of the Protestant Reformation. Other and independent influences had still more to do with it, but those influences were not, as in the case of Anabaptism, mystical and apocalyptic, but humanistic. There were humanists, to be sure, among the Anabaptists, but humanism had nothing to do with the Anabaptist movement as a whole, while in Socinianism its influence was all-controlling. Both the uncle, Lælius Socinus, and the nephew Faustus, who did much to give Socinianism its permanent character, were born and brought up in Northern Italy, where the humanistic spirit was strong, and in Poland, where the movement first gained a foothold, and enjoyed its largest development, humanism was widespread and influential. Socinianism, in fact, was the earliest organised expression of the humanistic spirit in religion. Its principles were largely of humanistic rather than Protestant origin, but many of its leaders, like large numbers of the Anabaptists, were originally Protestants who broke with the reformers because they believed the latter were not giving their own principles consistent application. This fact, together with the community of interest due to common opposition to the Roman Catholic establishment, led the Socinians to regard themselves as Protestants, even though they repudiated the fundamental doctrines of the reformers, and were condemned and disowned by all other Protestant bodies.

The Socinians were by no means the only anti-Trinitarians of the sixteenth century. As the fundamental dogma in the historic Catholic system, the Trinity had long been a favourite object of attack by theological radicals. The sixteenth century witnessed many such attacks, both from Catholics and Protestants. Most of them, however interesting and instructive, were of little historical importance, and none of them would have had any appreciable influence upon the development of Protestant thought had it not been for Faustus Socinus, who succeeded in gathering the Unitarians of Poland into a strong and compact sect which bore the name of Polish Brethren,' and which had a long and honourable history. He succeeded also in freeing the sect from the Anabaptist tendencies with which Unitarianism in Poland was widely involved, and in giving it an independent character of its own. He had himself no sympathy with the prevailing spirit of the Anabaptists. Neither their social ideals nor their ethical and religious principles appealed to him. There was nothing either of the mystic or of the fanatic about him, nor indeed of the social revolutionist or reformer, and the Socinian system which he impressed upon the sect he did so much to organise was in its dominating spirit and interest totally unlike Anabaptism, in spite of their common rejection of some traditional doctrines.

The principles of the Socinians may be gathered from the writings of their leaders, particularly of Faustus Socinus,[1] and also most easily from the *Racovian Catechism*,[2]

---

[1] The works of Faustus Socinus are published in the first two volumes of the *Bibliotheca Fratrum Polonorum*, Amsterdam, 1656.

[2] The first edition was published in 1605 in Polish. In 1608 a German translation was issued, and in 1609 a Latin version. An English translation by Thomas Rees, based upon a revised and enlarged Latin edition of 1680, was published in 1818. It is from this translation that the quotations in the text are taken.

which was published in 1605, shortly after Socinus' death.

Fundamental in the teaching of the Socinians was the moral ability of man. Like the humanists in general, they had a controlling ethical interest, and it seemed to them essential to moral living that a man should have adequate native power and freedom of will to choose and follow virtue for himself. Nothing could be more striking than the contrast between the Socinians and the Protestant reformers at this point, and nothing better illustrates their difference of spirit and interest. Upon the absolute bondage of the human will and the utter inability of the natural man to do anything good, Luther laid the greatest stress, and his attitude became characteristic of the Reformation movement as a whole. The Socinians, on the other hand, asserted man's freedom in the strongest possible terms (cf. *Racovian Catechism*, sec. 5, chap. x.). Unless he is free he is not responsible for his acts, and no moral quality can be ascribed to them.

Consistently with their attitude in this matter, the Socinians rejected the doctrine of divine predestination, which was a fundamental tenet with all the leading reformers. To quote from the *Racovian Catechism* (sec. 5, chap. x.) : 'If, as you state, there be free will, how comes it to pass that so many deny it ? They do this because they think they have certain testimonies of Scripture, wherefrom they imagine they can make it appear that there is no free will in those things of which I have spoken. What are those testimonies ? They are of two kinds : the one, from which they persuade themselves that they can infer this ; the other, by which they conceive that free will is expressly taken away. Which are those testimonies whence they endeavour to infer this ? All those that treat of the predestination of God. . . . What is your opinion of this matter ? That this notion of predestination is altogether false—and principally for two reasons, whereof one is that it would necessarily destroy all religion, and the other that it would ascribe to God many things incompatible with His nature. Show me how the admission of this opinion would altogether destroy true religion ? This is evident from hence, that all things relating to faith and religion would be in us from necessity ; and if this were the case, there would be no need of our efforts and labours in order to be pious. For all exertion and application is wholly superfluous where all things are done through necessity, as reason itself shows. But if exertion and application be taken away from piety and religion, piety and religion must perish ' (p. 332).

Similarly the Socinians rejected the traditional doctrine of original sin, as accepted both by Catholics and Protestants, asserting that man was created mortal, not immortal, and that he lost neither life nor freedom by Adam's fall.[1] He is still able to obey the commands of God as Adam was ; his nature is not corrupt any more than was Adam's ; and he, therefore, does not need to be regenerated and transformed by divine power. The whole Catholic system of redemption thus became unnecessary, and it is characteristic of the Socinian intellectualism that, finding it to be so, they repudiated it unhesitatingly.

An essential element in the Catholic theory of redemption was the traditional doctrine of the atonement, which the reformers took over from the theologians of the Middle Ages. This doctrine was one of the principal objects of attack on the part of the Socinians, and their criticism of it was often very acute.[2] God's nature, they claimed, is such that He is in no way bound to an atonement in order that He may forgive sin. He is free to forgive with or without conditions, and hence the most telling argument for the traditional substitutionary theory falls to

[1] Cf. *Racovian Catechism*, p. 325 *sq.* ; and Socinus's *De Statu primi hominis ante lapsum, Opera*, vol. ii. p. 253 *sq.*

[2] See Socinus's *De Jesu Christo Servatore, Opera*, vol. ii. p. 121 *sq.* ; and *Racovian Catechism*, sec. 5, chap. viii.

the ground. Christ's work consists in reconciling men to God rather than God to men; it is His influence on men rather than on God that is important.

With the necessity of transforming the nature of man by the divine indwelling, and of making atonement in order that God might forgive, went the traditional basis for the belief in the deity of Christ, and the Socinians were entirely consistent in attacking that belief. They carried their opposition so far as to reject also the doctrines of pre-existence and incarnation. They were more radical even than the Arians, setting over against the historic theory of Christ's person, not the doctrine of a pre-existent divine being lower than God, who became incarnate, but the man Jesus Christ, whose true humanity and genuine moral development gave His life a real ethical value for all His followers.

The deity of Christ constituted the essential element in the historic doctrine of the Trinity. With the former, therefore, went the latter.[1] Here we come upon the most notorious feature of Socinianism—the rejection of the dogma of the Trinity. It would be a mistake, however, to suppose that this was its fundamental interest. There were many anti-Trinitarians of the day who found in the doctrine of the Trinity their principal point of attack, and doubtless not a few of them became Socinians. But the interest which controlled Socinus himself, and the sect as a whole, was deeper than this. The assault upon the Trinity was only an incident in a much larger campaign. Socinus himself says that while he thinks it well to know the truth in this matter, no one will be lost because he accepts the doctrine so long as it does not interfere with his worship and service of the one true God.[2] And accordingly, while in the *Racovian Catechism* large space is devoted to showing that the traditional belief in the deity

---

[1] Cf. *Racovian Catechism*, sec. 3, chap. i.
[2] *Opera*, vol. i. p. 652; cf. also *Racovian Catechism*, p. 46.

of Christ is erroneous, the doctrine of the Trinity is dismissed in a few paragraphs (sec. 3, chap. i.). That the Socinians are known as Unitarians, and justly so, should not mislead us, therefore, into supposing that anti-Trinitarianism was their primary interest. It was only a corollary of positions much more vital and fundamental.

With the rest of the Catholic system of redemption went also the traditional doctrine of the Church and the sacraments as means of grace. The Church is simply the community of those who embrace saving doctrine.[1] Baptism is only a sign and pledge of faith and obedience on man's part, and the Lord's Supper nothing more than a commemoration of the death of Christ.[2]

It is evident that the Socinians were remarkably consistent in the application of humanistic principles to Christian theology, and yet their consistency was not complete. Their changed estimate of man led to the rejection of the traditional system of redemption with all that it involved, but the modern spirit which voiced itself in that estimate found only limited expression after all, for instead of declaring that man is entirely sufficient to himself, they asserted his absolute need of light from above in order that he might know the way of life and salvation, which would otherwise be hidden from him. In other words, while they insisted upon the moral ability of man, they denied the sufficiency of his knowledge. It is true that they made much of the power and authority of human reason. Like the humanists in general, they insisted that in religion, as in all other matters, human reason has a necessary place. In the *Racovian Catechism*, in response to the question, 'Of what use then is right reason, if it be of any, in those matters which relate to salvation?' it is said: 'It is indeed of great service, since without it we could neither perceive with certainty the authority of the sacred writings, understand their con-

[1] *Racovian Catechism*, sec. viii. chap. i.   [2] *Ibid.* sec. v. chaps. iii. and iv.

tents, discriminate one thing from another, nor apply them to any practical purpose. When, therefore, I stated that the Holy Scriptures were sufficient for our salvation, so far from excluding right reason, I certainly assumed its presence' (sec. 1, chap. ii.). In accordance with this principle the Socinians used rational arguments on a large scale in attacking traditional doctrines. Indeed, the irrationality of the existing system was one of their principal grounds of hostility to it. All would-be religious truth, like alleged truth in any other sphere, must submit to the judgment of the human mind. Nothing contrary to reason can possibly be true in religion any more than anywhere else. We have here another point of contrast between the Socinians and the Protestant reformers, particularly Luther. He spoke with great contempt of the human reason, and denounced both schoolmen and humanists because they depended upon it; and while in this he was more extreme than most of his associates, the depreciation of natural reason in connection with divine things was characteristic of the Reformation movement as a whole. As a consequence the rationalism of the Socinians was widely condemned by the Protestant divines of the day, and was made one of the chief counts in the orthodox indictment of them.

And yet, in spite of their rationalism, the Socinians denied that human reason is enough to guide a man in the way of life and salvation. Every one must be enlightened from above if he is not to perish eternally. In the *Racovian Catechism* it is said : 'As you stated at the commencement that the way which leads to immortality was pointed out by God, I wish to know why you made this assertion ? Because man is not only obnoxious to death, but could not of himself discover a way to avoid it, and that should infallibly conduct to immortality.' 'How do you prove that he could not of himself discover the way by which he might avoid death, and which would infallibly conduct him to immortality ? This may be seen from hence, that so glorious a recompense, and the sure means of obtaining it, must wholly depend on the will and counsel of God. But this will and counsel, what human being can explore and clearly ascertain, unless they be revealed by God Himself ? ' (sec. 2, chap. i.).

It was in accordance with this conception of human need that the Socinians interpreted Christianity. The *Racovian Catechism* opens with the words : ' I wish to be informed by you what the Christian religion is ? The Christian religion is the way of attaining eternal life which God has pointed out by Jesus Christ, or, in other words, it is the method of serving God which He has Himself delivered by Jesus Christ.' Man's supreme duty is to serve God, who will reward the obedient with eternal life, and punish the disobedient with eternal death. How God is to be served no one can discover for himself; He is an absolute sovereign, and has the right to demand such service as He pleases, so long as it is not ' in its own nature evil and unjust ' (sec. 3, chap. i.). What that service may be we can learn only from God. Divine revelation is, therefore, unconditionally necessary, and is supplied by Christianity. Christ's supreme work was that of a prophet, to declare both by precept and example God's will for men. That it was truly the divine will which he declared is proved by the holiness of his life, by His miracles, and by His death and resurrection. To the Christian conscience, or to the inner experience of forgiveness and salvation, no appeal is made in support of Christianity. The evidences that it is of God are wholly external, particularly the supernatural elements in the life of Christ.

Consistently with the conception of Christ's work as chiefly that of a revealer of God's will, more than half of the *Racovian Catechism* is devoted to his prophetic office, under which head are treated such subjects as the precepts of Christ, including the Ten Commandments as interpreted by Him, Baptism, the Lord's Supper, eternal life, the promise of the Holy Spirit, the death of Christ, faith, free will, and justification. The attempt was made—though it was not carried through consistently at all points—to view the whole Christian system under this aspect; its one great significance is that it is a revelation of the will of God and a promise of a blessed immortality to those living in accordance therewith. The Socinian notion of the Christian life was legal to the last degree. To be a Christian is simply to know and do the will of God revealed by Christ. Faith is a motive leading man to obedience, and unless followed thereby it is of no avail. Knowledge and conduct are the two essential elements. For them who know and do is the reward, but only for them.

The Christian revelation, a knowledge of which is necessary to salvation, is contained in the Scriptures alone. The Bible, especially the New Testament, is a divine book, authoritative in all its parts, and from it alone the will of God can be learned. Extended arguments for the authenticity of the New Testament, all of an external character, are given in the first section of the *Catechism*, and the Old Testament is accepted on the testimony of the New. Both are appealed to in support of the teachings of the *Catechism*, but the New Testament far more largely than the Old. The Socinians made thoroughgoing work of the principle of Biblical authority. It was no mere form of speech with them; it was taken in the most serious possible way. Christianity became in their hands more completely than ever before a book religion. Not from the traditions of the Church, not from communications of the Spirit to this or other ages, and not from the Christian consciousness, individual or collective, is the will of God to be learned, but from the Bible alone, the one and only revelation vouchsafed to men.

The rationalism of the Socinians did not in any way

interfere with their recognition of the authority of the Scriptures, but it did affect their interpretation of them. Whatever God has revealed must be rational. The Scotist divorce between the reason of man and the reason of God, the Socinians did not admit. It is often said that their view of God was taken from the Scotists, but this is an error. They emphasised God's absolute will, and unconditional sovereignty, but they denied that He could act inconsistently with sound reason any more than with right and justice, and they believed that sound reason is one in God and man. The Bible, therefore, must be interpreted by the light of reason. It can contain nothing irrational, and to deduce from it teaching that does violence to our sense of the fitness of things is to misinterpret it. The application of this criterion to the reading of the Scriptures meant in many cases a decided advance upon traditional exegesis, but in other cases flagrant misunderstanding. In their interpretation of the synoptic gospels, for instance, the Socinians were as a rule far sounder than most Catholic and Protestant exegetes. But when it came to Paul and John, their mysticism was so foreign to the Socinian way of looking at things that they were very commonly misinterpreted. With the miraculous element in the Biblical records, the Socinians had no trouble; they believed in the supernatural as firmly as any of their contemporaries. But they were ethically, not religiously, interested, and with the mystical element in Christian experience they had no sympathy. It was, therefore, inevitable that they should be quite blind to certain features of Biblical teaching. But they were none the less sincere in their recognition of Scriptural authority, and none the less zealous in their conformity to what they believed to be the meaning of the word. In fact, they carried their loyalty to the Scriptures so far that they accepted many doctrines, and retained many practices, simply because they found them in the Bible.

and not a few of these were out of line with their controlling principles. Thus, for instance, although they denied Christ's pre-existence, and insisted that the one important thing to know about Him was that He had a real human nature,[1] they yet accepted the Virgin birth,[2] and held that Christ ascended to heaven before His public ministry, and there learned the revelation which He afterward communicated to the world.[3] They also taught that He was exalted to the right hand of God after His resurrection, and became Priest and King and Judge of all men, and they insisted that divine worship should be paid Him. On this last point there was a difference of opinion among the early Unitarians of Poland, but the worship of Christ was maintained by Socinus himself and the majority of the Socinian sect.[4]

Upon the authority of the Bible, too, they made many statements about the work of Christ, which it is difficult to harmonise with their general attitude upon the subject. They spoke of Him as a mediator, a propitiation, an expiation, a satisfaction, an offering, a sacrifice, and so on.[5] They also made use of the conception of the Holy Spirit, though they denied his personality, and they talked about the inspiration and strength for virtuous living which the Spirit imparts to Christian believers.[6] They likewise retained baptism, and the Lord's Supper, evidently only because found in the New Testament. In all these cases they attempted to interpret the phrases they quoted, and the ideas and practices they adopted, in accordance with their general view of Christianity, and even in some cases to give them a real significance. But often the disparity was too great and the inconsistencies were left unresolved. Their effort to see in Christianity nothing but a revelation of the divine will, and to reconstruct the whole Christian

---

[1] *Racovian Catechism*, p. 51 *sq.*
[2] *Ibid.* p. 53.
[3] *Ibid.* p. 170.
[4] Cf. *ibid.* p. 189 *sq.*
[5] *Ibid.* pp. 297 *sq.*, 349 *sq.*
[6] *Ibid.* pp. 284 *sq.*, 324 *sq.*

system from that point of view, broke down, in fact, simply because of their loyal adherence to the text of the Scriptures, and the result was a curious medley of disparate and often inconsistent elements.

Socinianism was condemned by the Protestant Churches, both Reformed and Lutheran, but it left its mark upon them. After being driven out of Poland in 1661, when the Government became Roman Catholic, the sect lost its corporate existence, but many found their way to Holland, where their principles bore considerable fruit. Their respect for the Bible, and their rejection of a large part of the traditional system because of its un-Biblical character, tended to enhance the credit of the Scriptures, whose authority was recognised even by so radical a sect, and at the same time provoked inquiry as to the Scriptural basis for existing doctrines. Biblical study was thus greatly forwarded by their challenge.

On the other hand, wherever they went they promoted a more humanistic way of looking at things. Unconditional election and the complete bondage of the will came to be questioned far beyond the confines of Socinianism itself. There can be no doubt for instance that Arminianism was, in part at least, the fruit of Socinian influence. In general it may be said that the rationalism of the Socinians, limited as it was, yet made its influence widely felt, fostering in some cases a more, in others a less, extreme radicalism than they themselves represented. By their criticism of the existing theological system, both on Biblical and rational grounds, they undermined its credit in many quarters, and hastened the day of its disintegration.

CHAPTER VII

THE ENGLISH REFORMATION

ENGLAND's break with Rome, which came under Henry VIII., and at his instance, was made possible, if it was not directly caused, by many influences. Discontent with the encroachments of the papacy, growing national feeling, popular dislike of the clergy, united to weaken the hold of the old Church. Lollardy, with its anti-ecclesiasticism, and its emphasis upon the authority of the Bible, in spite of repression and persecution, was still a force in many quarters, and humanism had its representatives and champions in England as well as on the Continent. The writings of Luther were widely read, and his opinions early gained considerable vogue, especially in university circles. Henry was, therefore, acting in accordance with a widespread and growing sentiment among his subjects when he forced the break with Rome, and the establishment of a national Church of England. Religiously and theologically, he was a conservative. He wished to be recognised as the supreme head of the English Church, but he desired no change in either doctrine or worship. Had it been possible he would have retained the old system in its completeness with the single exception of the papacy. This, however, he could not do. It was natural that the chief supporters of royal supremacy should be those most imbued with Protestant principles; to disregard altogether their desire for a reform of the existing system, both in doctrine and in worship, was out of the question.

In 1536, two years after the adoption by Parliament of the Act of Supremacy, which completed the schism with the Church of Rome, there was drawn up a set of ten articles, the first five doctrinal in character, the others dealing with ecclesiastical rites and ceremonies. They were published under the title of 'Articles devised by his King's Highness Majesty to establish Christian Quietness,' and were ordered to be read in the churches. They were conservative in spirit and denounced radicalism, both in doctrine and worship, but they emphasised the free grace of God in justification, they omitted all mention of transubstantiation in the account of the Mass, and they spoke of the Bible, the three ecumenical creeds, and the decisions of the first four councils as the supreme doctrinal standards. They thus looked in a hesitating way in the direction of Protestantism without breaking at any decisive point with traditional principles.

In the royal Injunctions of 1538 the clergy were directed to see that a copy of the Bible in English was placed in every parish church, where it might be read by the people, and to 'provoke, stir, and exhort every person to read the same as that which is the very lively word of God that every Christian man is bound to embrace, believe and follow if he look to be saved.'[1]

In 1537 there was issued by the archbishops and bishops, a work entitled *The Institute of a Christian Man*, and commonly called the Bishops' Book, which consisted of an exposition of the Creed, the sacraments, the Ten Commandments, and the Lord's Prayer.[2] It represented very much the same point of view as the Ten Articles, but went beyond them in denying the doctrine of Purgatory.

In 1539, on the other hand, in consequence of popular insurrections caused in part by the religious innovations, particularly the dissolution of the monasteries, Parlia-

---
[1] Quoted from Gee and Hardy's *Documents*, p. 276.
[2] Reprinted in *Formularies of Faith put forth by authority during the reign of Henry VIII*. Oxford, 1825.

THE ENGLISH REFORMATION

ment passed a reactionary act 'for the abolishing of diversity in religion,' commonly known as the Six Articles' Law. In it transubstantiation was explicitly affirmed, and the denial of it made punishable by death; the needlessness of communion in both kinds, and the binding character of vows of chastity were asserted, private Masses approved, and the celibacy of the clergy and auricular confession made obligatory. In 1543 a revised edition of the Bishops' Book was published under the title of *The Necessary Erudition of a Christian Man*.[1] This was known as the King's Book, and was intended to supersede the earlier work. It was thoroughly Catholic in its spirit and tendency, and lacked all the traces of Protestantism which had marked the Bishops' Book.

The *via media* thus established the king succeeded in maintaining during the rest of his reign, though it probably satisfied very few of his subjects. On the one hand, devout Catholics wished to restore the papal supremacy, and on the other hand convinced Protestants, whose number was steadily increasing, wished to revolutionise the traditional system.

Under Edward VI. the Protestant party had the ascendency in the government, and the new faith was given practical expression in many ways. The Six Articles' Law was repealed, images were removed from the churches, and the invocation of saints forbidden. A book of homilies was published, similar to the Bishops' Book, but more decidedly Protestant, the administration of the Communion in both kinds was commanded, clerical marriage was permitted, and the Book of Common Prayer was issued and made the only lawful service book of the English Church.[2] Finally, forty-two articles of religion were framed and put

---

[1] Also reprinted in *Formularies of Faith*, etc.
[2] By Edward's first Act of Uniformity passed by Parliament in January 1549. A second and revised edition of the Prayer Book was substituted for the first by the second Act of Uniformity, January 1552. The two Acts are given by Gee and Hardy, pp. 358 ff. and 369 ff.

forth by royal authority as the official confession of faith.[1] Before they got into general use, Edward's elder sister Mary, a devout Catholic and papist, came to the throne, and a reaction took place, resulting in the temporary re-establishment of the old system and the bitter persecution of the adherents of the new régime.

Mary was succeeded in 1558 by her half-sister Elizabeth, daughter of Anne Boleyn, the necessities of whose position required her to repudiate the authority of the Pope, and to maintain the royal supremacy and the independence of the English Church. It was impossible, even had it been desired, to restore the condition of things that existed in the later years of Henry VIII. Protestantism had grown so strong in the country at large that it was necessary to give the English establishment a far more Protestant character than Henry would have approved. It is true that both Elizabeth and her government were more conservative than Edward's Council of Regency, and the Protestantising process was not carried so far as it doubtless would have been had Edward remained longer on the throne. Still, practically all that was accomplished under Edward was ratified under Elizabeth, and in polity, worship, and doctrine, the English Church was given the general character which it has borne ever since. Episcopacy was retained. The Prayer Book was re-issued with some minor changes, its use was made obligatory in all churches, and worship by any other form was prohibited.[2] The forty-two articles were revised and reduced to thirty-nine, and assent to them was required of all clergymen.[3]

[1] The forty-two articles received Edward's signature in June 1553 and he died the following month. On the articles see Hardwick's *History of the Articles of Religion*, revised edition, 1859.

[2] By the Act of Uniformity of 1559, given by Gee and Hardy, p. 488 *sq*.

[3] The thirty-nine articles were approved by Convocation in 1563, and issued by royal authority without the twenty-ninth article on the eating of Christ's body by the wicked. In 1571 Parliament passed the Subscription Act by which the articles, with the twenty-ninth restored, were made permanently binding (see Gee and Hardy, p. 477).

The Thirty-Nine Articles in which the theology of the English Reformation received final expression, were simply a revision of the forty-two of Edward, and represented the same general type of doctrine. There was no independent theological thinking in England during the period of the Reformation. The leaders of the English movement were largely engrossed in matters of government and worship. There was indeed no important theologian among them. In doctrinal matters they followed the Continental reformers, emphasising the positions common to all of them, and minimising the matters in which the Lutheran and Reformed theologians disagreed. They adopted the common Augustinian platform, upon which Luther, as well as Zwingli and Calvin, stood, and the common doctrine of justification by faith. They were Calvinistic rather than Lutheran in their view of the Lord's Supper, perhaps in part because Bucer spent the last three years of his life as a professor at Cambridge, during the reign of Edward VI., and came into close relation with the Protestant leaders of the day. On the other hand, it was the more conservative Lutheran rather than the more radical Reformed idea of the authority of the Church that finally prevailed. As a result, the English Reformation bore a less advanced character than the Swiss. Moreover, the theory of the relation of Church and State was Luther's rather than Calvin's. The supreme authority of the civil power in ecclesiastical affairs was established permanently, not, to be sure, as a result of Luther's teaching, but as a natural consequence of the situation under Henry VIII.

The forty-two articles of Edward, which were in the main reproduced in the thirty-nine of Elizabeth, were based upon the Augsburg Confession of 1530, through the medium of fifteen articles drawn up in 1538 by a committee of German and English theologians, but not published. In the revision under Elizabeth, use was also made of the Württemberg Confession of 1552, framed by Brentius and other Lutheran theologians for presentation to the Council of Trent. Both the Augsburg and Württemberg confessions were purposely made as conservative and conciliatory as possible, their aim being to show Protestantism in the most favourable light. The English articles bear in part the same general stamp, but there is more evangelicalism in them, and they are explicit and outspoken on some subjects not touched in the two German confessions. In general, it may be said that they were intended to be a reasonably complete statement of the Protestant faith as accepted by the Continental churches, and interpreted in England, that they are genuinely Protestant, but emphasise, like the Augsburg Confession, the common Catholic faith, and warn against Protestant radicalism, that they are Augustinian, but moderately so, and that they belong exclusively to neither the Lutheran nor Reformed wing of Protestantism, except in the doctrine of the Eucharist, where the Calvinistic view is stated without repudiating the Lutheran opinion. The statements concerning the rule of faith, which are not found in the Augsburg Confession, also show Reformed influence, as does the careful and judicious article on predestination, which is likewise lacking in the earlier creed. Finally, it is to be noticed that the articles are eminently practical, not speculative in interest, and guard carefully against practical radicalism, particularly antinomianism. On the whole, they constitute one of the very best symbols of the Reformation, and, at the time they were framed, were admirably adapted for a State church, in which it was necessary to comprehend as many divergent views as possible. There would have been no serious Protestant nonconformity in England in the sixteenth and seventeenth centuries on the ground of the articles alone. They stated the common platform so sanely and moderately that most Protestants could find no particular fault with them.[1]

It was during the reign of Elizabeth that the Puritan controversy began to distract the English church. From the beginning of the Reformation there were two divergent opinions as to the proper attitude toward the old system. Some believed that only by complete repudiation of traditional forms and ceremonies could Protestantism permanently maintain itself, while others dreaded the unsettling effects of too radical a change. The former maintained that nothing should be allowed in doctrine, worship, or polity which was not approved by Scripture or fairly deducible therefrom. The latter, while recognising the binding authority of the Bible in the matter of doctrine, held that in worship and polity the Church had the right to determine its own conduct provided it did not contradict Scriptural teaching. The latter was Luther's principle, the former Zwingli's and Calvin's. In England the more conservative position prevailed in the beginning, but there were not wanting representatives of the other view, and already in the reign of Edward VI. they began to cause trouble. Under Elizabeth the controversy waxed warm. It was originally confined for the most part to the sphere of worship, and had to do with forms, ceremonies and vestments, but gradually it involved the whole question of the nature and government of the Church and its relation to the State. In the first of the Admonitions to Parliament (1572), which was written by Field and Wilcox, and constituted one of the most important Puritan manifestoes of the day, although there was a discussion of forms of worship and clerical vestments, it was said, 'Neither is the controversy between them

[1] Compare for instance the remark on the last page of the first of the famous Puritan Admonitions to Parliament of the year 1572: 'For the articles, concerning the substance of doctrine, using a godly interpretation in a point or two, which are either too sparely or else too darkly set down, we were and are ready according to duty to subscribe unto them.'

and us as for a cap, a tippet, or a surplice, but for great matters concerning a true ministry and regiment of the Church according to the Word. Which things once established, the others melt away of themselves.' And in the second Admonition of the same year from the pen of Thomas Cartwright, the polity of the Church was made the principal subject of discussion. In this document prelacy was attacked, and presbyterianism declared to be the only lawful government because taught in the Scriptures, the independence of the Church was asserted, and its subjection to the State rejected in good Calvinistic fashion. Strict ecclesiastical discipline was also insisted upon in the spirit of Calvin. The same general position appears in a work by Walter Travers, published in 1574, under the title *A Full and Plain Declaration of Ecclesiastical Discipline out of the Word of God, and of the Declining of the Church of England from the same*.[1]

The classical defence of the established Anglican position against the attacks of the Puritans is found in Richard Hooker's great work on *Ecclesiastical Polity*.[2] In opposition to the Puritan insistence upon the Scriptures as the sole rule of conduct, Hooker maintains that the Bible, the tradition of the Church, and the human reason all have their places in determining what is right, both for the individual and for the Church. 'For whereas God hath left sundry kinds of laws unto men, and by all those laws

[1] This became the recognised text-book of puritanism. It was written in Latin and issued by Cartwright in an English translation. In the same connection may be mentioned a brief book of discipline drawn up about 1580 on the basis of Travers' work and widely used by Puritan clergymen in the effort to reform the English Church from within, and to make it Presbyterian in government and discipline. An English translation of it was found among Cartwright's papers and published in 1644 (reprinted in the appendix of Briggs's *American Presbyterianism*). The Latin original has finally come to light, and is given in Paget's *Introduction to the Fifth Book of Hooker's Ecclesiastical Polity* (1899).

[2] The first four books were published in 1594, the fifth and longest in 1597, the sixth, seventh, and eighth after the author's death, from notes found among his papers. The sixth book, as it stands, has no relation to the Puritan controversy, in spite of its title, and should not constitute a part of the *Ecclesiastical Polity*.

the actions of men are in some sort directed; they hold that one only law, the Scripture, must be the rule to direct in all things, even so far as to the taking up of a rush or straw, about which point there should not need any question to grow, and that which is grown might presently end, if they did but yield to these two restraints. The first is, not to extend the actions whereof they speak so low as that instance doth import of taking up a straw, but rather keep themselves at the least within the compass of moral actions, actions which have in them vice or virtue. The second, not to exact at our hands for every action the knowledge of some place of Scripture out of which we stand bound to deduce it, as by divers testimonies they seek to enforce; but rather as the truth is, so to acknowledge, that it sufficeth if such action be framed according to the law of reason' (Book II., Introduction).

In matters of faith, Hooker held that the Bible alone should be followed, but in the sphere of polity and worship the Church might adopt such forms as she pleased, and might change them when she saw fit, provided she did not contradict the principles of religion laid down in Scripture.[1]

In discussing the details of the Anglican system which were criticised by the Puritans, Hooker maintained that the question in every case is not whether the particular forms and ceremonies are of Popish origin, but whether they are bad in themselves. Even if they cannot be shown to be positively good and useful, if they are not injurious, they should be retained. Moreover, even harmful things should be kept if not too harmful, for the evil of changing the established order may prove greater than the evil involved in retaining the thing complained of.[2]

The seventh book contains an elaborate defence of

---

[1] Cf. bk. III. chaps. iii. and x.; and bk. V. chap. viii.
[2] Bk. IV. chap. xiv.

episcopacy on the basis of the Bible and the tradition of the Church. In the first chapter it is said, 'A thousand five hundred years and upward the church of Christ hath now continued under the sacred regiment of bishops. Neither for so long hath Christianity been ever planted in any kingdom throughout the world, but with this kind of government alone; which to have been ordained of God, I am for mine own part even as resolutely persuaded as that any other kind of government in the world whatsoever is of God.' But the book must be read in the light of Hooker's general position touching the authority of the Church to fix and to alter its government and worship, and particularly in the light of such a passage as the following from the third book: 'If therefore we did seek to maintain that which most advantageth our own cause, the very best way for us and the strongest against them were to hold even as they do that in Scripture there must needs be found some particular form of Church polity which God hath instituted, and which for that very cause belongeth to all churches, to all times. But with any such partial eye to respect ourselves, and by cunning to make those things seem the truest which are the fittest to serve our purpose, is a thing which we neither like nor mean to follow' (chap. x.).

The eighth book is a defence of the royal supremacy on the ground that the Church of England is a national institution to which every Englishman belongs, and therefore is subject to the same authorities which the nation as a whole is subject to. The work constitutes an admirable presentation of the Anglican point of view, and rises far above the level of contemporary controversy in loftiness of style, breadth of outlook, kindliness of temper, general moderation and avoidance of all extremes. In its emphasis on the dignity of human reason, in its insistence on the authority of tradition, and in its recognition of the value of rites and ceremonies, and of the importance of uniformity of worship and order and propriety in the services, it is representative in the highest degree of the best type of historic Anglicanism.

The Presbyterian principles of Cartwright were not shared by all the Puritans, but they became increasingly common, and as time passed the controversy was more and more confined to questions of polity and discipline. Doctrine, too, became involved as the Puritans, in opposition to the growing Arminianism of their opponents, emphasised a high and rigid Calvinism. When they gained control of the government under the Commonwealth, they immediately undertook to put their principles into practice and to reform the Church in accordance with their long-cherished ideas. The Westminster standards (1645 ff.) were for a short time the official standards of the English Church. They represented an extreme Calvinism in theology, Presbyterianism in polity (though without the assertion of its exclusive divine right), and Puritanism in worship. With the Restoration in 1660 the old Anglican order was re-established, and Puritanism was again proscribed, and since the Revolution of 1688 it has existed only in the form of legalised dissent.

In Scotland, meanwhile, under the leadership of John Knox, Calvinism in doctrine, Presbyterianism in polity, and Puritanism in worship were permanently stamped upon the Protestantism of the country,[1] and in 1690, after the English revolution, the Westminster standards were made binding by law upon the Scottish Church.

As already seen, the great Puritan leaders of the late sixteenth and early seventeenth centuries desired to reform the English Church from within. They had no quarrel with the idea of a national church, though they would make it independent of State control. But there

[1] See the first Scottish Confession of 1560, the *First Book of Discipline* of the same year, and the Genevan *Book of Common Order* of 1556, which was used also in Scotland.

were others who repudiated the idea altogether, and withdrew from the establishment and undertook to form independent churches of their own. The most important of these were the early Independents or Congregationalists, whose principles were first set forth by Robert Browne in a number of remarkable tracts.[1]

Browne's theory of the Church was that of the Continental Anabaptists. The Church is a community of saints constituted by a voluntary covenant taken by Christian believers with God and with each other. It must keep itself free from all outside control, must be independent of the State, and must be preserved from impurity by the exercise of the strictest discipline. Browne was apparently moved originally by the desire, not to frame a novel ecclesiastical polity, but to promote the spiritual life of believers. To this end it seemed to him necessary that they should separate from their ungodly fellow-members of the Established Church, and should have communion and worship only with the truly regenerate. It was impossible, he believed, to make the Church of England a really spiritual institution, including as it did all baptized persons, and the course of his fellow-Puritans in looking for its reformation to the civil government, and waiting until their principles found acceptance in Parliament, seemed to him futile. He adopted the Anabaptist principle of the complete separation of Church and State, and advocated the Reformation of the Church 'without tarrying for any,' to quote from the title of one of his most famous tracts; or in other words, the formation of a new church, or new churches, composed wholly of

[1] The most important of his tracts are 'A Book which Showeth the Life and Manners of all True Christians' (1582), 'A Treatise of Reformation Without Tarrying for Any' (1582), 'A Treatise upon the Twenty-third of Matthew' (1582), and 'A True and Short Declaration both of the gathering and joining together of certain Persons, and also of the Lamentable Breach and Division which fell among Them' (1583?) On Browne see especially Dexter's *Congregationalism of the Last Three Hundred Years as seen in its Literature*, and Burrage's *The True Story of Robert Browne* (Oxford, 1906).

true believers, and patterned in all matters strictly after the word of God.

Browne's position touching the relation of Church and State is set forth in such passages as the following :—' My kingdom, saith Christ, is not of this world, and they would shift in both bishops and magistrates into his spiritual throne to make it of this world ; yea to stay the church government on them, is not only to shift but to thrust them before Christ. Yet under him in his spiritual kingdom are (1 Cor. xii.) first Apostles; secondly Prophets ; thirdly teachers, etc. Also helpers and spiritual guides : But they put the magistrates first, which in a commonwealth indeed are first, and above the preachers, yet have they no ecclesiastical authority at all, but only as any other Christians, if so be they be Christians.' [1] ' We know that Moses might reform, and the judges and kings which followed him, and so may our Magistrates : yea they may reform the Church and command things expedient for the same. Yet may they do nothing concerning the Church, but only civilly, and as civil Magistrates, that is, they have not that authority over the Church, as to be Prophets or Priests, or spiritual Kings, as they are Magistrates over the same : but only to rule the commonwealth in all outward justice, to maintain the right welfare and honour thereof, with outward power, bodily punishment, and civil forcing of men. And therefore also because the Church is in a commonwealth it is of their charge : that is concerning the outward provision and outward justice, they are to look to it, but to compel religion, to plant churches by power, and to force a submission to ecclesiastical government by laws and penalties belongeth not to them, as is proved before, neither yet to the Church.' [2]

[1] 'Reformation without Tarrying for Any'; reprint in 'Old South Leaflet,' No. 100, p. 4.
[2] *Ibid.* p. 13. Browne's attitude in this matter seems clear, but in his article on 'Brownism' in Hastings's *Encyclopædia of Religion and Ethics*,

In Browne's theory of the Church the primitive idea of it as a community called out of, and set apart from, the world, came to extremest expression. Nowhere else in history has it been more consciously held and consistently realised. The Church is a company of saints, and its purpose is not the salvation of the world, or the transformation of the world into the Kingdom of God, but the communion of its members with God and with each other, and their growth in grace. The Church exists primarily for common worship and mutual edification. Not even

Powicke says, referring to Browne: 'But on the Continent he had been more than anticipated by the Anabaptists; for, in one respect at least, his plea, as compared with theirs, presents a remarkable limitation, viz. that he seems to permit, if not to oblige the Prince—after the examples of "the good kings of Juda"—not indeed to "force the people by laws or by power to receive the (true) church government," but yet, when once they had received it, to keep them to it, and even to "put them to death" if "then they fell away."' The whole passage from which Powicke quotes runs as follows:—'The Lord's kingdom is not by force, neither by an army or strength (Zach. iv., Hosea ii.), as be the kingdoms of this world. Neither durst Moses nor any of the good kings of Juda force the people by law or by power to receive the church government, but after they received it, if then they fell away, and sought not the Lord, they might put them to death. For the covenant was first made, as it is written (2 Chron. xv.), they made a covenant to seek the Lord God of their fathers, with all their heart, and with all their soul. And then follow the next words which are to be understood of them which made the covenant, for of them which so sware unto the Lord, whosoever did not seek the Lord God of Israel, should be slain, whether he were small or great, man or woman. And therefore did the whole congregation of Israel gather them together, to war against the children of Reuben and Gad, because they seemed to forsake the covenant (Joshua xxii.). Yet would not Hezekiah fight against Israel, though they laughed him to scorn and mocked at his doings (2 Chron. xxx.), for they had not received the covenant, but their forefathers, and they were now called to the covenant again, which the Lord had disannulled with their forefathers; as it is written (2 Chron. xv.), that for a long season Israel had been without the true God, and without priest to teach, and without law' (p. 10 ff.).

Moses' action was evidently justified according to Browne, not because, in general, magistrates have power to compel religious conformity, but because the people in this case had taken a covenant and he had the right to require fulfilment of it, the breaking of the covenant being properly a crime cognisable by the authorities. Moreover, Browne claimed that the Jewish commonwealth could not be made a model for England in the matter of a connection between Church and State. 'But if Zachariah or Haggai had tarried, it proveth not that we must tarry for our magistrates. For both Jehoshua the high priest, and Zerubbabel the Prince, were figures of the high priesthood and princedom of Christ, and also had an ecclesiastical government over the church which our magistrates have not' (p. 13).

monasticism was in principle less regardful of the welfare of the world at large than those who held this theory. In it the old Jewish idea of election as a privilege rather than a responsibility found its most consistent utterance, and religious exclusiveness of an extreme type was the result. It is true that Browne and the early Congregationalists, like the Anabaptists in general, did not deny the salvation of men outside of their particular communions; indeed, church membership was not necessary to salvation except as it was a part of the Christian's duty which he could not with impunity neglect. But only such pure communities as they were standing for could be regarded as genuine churches, and hence the obligation of every true Christian was to connect himself with one of them. The consequence was an exclusiveness in effect as complete as if they had denied salvation to any but themselves.

Consistently with this theory of the Church, Browne followed the Anabaptists in insisting upon strict discipline. Here he was at one with Calvin and the Puritans in general. One of the chief criticisms passed upon the English establishment by the Puritans was its neglect of discipline, and the consequent presence within it of a multitude of unworthy members. But Browne went even further than they, and insisted on excluding many whom they would have allowed to remain within the Church; and the difference was not merely one of degree, but of underlying theory. If the Church be a State institution, and all baptized citizens belong to it, as Browne's Puritan contemporaries commonly agreed, then the test to be applied to church members is of a different kind from Browne's test. Open and flagrant immorality, scandalous living of any kind, might fairly lead to excommunication, but more than this could hardly be demanded. But where the Church is supposed to be composed only of the truly regenerate, any valid evidence of the lack of a new birth must in consistency mean exclusion from membership. There might be differences of opinion as to the way in which this principle should be applied in particular cases, as there actually were, both among the Anabaptists and the early Independents, but the principle itself is clear enough, and differs radically from the common Puritan and Anglican position.

Another Anabaptist tenet adopted by Browne, and made one of the fundamental planks of Congregationalism, was the independence of the local church. According to Browne, ' Christians are a company or number of believers who, by a willing covenant, made with their God, are under the government of God and Christ, and keep his laws in one holy communion.' And throughout his *Book which Showeth the Life and Manners of all true Christians,* from which this quotation is taken, the independence and autonomy of the local church are assumed. Indeed, on Browne's theory of the Church as constituted by a voluntary covenant taken by Christian men with God and with each other, anything else than independency was impossible. According to this theory, the Church can be nothing but a local company of Christians, who enter into covenant and carry on their Christian life and work together. It is not the only church; wherever the truly regenerate thus enter into covenant, there is a true church, and hence there are many churches of Christ, each possessed of all the rights and privileges and powers of such an institution.

Still another feature of Anabaptism which was taken over and made their own by Browne and the early Independents was the democratic organisation of the Church. Ecclesiastical officers are not self-appointed nor imposed upon the Church from without, but are chosen by the congregation itself, and are responsible to their brethren, and may at any time be deposed by them. They do not constitute a special clerical class possessed of inalienable rights and independent of the people.

In even sharper contrast with traditional theory was the principle that the ordination as well as the appointment of its pastors, teachers, and other officers lay in the hands of the congregation. Ordination is not a sacrament, and does not convey grace, nor does it create a special ministerial class. It is simply the recognition of a man's divine gift to teach or rule, and of his choice by the congregation to exercise that gift within its bounds. In this the Reformation principle of the priesthood of all believers, and of their direct access to God in Christ without any human intermediary, found clear and consistent exhibition, as it did not in the churches of Luther, Calvin, and the other great Reformers.

In all the matters referred to, Browne and his early followers agreed with the Anabaptists, whose principles they had largely adopted. But there was one important difference. According to the Anabaptists, infant baptism is no baptism; only true believers are to be baptized, and their baptism constitutes the pledge of their Christian discipleship and their covenant with God, which makes them members of His Church. Browne, on the other hand, retained infant baptism. In his *Book which Showeth the Life and Manners of all true Christians*, apparently with the Anabaptist position distinctly in mind, he says: 'The children of the faithful, though they be infants, are to be offered to God and to the church that they may be baptized. Also those infants or children which are of the household of the faithful and under their full power.' The ceremony evidently meant primarily that believers took a pledge to bring up all those dependent on them in the admonition of the Lord. It thus lost all sacramental character, and its retention was not inconsistent either with fundamental Protestant principles or with Browne's own theory of the Church. But the continuance of the practice made it necessary to lay greater stress than the Anabaptists did upon the covenant whereby believers bound themselves together in a church. They did not become church members by baptism, as the Anabaptists held, they were baptized long before they believed, and the Church was composed only of believers. A further and independent step was, therefore, necessary to make them its members. Unless baptized believers entered into voluntary covenant with each other and with God—a covenant not involved in baptism, and entirely detached from it—there was no church, though there might be true believers. Thus the covenant idea became more controlling than in Anabaptism, and may be regarded as the most distinctive element in the Congregational theory of the Church. By it the Church is made more emphatically than ever before a company of men voluntarily bound to one another as well as to God. This separation of baptism from the covenant brought out with greater clearness than ever the fundamental difference between the traditional doctrine of the Church, both Catholic and Protestant, and the theory of the Separatists. To the former the Church is first, and the believer second; only in the Church is salvation to be found. To the latter, on the contrary, and even more clearly and emphatically to Browne than to the Anabaptists that preceded him, the believer is first, and the Church second, for the Church is nothing else than a community or assembly of those already saints.

The retention of infant baptism by Browne was productive of much confusion among his followers. It led almost inevitably to the notion that baptized infants are in some sense members of the Church, a notion quite inconsistent with his fundamental theory. As a consequence, some of his followers, feeling the difficulty, followed the Anabaptists in rejecting infant baptism, and united to form a separate organisation, which became the parent church of English Baptists. Among them the congregational principle of the strictly voluntary character of the Church has been kept alive more generally than among those who bear the name of Congregationalists.

At another important point many of Browne's early followers differed both with him and with the Anabaptists. Instead of insisting upon the complete separation of Church and State, they approved a certain degree of connection between them. In the London-Amsterdam Confession of 1596, it is said ' That it is the office and duty of princes and magistrates, who, by the ordinance of God, are supreme governors under him over all persons and causes within their realms and dominions, to suppress and root out by their authority all false ministries, voluntary religions and counterfeit worship of God. . . . And on the other hand to establish and maintain by their laws every part of God's word, his pure religion and true ministry, to cherish and protect all such as are careful to worship God according to his word, and to lead a godly life in all peace and loyalty ; yea to enforce all their subjects, whether ecclesiastical or civil, to do their duties to God and men, protecting and maintaining the good, punishing and restraining the evil, according as God hath commanded, whose lieutenants they are here on earth.'[1]

Under the Commonwealth the Independents advocated a degree of religious liberty far greater than most believed in, but by no means complete, as the following passage from the famous Savoy declaration of 1658 abundantly shows :—' Although the magistrate is bound to encourage, promote, and protect the professor and profession of the gospel, and to manage and order civil administrations in a due subserviency to the interest of Christ in the world, and to that end to take care that men of corrupt minds and conversations do not licentiously publish and divulge blasphemy and errors in their own nature, subverting the faith, and inevitably destroying the souls of them that

[1] § 39 ; quoted from Walker's *Creeds and Platforms of Congregationalism*. p. 117.

receive them; yet in such differences about the doctrines of the gospel, or ways of the worship of God, as may befall men exercising a good conscience, manifesting it in their conversation, and holding the foundation, not disturbing others in their ways or worship that differ from them; there is no warrant for the magistrate under the gospel to abridge them of their liberty.'[1] In New England even so large a measure of liberty as this was not granted in the early days to those who were of a different mind from the authorities in religious matters. Evidently the difference between these Independents on the one side, and Calvin and the Puritans in general on the other, was at this point simply a matter of degree. All believed in some connection between Church and State, but the Independents reduced it to lower terms than Calvin and most of the Puritans. In recognising the possibility of any connection whatever they were quite untrue to the underlying principle upon which their theory of the Church rested, and their inconsistency did much to obscure and hinder its influence, opening the way to the dominance of another and totally different theory of the Church.

On the other hand, many of the early English Baptists, apparently under the influence of the Anabaptists of Holland, whose theory of baptism they adopted, were thoroughgoing in their assertion of the principle of religious liberty, and of the complete separation of Church and State, showing again their greater consistency with the underlying Congregational theory of the Church.[2]

At the opposite pole from the Independents in their doctrine of the Church were the representatives of the High Church party, which took its rise before the end of Elizabeth's reign, and was very strong during the greater part of the seventeenth century.

---

[1] Chap. xxiv. § 3; quoted from Walker, *ibid.* p. 393.
[2] See the 'Tracts on Liberty of Conscience and Persecution, 1614-1661'; edited for the Hansard-Knollys Society by E. B. Underhill (London, 1846).

Hooker, as we have seen, while maintaining that episcopacy was the primitive form of Church government, did not make it necessary to the being of the Church. But in opposition to the narrow Presbyterianism of Cartwright and his Puritan associates, the tendency arose to claim the same sort of exclusive divine right for episcopacy, and thus to fight fire with fire. The result was the rapid spread of the traditional Catholic theory of the Church and the rejection of the distinction between the visible and the invisible Church, which the early English divines had shared with the Continental Reformers. In Hammond's *Practical Catechism* (1644), it is said that the 'Church is a society of believers under bishops and pastors, succeeding those on whom the Holy Ghost came down, and (by receiving ordination of those that had that power before them, that is of the bishops of the church, the continued successors of the Apostles) lawfully called to these offices' (p. 329).

Perhaps as good and elaborate a statement of the High Church position as is to be found anywhere is given by Herbert Thorndike in his *Rights of the Church in a Christian State*, his *Laws of the Church*, his *Just Weights and Measures*, and other works. According to him establishment by the apostles and control by the bishops, their successors, are necessary to the very being of the true Church, without which salvation is quite impossible. Baptism itself is not effectual to salvation unless administered within the unity of this Church. To suppose that Christians can join together to form a true church is preposterous; there can be no true church except this apostolic episcopal church, into which Christians must enter and within which they must remain if they would be saved.[1]

This church has alone the right to interpret the word of God, for only to it have the apostles entrusted the deposit of truth, whose acceptance is necessary to salva-

---
[1] Thorndike's *Works*, vol. ii. p. 386 ff.

tion.[1] It is always visible, and its indispensable marks, in addition to apostolic succession, which is invariably necessary, are not only the word and the sacraments, but 'that preaching of the word and that ministering of the sacraments which the tradition of the whole church confirmeth the sense of the Scriptures to intend.'[2]

This, of course, is the genuine Catholic theory of the Church and differs from the Roman Catholic only in rejecting the papacy. The rejection of the papacy and separation from the Church of Rome were justified by Thorndike, as by his fellow-apologists for Anglicanism, by the departure of Rome from the true doctrine of the apostles as interpreted by the universal Church of the first six centuries.[3] Presbyterian and Independent bodies are not the true Church, because they lack apostolic succession.[4] The Roman Catholic body, on the other hand, is a true and Catholic church, within which salvation may be obtained; but at the same time it is corrupt, and its abuses are so great that salvation is made difficult, and the Church of England's separation from it is therefore abundantly justified.[5]

This genuinely Catholic but non-papal theory was maintained by many churchmen of the seventeenth century, and has continued ever since the theory of the High Church party within the Anglican communion.

[1] Thorndike's *Works*, vol. ii. p. 110 ff.
[2] *Ibid.* vol. iv. p. 895; cf. p. 905 and vol. v. p. 126.
[3] *Ibid.* vol iv. pp. 399, 436.
[4] *Ibid.* vol. v. p. 71 ff.
[5] *Ibid.* vol. iv. p. 910 ff.; vol. v. p. 280 ff.

CHAPTER VIII

PROTESTANT SCHOLASTICISM

UPON the creative period of the Reformation there followed a period of formulation in the sphere of theology. It was the common conviction of Protestant theologians that one of the most important results of the Reformation, many said its most important result, was the purification of Christian doctrine. Protestantism, it was claimed, maintained the true Catholic faith from which the Roman Church had wandered. To restore this true faith and to purge it of all error was widely regarded as the Protestant theologian's supreme duty.

As remarked in a previous chapter, the foundations of Protestant scholasticism were laid by Philip Melanchthon. His idea of the Church as a school for the teaching of sound doctrine, his recognition of reason and revelation as the two sources for a knowledge of religious truth, and his own labours in the field of dogmatic theology, all contributed to the rise and spread of scholasticism within the Lutheran Church, and the similar views and labours of his younger contemporary, Calvin, did the same for the Reformed churches. During the early years of the Reformation there was too much work of a practical character to be done in spreading evangelical principles, and in laying the foundations of Protestantism to leave much time or leisure for strictly theological work. But when the Protestant State churches of Germany were once firmly established, and the Reformation had gained a permanent footing in Switzerland, the labour of systematising Protestant theology was taken up by many hands. The latter part of the sixteenth century and the major part of the seventeenth constituted the great theological period of Protestantism upon the Continent, both Lutheran and Reformed—the period of Protestant scholasticism in a pre-eminent degree.

The theological conception of the new movement led naturally to serious and long-continued controversy. If the great purpose of the Reformation was to restore sound doctrine, it became of cardinal importance to discover and conserve such doctrine in all its parts. To allow error to prevail was to defeat the end for which Protestantism existed. Already before the death of Luther divergencies had appeared between his own and Melanchthon's interpretations of certain elements of the traditional faith. The seeds of controversy were thus sown at an early day, and while the disagreements were often from a practical point of view of little consequence, they had large theological implications, and it was impossible under the circumstances to overlook them. Into the details of the numerous controversies which distracted both wings of Protestantism it is out of the question to enter here. The Lutheran churches suffered from them more than the Reformed. The theology of the latter was based upon one great controlling principle to a degree not true of the former. Luther's conception of saving faith had tremendous practical value, both religious and ethical, but as an effective principle of organisation in dogmatic theology it did not compare with Calvin's conception of the omnipotent will of God. It was widely interpreted indeed to mean the acceptance of sound doctrine, and thus had only preliminary and formal value for theology. Moreover, the Reformed churches had, in Calvin's *Institutes*, a system of dogmatics unmatched in the other camp, and in Calvin himself a leader who divided his authority with no other, while Lutheran theologians looked back to two leaders of diverse tendencies.

Melanchthon's disagreements with Luther, and particularly his conduct in connection with the Leipzig Interim of 1548, when he yielded to the Catholics far more than most Lutherans thought justifiable, brought widespread hatred upon him, and two parties speedily arose—the Philippists, as Melanchthon's supporters were called, and the Genuine Lutherans, as his opponents styled themselves. Between these parties bitter enmity reigned for some years, and its effects were felt for a much longer time. The most important controversies in which the two parties aligned themselves upon opposite sides were the Synergistic, Melanchthon's synergism being set over against Luther's doctrine of the bondage of the will and unconditional predestination; and the Crypto-Calvinistic, in which the subject of dispute was the nature of Christ's presence in the Lord's Supper, the followers of Melanchthon being accused by their opponents of secretly maintaining Calvin's doctrine of the eucharist. Other controversies were the Antinomian, concerning the place of the law; the Majoristic, concerning the relation of good works to salvation; and the Osiandrian, concerning the nature of justification.[1] In these and other less important controversies the alignment of parties was not always identical.

More than one German prince, and not a few theologians, deprecated the constant theological strife and the resulting divisions, and many efforts were made to bring about

[1] Of all these controversies the Osiandrian is the most interesting. Osiander, one of the greatest Lutheran preachers of the sixteenth century, and at the time of his death Professor of Theology at Königsberg, reproduced the genuine Pauline position that the sinner is made righteous (not merely declared so), and that instantaneously, by the indwelling of Christ, who becomes Himself the sinner's righteousness. See his *Disputationes duæ: una de lege et evangelio* (1549); *Altera de justificatione* (1550); his *De unico mediatore Christo et justificatione fidei* (1551); and see M'Giffert's *Apostolic Age*, chap. iii., for this interpretation of Paul.

The position of Osiander found little favour. Its Pauline character was not recognised then, and has seldom been recognised since, and Osiander's real significance has consequently been generally overlooked.

reconciliation and reunion. Finally, in 1580, there was published by the Elector of Saxony the famous *Formula of Concord*, a confession of faith drawn up by representatives of the Lutheran party, which had succeeded in gaining the upper hand in Saxony as well as in the greater part of Germany. The formula did not attempt to reconcile the Philippists and the Genuine Lutherans, but only divergent views within the ranks of the latter party. In this aim it was eminently successful. Its statements were moderate, and represented, in some cases, a compromise, not always consistent, between two divergent opinions. It did not deal with the whole range of theology, but only with such subjects as the following, all of which had been matter of controversy:—original sin, free will, the righteousness of faith, good works, the law and the gospel, the Lord's Supper, the person of Christ, His descent into hell, adiaphora or indifferent things, and predestination. It asserted the supreme authority of the Bible, and the authority in a secondary sense, as containing the proper interpretation of the Scriptures, of the three ancient creeds (the Apostles', the Nicene, and the Athanasian), the Augsburg Confession, Melanchthon's Apology for the Confession, the Smalcald Articles, and Luther's two Catechisms. These, with the *Formula of Concord* itself, were published together under the title of *The Book of Concord*,[1] which was widely adopted as the official doctrinal standard of the Lutheran churches. The *Formula of Concord* served to compact the conservative wing of Lutheranism, and to stereotype its theology. Thenceforth the lines were fixed within which orthodox theologians moved, and scholasticism developed rapidly.

Like the schoolmen of the Middle Ages, the Lutheran theologians had, in the *Formula of Concord*, a closed system. Its acceptance was regarded as necessary to

[1] For the text of *The Book of Concord* see Mueller's *Die symbolischen Bücher der evangelisch-lutherischen Kirche*; for an English translation see Jacob's *Book of Concord*. On the controversies leading up to it see Schaff's *Creeds of Christendom*, vol. i.

salvation, because it set forth the true interpretation of the Bible. To depart from it or correct it in any way was out of the question. Theological speculation must take it for granted, and the duty of the theologian was to move always within set bounds, systematising, elucidating, and defending truth already fully given and unalterably fixed. As in all scholasticism the importance of a particular doctrine came to depend upon its place in the system rather than upon its practical relation to life. Truth was gained, not from the religious and moral experience of individual or church, but by logical deduction from the accepted system, and it was tested by its consistency with the larger whole.

There was little new in the scholasticism of the period. The theology, in spite of many differences in detail, was very largely that of the Middle Ages. Reason and revelation were employed in a similar way, and the method of treatment was identical. The reigning philosophy was still that of Aristotle, as understood by the mediæval schoolmen, and the supernatural realm was conceived in the same objective and realistic fashion. Compared with that of the Middle Ages, Protestant scholasticism was much more barren, and at the same time narrower and more oppressive. Instead of attempting to cover the whole field of human knowledge, and bring science and philosophy and politics under the dominion of religion, the schoolmen of the seventeenth century confined themselves strictly to the sphere of theology. Of the new science and philosophy that were making headway in the world outside they took no account. They were not in any sense leaders of world-thought as the great mediæval schoolmen were. Moreover, their theology itself, at least in many of its details, was that of a sect not of the world-church. The *Formula of Concord* was rejected, not only by all Catholics, but by Reformed Protestants, and by many Lutherans as well. There was also much less freedom and room for speculation under its control than in the Middle Ages. It was elaborate and exhaustive in its treatment of a great variety of topics, while in the Middle Ages the official dogmas were few and, for the most part, of a very general character. It is not surprising that, in spite of the immense amount of work done, and the elaborate dogmatic systems produced by the Lutheran theologians of the seventeenth century, the period, even from a theological point of view, was barren and dreary to the last degree. Of dogmatics there was plenty, for it was regarded as the principal theological discipline, and completely overshadowed Biblical, historical, and all other studies. But it was a dogmatic of the narrowest type, without relation to the thought of the world at large, and without effect upon the religious and moral life of Christian people.

The most original part of the theology of the day was the doctrine of the Bible, which was worked out more carefully and elaborately than ever before.[1] In opposition to the Catholic dependence upon the authority of tradition, it became necessary, in order to guarantee the truth of Lutheran theology, to treat the Bible as an external and objective standard, possessing independent value of its own quite apart from its effect upon the mind and heart of the reader. The notion of the *testimonium Spiritus Sancti* as the witness of the Spirit in the heart of the individual believer was rejected as dangerously subjective. The canonicity of a book was proof that its divine character had been attested to the Church, and back of this the individual had no right to go. The same kind of an *ex opere operato* theory was attached to the Bible as the Catholics attached to the sacraments. It came to be viewed exclusively as a doctrinal code instead of a means of grace, and its primary quality was infallibility. The

---

[1] See *e.g.* Gerhard's *Loci Theologici*, locus i. ; Calov's *Systema Locorum Theologicorum*, tom. I. c. iv. ; Quenstedt's *Theologia Didactico-polemica*, pars. I. c. iv.

Catholic nature of the doctrine, though it was a doctrine peculiar to Protestants, is very apparent.

In their effort to guarantee the absolute infallibility of the Bible some of the theologians of the day were carried to the furthest possible lengths. The Bible is not in any sense a human book; it is the literal word of God in all its parts, having been dictated by the Holy Spirit to men acting only as amanuenses. Who the author of this or that book might be was of no consequence, and all questions as to date and circumstances of composition, or as to authenticity and integrity became unimportant and irrelevant. Not simply is the Bible as a whole, or the truths which it contains, from God, but every phrase, word, and letter, including even the vowel points of the Hebrew Massoretic text. It is infallible, not alone in the sphere of religion and morals, but in history, geography, geology, astronomy, and every other field upon which it touches. There can be no inaccuracies and no discrepancies anywhere, and the most violent hypotheses are made in the effort to reconcile and harmonise. Never before, indeed, was the harmonising process carried out in so great detail, and with so little regard to the probabilities of the case. All notion of historic development was lost, and all idea of successive stages in the process of divine revelation. The Bible was treated simply as a collection of proof texts for the doctrines of Protestant theology, more particularly for those contained in the *Formula of Concord*, and one part of it was given the same weight as any other part. The whole treatment of the subject was *a priori* to the last degree. The Bible must be an adequate authority, and hence it must be absolutely infallible and perfect in all its parts and in all respects. Even the quality of divinity was ascribed to it by some, and the most crass and magical ideas of its virtue and efficacy became common among the rank and file.

Another matter in which the scholastic spirit and method

had large play, and the Lutheran theologians went beyond the schoolmen of the Middle Ages, was the doctrine of the person of Christ. Luther insisted most earnestly upon the complete union of His divine and human natures, because without it His work would be vain and man's redemption a delusion. It was not a speculative affair with him, but a thing of profound and immediate religious concern. A similar interest caused him to lay stress upon the real presence of Christ in the eucharist, but in the controversy over the matter with Zwingli and others he was led rather deeply into metaphysical and theological speculation, and into scholastic subtleties quite unlike his usual vein. To explain the real presence, he invoked the theory of the ubiquity of Christ's body, and to justify ubiquity the theory of the *communicatio idiomatum*, or the communication of the attributes of Christ's divine nature to His human nature, imparting to it the qualities of omnipotence, omniscience, and particularly omnipresence. By the Lutheran theologians of the sixteenth and seventeenth centuries the subject was discussed in great detail. What was secondary with Luther they made primary, and theories which he had appealed to only to justify and explain vital religious values were treated by them as independent theologumena detached from all experience. Thus viewed, they became excellent material for scholastic discussion, and much was made of them both before and after the adoption of the *Formula of Concord*. What is the extent of the *communicatio idiomatum*? Does it embrace all the divine attributes, or only a part of them? Is ubiquity to be taken in the sense of omnipresence, or only multipresence? Is it absolute or only relative, necessary or dependent on the will? These and other similar questions were eagerly discussed in connection both with Christology and with the doctrine of the eucharist.[1] Because of their bearing upon the latter,

[1] Cf. the *Formula of Concord*, chaps. vii. and viii.

in fact, they had more than merely speculative importance, particularly in the controversy between the Genuine Lutherans and the Calvinists and Crypto-Calvinists. It is impossible here to enter into the details of these and similar discussions. I have referred to them only to illustrate the scholastic character of the theology of the day and the kind of questions that engaged chief attention.

In the Reformed churches the conditions were much the same. The theory of the Bible, elaborated by such theologians as the older and younger Buxtorf, was to all intents and purposes identical with the theory of their Lutheran contemporaries, though less magical and materialistic. In Christology, on the other hand, the Reformed theologians stood commonly at the opposite pole from the Lutherans. Instead of emphasising the union of the divine and human natures in Christ, they were inclined rather to emphasise their distinction, following in this the lead of Calvin. And so the *communicatio idiomatum* and the ubiquity of Christ's body were rejected, and tendencies akin to the modern theory of kenosis were not uncommon.

More important in the Reformed churches of the period was the doctrine of predestination. It was generally accepted from the time of Zwingli on, and gained entrance, though in a comparatively mild form, into a number of Reformed confessions. It was first made the subject of serious controversy at the beginning of the seventeenth century in Holland, where liberalism was more or less in the air. Prominent among the critics of Calvinism there was Jakob van Herman, or Arminius, the principal theologian of the opposition, whose name was ultimately given to the whole movement;[1] Simon Episcopius, Jan Uyttenbogaert, and the great lawyer and statesman, Hugo Grotius. Their position was set forth in 1610 in a document known as the Remonstrance.[2] It con-

---
[1] English translation of Arminius's *Works* by Nichols, 1825 *sq.*, in 3 vols.
[2] See Schaff's *Creeds of Christendom*, vol. iii. p. 545 *sq.*

sisted of five negative and five positive articles, the former rejecting unconditional predestination, both in its supra- and infra-lapsarian forms, limited atonement, irresistible grace, and perseverance of the saints, and the latter maintaining conditional predestination, universal atonement, and the necessity but resistibility of grace. In the last article the possibility of falling from grace is referred to, but not positively asserted.

The party suffered a complete defeat at the Synod of Dort in 1619, and the canons adopted there contain a clear and definite though not extreme statement of the Calvinistic position upon the matters in dispute. They teach unconditional predestination, limited atonement, human inability, the irresistibility of grace, and the perseverance of the saints—the so-called five points of Calvinism.[1]

In this connection attention may be called to an interesting modification of the traditional doctrine of the atonement introduced by Grotius in his work, *On the Satisfaction of Christ*, published in 1617.[2] In this work it is maintained that Christ died, not because God could not forgive sin unless atonement were made and His justice satisfied, but in order to show the heinousness of sin. If it were forgiven without penalty it might seem of little consequence. In place of the commercial relationship of creditor and debtor, which Anselm had conceived to exist between God and man, the lawyer and statesman, Grotius, put the governmental relationship. A ruler has the right to remit a penalty provided the end for which it was fixed can be attained in another way. The end of all penalty is not to avenge sin, but to preserve order and deter from transgressions. It looks to the future, not to the past. And hence Christ died in order that the

---

[1] See Schaff's *Creeds of Christendom*, vol. iii. p. 550 *sq.*
[2] *Defensio fidei Catholicae de satisfactione Christi adversus Faustum Socinum; Opera theologica* (Amsterdam, 1679), tom. iii. col. 297 *sq.* English translation by F. H. Foster (Andover, 1889).

awfulness of sin might be exhibited, and thus men restrained from it.

The artificial character of the doctrine is manifest at a glance. It is a capital example of the scholastic method of meeting difficulties by framing an abstract theory which has no basis in fact and no contact with reality. The theory was considered by Grotius' opponents a fatal error, completely undermining the doctrine of the atonement, and it found no favour except among the Arminians, and was not universally adopted even by them. But that it may be held by high Calvinists is proved by its vogue among the Edwardean theologians of New England, beginning with the younger Edwards.

The high Calvinism formulated at the Synod of Dort prevailed almost unquestioned in Holland, France, Switzerland, Scotland, and among the Puritans of England for some generations. At the Protestant college of Saumur, in Central France, the effort was made by certain theologians to render the system less offensive and more comprehensible at two or three points. Moses Amyraut, for instance, taught that divine grace acts not directly upon the will, but upon the intellect which controls the will; and his pupil, Pajon, maintained that it acts only indirectly even upon the intellect. Thus it was thought that the divine activity was made less arbitrary and mechanical, and its relation to human activity rendered psychologically explicable. Amyraut also drew a distinction between natural and moral inability, which later became famous in the Edwardean theology of New England. He declared that every man has the natural ability, but lacks the moral ability, that is, the will, to believe, until moved thereto by regenerating grace. More interesting and pregnant was the suggestion made in connection with his theory of hypothetical universal grace that God's end in creation and redemption was not the exhibition of His glory, but the exercise of His goodness.

This was fitted to transform the Calvinistic system, had it been followed up, as it was not.[1]

A colleague of Amyraut, Joshua La Place, introduced a modification into the current doctrine of original sin by substituting what is known as mediate for immediate imputation. Immediate imputation means that the primary ground of our condemnation is Adam's sin, the guilt of which is reckoned to us by God. The actual sinful nature with which every man is born is a part of the consequent punishment. La Place, on the contrary, taught that men are condemned primarily for their own sin, and that the guilt of Adam's fall is counted to them as a penalty therefor. Thus he thought the justice of God was safeguarded, and the whole doctrine of original sin made more comprehensible and reasonable.[2]

The scholasticism of all this kind of thing is very evident. The modifications of current views suggested by Amyraut and La Place were, for the most part, simply verbal. An indirect instead of a direct divine control, moral instead of natural inability, a universal grace, which is hypothetical only, instead of a limited atonement, mediate instead of immediate imputation—all this is possible only when form means more than substance and appearance more than reality. The practical effect in every case is recognised to be the same as on the older view, but it is supposed that difficulties are met by changes of statement. The difficulties so met are only formal, not real. They lie in the sphere of logic, not of life, the sphere to which scholasticism belongs.

The innovations of Amyraut and La Place were not intended to undermine or weaken Calvinism in any way, but they were symptomatic of a growing spirit of dis-

---

[1] Among Amyraut's writings the most important are his *Traité de la Prédestination* (1634), his *De la Justification* (1638), and his *Exercitatio de Gratia universali* (1646). See Saigey's *Amyraut, sa vie et ses écrites* (1849), and Haag's *La France Protestante*, vol. i. 72 sq. (1846).

[2] See his *De imputatione primi peccati Adami* (1655).

content with the current statements of the system, and slight and, for the most part, only formal as they were, they caused great excitement both in France and Switzerland. The Saumur theologians succeeded in convincing their Protestant countrymen of their orthodoxy, but in Switzerland feeling against them ran high, and in 1675 the famous *Formula Consensus* was drawn up by Heidegger of Zurich, as a protest against their teachings, and was adopted by a number of Swiss cities. In it the current Calvinism of the day was given its most elaborate and scholastic official expression.[1]

More profoundly than by the teaching of the Saumur school scholastic Calvinism was affected by the so-called Federal theology, or the theology of the covenants, which was taught in the sixteenth century by Bullinger of Zurich, Olevian, one of the authors of the *Heidelberg Catechism*, and others. It had its largest development in the following century in Holland at the hands of Cocceius,[2] and from him it gained the name Cocceianism, by which it was widely known. It was Biblical rather than speculative in character. It taught, upon the basis of the Scriptures, a covenant of works and a covenant of grace which God made successively with man, and by which He carried out His eternal purpose for the redemption of the elect. Cocceius was an orthodox Calvinist, and the doctrine as he taught it was entirely in accord with the Calvinism of the day, but it meant a new emphasis and a new point of view. Instead of centring attention upon the eternal decree of God, the covenant theology laid stress upon His historical activity in dealing with men first in one way, and then when that failed, in another. The tendency of such a change of interest was inevitably

---

[1] For the text of the *Formula Consensus* see Müller's *Die Bekenntnisschriften der reformierten Kirche*, p. 861. The assertion of the inspiration of the Hebrew vowel-points in Article II. was due to the denial of it by Louis Cappel, a colleague of Amyraut and La Place.
[2] See his *Summa Doctrinae de Foedere et Testamentis Dei* (1648).

to weaken the dominance of the scholastic orthodoxy of the day, though it was not realised for a long time. Indeed, the doctrine of the covenants was widely accepted by orthodox Calvinists, and found its way into the Irish articles of 1615, the Westminster Confession of 1645, and the Swiss *Formula Consensus* of 1675, all of them strongly and emphatically Calvinistic, and the last of them, at any rate, genuinely scholastic.

In spite of the various influences tending to undermine the sway of the scholastic spirit and method, Reformed theology, like Lutheran, continued in most quarters to be controlled by both until almost the close of the seventeenth century. When the break came it was due, not to modifications of the existing systems, painfully and laboriously wrought from within, but to extraneous forces altogether. Some of those forces will be considered in the following chapters.

CHAPTER IX

PIETISM

I. *German Pietism*

PIETISTIC tendencies appeared both in Lutheran and Reformed circles before the end of the sixteenth century, but they had their largest development in the late seventeenth and early eighteenth centuries. At the close of the Thirty Years' War religious life in Protestant Germany was at a low ebb. The control of the Church by the civil government in the various principalities did not make for spirituality. The interpretation of saving faith in terms of intellectual assent, the prevalence of scholasticism, the emphasis upon formal orthodoxy, the absorption of the leading men of the Church in theological controversy, all tended to depress the religious and moral life of the country, and the war itself had demoralising effects and accentuated conditions already widespread.

The specific movement known as German Pietism began only as an effort to improve local religious and moral conditions in Frankfort-on-Main, but it soon spread throughout the country. Its great protagonist was Philip Jacob Spener, who was born in 1633, and held important clerical positions successively in Frankfort, Dresden, and Berlin, until his death in 1705. Spener was a man of mystical, but practical, temperament, and had read widely in devotional literature, both mediæval and modern. It was not the theosophy or the quietism of the mystics that attracted him; he was too sober-minded to feel sympathy with the former, and of too active a temperament to find the latter congenial; but their emphasis on inner vital Christianity and their hostility to a formal and dead theology. He felt the influence particularly of the famous German mystic, Johann Arndt, whose *Wahres Christenthum* was perhaps the best known devotional work of the day in Germany.

In Frankfort, Spener became aroused by the low religious and moral tone of the city, and he undertook to raise it by making his preaching more directly practical, by laying emphasis upon life rather than doctrine, by multiplying his pastoral labours, and particularly by holding meetings in his own house for the devotional study of the Bible, and for prayer and edification. A marked feature of his preaching was his strong eschatological emphasis. He believed that the last times were at hand, and that the return of Christ and the establishment of the Messianic Kingdom would take place in the near future.[1] This gave to much of his work an enthusiastic and somewhat feverish character not unlike that which marked the primitive days of the Christian Church.

In 1765 he wrote a preface to an edition of Arndt's sermons, which was issued separately a few months later under the title of *Pia Desideria*, and was read very widely. With its publication Spener sprang at once into prominence, and his influence began to be felt throughout the country. The book is in two parts, the first portraying the evil conditions of the day—religious indifference, absorption in scholastic theology, and the wide prevalence of immorality—and maintaining the possibility of better things; the second setting forth the methods to be employed in effecting a reformation. The second part contains what may be called the programme of the pietistic movement. The following matters are emphasised as particularly important:—First, the study of the Scriptures by

[1] Cf. especially his *Behauptung der Hoffnung künftiger besserer Zeiten*.

all classes of Christians. In this connection Spener recommends meetings for Bible-reading and spiritual edification such as he was holding in Frankfort. These were to be made centres of religious life for the leavening of the whole Church. They became very common among the Pietists, and were known commonly as *collegia pietatis*. Secondly, the universal priesthood of believers, involving the duty of mutual instruction, inspiration, and reproof. Thirdly, the practical nature of Christianity, which consists not in the knowledge, but in conduct, and particularly in the exercise of mutual love and service. Fourthly, the evils of religious controversy and the duty of dealing with unbelievers and heretics in the spirit of love. Fifthly, the importance of piety as well as of learning in candidates for the ministry. It is urged that theological professors should be examples of piety, and should train their students in practical religion as well as in theology. The study of such books as the *Theologia Germanica, Tauler's Sermons*, and the *Imitation of Christ* is recommended, as also practice in pastoral work during the period of preparation. These were unheard-of innovations in theological education. Finally, Spener insists upon the necessity of making preaching more simple and practical. The following quotation from his discussion of the last point shows his general interest with sufficient clearness:—'Since our entire Christianity consists in the inner or new man, and its soul is faith, and the effects of faith are the fruits of life, I regard it as of the greatest importance that sermons should be wholly directed to this end. On the one hand they should exhibit God's rich benefits, as they affect the inner man, in such a way that faith is advanced and the inner man forwarded in it. On the other hand they should not merely incite to external acts of virtue and restrain from external acts of vice, as the moral philosophy of the heathen does, but should lay the foundation in the heart. They should show that all is pure hypocrisy, which does not come from the heart, and so accustom the people to cultivate love to God and their neighbours and to act from it as a motive.'[1]

The book suggested, or at any rate foreshadowed, most of the points which were later emphasised by the Pietists, and became characteristic of the pietistic movement. Biblical study for devotional and practical purposes, depreciation of scholastic and polemic theology, emphasis of the feelings and will at the expense of the intellect, love for devotional literature, especially of a mystical type, insistence upon the necessity of personal faith and growth in Christian perfection, the recognition of a true kernel within the Church, an *ecclesiola in ecclesia* made up of the truly regenerate, and the new independence given the laity by the formation of the *collegia pietatis*, in which their religious life found expression apart from the Church and its organised ministrations. The last point is of especial importance. The pietistic movement was largely a lay movement. Not that the clergy held aloof and bore no share in it, but that the principle of the universal priesthood of believers underlay it, and expressed itself in new religious activities on the part of the people.

Spener was an orthodox Lutheran, and made no attack upon current theology. Nevertheless his theological attitude was very different from that of most of his contemporaries. He deprecated what seemed to him an over-emphasis upon the theoretical side of religion, and insisted that personal piety, the bent of the heart and life, was far more important than doctrinal soundness. He felt, too, that the theologians of the day were interested in the less rather than the more important doctrines, and he wished

[1] P. 101, Leipzig edition of 1841. In addition to the *Pia Desideria* Spener published in 1677 a book on the spiritual priesthood (*Das Geistliche Priesterthum*), and this was followed in the same year by a *Letter to a Foreign Theologian* (*Sendschreiben an einen Christeifrigen ausländischen Theologen*). These three books set forth adequately his controlling principles. For an exhaustive bibliography of Spener's writings see the *Life* by Gruenberg, vol. iii.

to bring into prominence those which had direct effect upon the personal religious life, particularly the doctrines of salvation. The value of a belief, he maintained, depended wholly upon its practical bearing. He distinguished between essential and non-essential elements in the traditional faith, and assumed a freer attitude than was customary toward the official symbols.

One of the principal causes of the low spiritual and moral tone of the Church, he felt, was a misunderstanding of the nature of saving faith, leading to an unfortunate divorce between justification and sanctification, between belief and life. In his desire to meet this fundamental error he emphasised the doctrine of regeneration, and insisted that the all-important thing was the transformation of character through vital union with Christ. Only where the life is actually changed and the spirit and motive of Christ control one's conduct, has a person any right to think that he has been born again and is to be counted of the number of the saved. Christian conduct Spener interpreted in other-worldly terms. Not, as with Luther, victory over the world, but escape from it was his ideal. Piety was to show itself in devotion to spiritual and supernal things, and in the transfer of affection and interest from this world to another. In general, it may be said that pietism, whether in Holland, Switzerland, Germany, or elsewhere, represented an ascetic reaction against the common worldliness of the average Christian, a reaction similar in principle to that involved in monasticism, but less thoroughgoing in practice.

Spener felt that the Protestant Reformation had not completed its work, that the purification of doctrine needed to be followed by the sanctification of life. He emphasised faith as the condition of salvation in good Lutheran fashion, and yet his interpretation of the Christian life was more Catholic than Protestant. He saw to what indifference and carelessness the current notions of justification and of assurance were leading, and he took issue with both, insisting that justification means nothing without regeneration and sanctification, and that assurance is a dangerous thing if based upon aught but the evidence of a transformed and holy life. It is clear that the controlling interest throughout was not religious, as with Luther, but moral. Not a man's relation to God was the important thing, but his character and conduct. Salvation is a present reality, but it is not so much peace with God and the consciousness of divine sonship as holiness of life wrought by the indwelling of the Spirit. In this connection Spener insisted upon the possibility and importance of Christian perfection, by which he meant not a strict legal sinlessness, but the constant direction of the heart toward holiness, and continual and undeviating progress in it. To be content with anything less was a mark of an unregenerate heart. Introspection and self-examination became under these circumstances almost inevitable, and found constant encouragement and exercise in the *collegia pietatis*.

The pietism of Spener and his followers was essentially mediæval in its estimate of man and the world. Distrust of human nature and despair of the salvability of society were both characteristic of it. Salvation meant escape from an evil world for a few elect souls who banded together for spiritual communion and mutual edification, and these elect souls were not the Christian Church, but a small circle within the larger body. Spener, to be sure, was very eager and zealous to enlarge this circle, to extend the benefits of the great revival of religion to the entire membership of the Church, and to permeate the whole community with its principles; but after all conversion meant a selective process, and withdrew a man's interest not simply from the world, but also, to some degree at least, from the Church.

Though mediæval, both in its estimate of the world

and man, and in its conception of salvation, pietism was a decided advance upon the Protestantism of the day and a prophecy of a new age to come. The vitalising of Christian piety, the breaking of scholasticism's control, the recognition of religious experience as the chief basis of theology, the emphasis of the will instead of the intellect in religion, the prominence given to the emotions, and above all the individualism of the whole movement and its hostility to ecclesiasticism, sacramentarianism, and sacerdotalism, meant much for days to come. Pietism was one of the forces which brought the modern age in the religious life of Germany. It preceded rationalism, and, unlike the latter as it was in spirit and interest, it yet prepared the way for it by weakening the hold of the ecclesiastical institution with its creeds and sacraments. It was as individualistic as rationalism, though in a very different way, and in Germany at least it represented, on the whole, advance not reaction in the development of religious thought.

In spite of the contrast in spirit and tendency between the Pietists and their Lutheran brethren, and in spite of the bitter controversy to which the movement gave rise, most of the Pietists remained within the Lutheran body (separation taking place only in the case of the Moravians), and before the death of Francke, the second great leader of the party, which occurred in 1727, pietism had become the dominant force in German religious life. Of its immense services in the field of charitable and religious work—the foundation of orphan asylums, the education of the young, the care of the poor, the promotion of foreign missions—it is impossible to speak here. Its great influence was before long undermined by rationalism, which spread rapidly after the middle of the eighteenth century, but it never ceased to make itself felt, and it became one of the factors in the revival of religion, and the reconstruction of theology at the beginning of the nineteenth century.

II. *English Evangelicalism*

In England pietism came to most striking expression in the great evangelical revival of the eighteenth century. Mystical tendencies had appeared in the previous century, most notably in the Society of Friends, in which the immediate presence of the Holy Spirit, making all external forms and ceremonies, sacraments and priesthood unnecessary, was emphasised as it had not been since the primitive days of Christianity.[1] Mystical piety of a somewhat extreme type was exemplified also by the non-juror William Law, the author of two famous devotional works, *A Practical Treatise upon Christian Perfection*, and *A Serious Call to a Devout and Holy Life*.

John Wesley, to whom the evangelical revival was chiefly due, was greatly influenced by Law's writings, but the determining impulse came from German pietism through his association with a small company of Moravians in London. Under their influence he passed through a religious experience in 1738, which he always referred to afterwards as his conversion, although he had already been for some years an ordained clergyman of uncommon piety and devoutness. This experience he relates in his *Journal*, giving a detailed account of the steps that led up to it. The climax is described in the following words: 'In the evening I went very unwillingly to a society [2] in Aldersgate Street, where one was reading Luther's preface to the *Epistle to the Romans*. About a quarter before nine, while he was describing the change which God works in the heart through faith in Christ, I felt my heart strangely warmed. I felt I did trust in Christ; Christ, alone for salvation; and an assurance was given me that he had

[1] See the *Journal* of George Fox (1694 *sq.*), and Robert Barclay's *An Apology for the True Christian Divinity, as the same is held forth and preached by the People, called in scorn, Quakers* (1676).
[2] Compare Wesley's description of the institution of a society for prayer and mutual edification, similar to the *collegia pietatis* of the German Pietists, in his Journal, *Works*, vol. i. p. 186.

taken away *my* sins, even *mine*, and saved me from the law of sin and death.'[1]

This event was epochal in Wesley's life. It meant a transfer of emphasis from baptism to conversion, from the Church as an institution to the personal religious experience of the individual Christian. It meant also a return to the genuine but practically forgotten Reformation platform of a present salvation by faith alone, through grace, and not through works. This was the birth of English evangelicalism, and the beginning of the great evangelical revival, for the preaching of Wesley's new-found gospel followed as a matter of course. Joined by his brother Charles, and by his friend, George Whitefield, who had passed through a similar experience, Wesley commenced that extraordinary career of evangelism which lasted for fifty years, and transformed the religious life of England.

Like German pietism, English evangelicalism was practical in its aims and methods, but it had great influence in the sphere of religious thought. It is a fact of cardinal importance that it took its rise in a period dominated, not by scholasticism, but by rationalism. It was, in fact, in no small part a reaction against rationalism in all its forms.[2] This gave it, in spite of its kinship with German pietism, a very different character in many respects. Doctrines which were largely taken for granted by the Pietists of Germany, as being the common property, both of themselves and of the orthodox, received chief emphasis from Wesley and his associates, because they were denied or minimised by the rationalists of the day.

[1] *Works*, vol. i. p. 194. I have used the first American edition of Wesley's *Works*, New York, 1827, in ten volumes.
[2] There is an infelicity in treating evangelicalism before rationalism. It can be fully understood only in the light of the rationalism against which it was a protest. At the same time, even though it mean some violation of the chronological order, it seems important to deal with the various pietistic movements, which are so closely akin, in a single chapter. But the anti-rationalistic reactionary character of evangelicalism should not be forgotten for a moment.

Thus the doctrine of the Fall gained a peculiar prominence, and human depravity and inability were preached with an earnestness seldom equalled. 'The fall of man,' Wesley says, 'is the very foundation of revealed religion. If this be taken away the Christian system is subverted, nor will it deserve so honourable an appellation as that of a cunningly devised fable.'[1] It was at this point that the fundamental contrast between the Evangelicals and their rationalistic contemporaries appeared most clearly. The tendency of the age was to recognise the natural worth and ability of man, both intellectual and moral. This the Evangelicals felt was the great foe which had to be met if Christianity were actually to lay hold upon the hearts and lives of men. In a sermon on Original Sin, Wesley says, 'This, therefore, is the first grand distinguishing point between heathenism and Christianity. The one acknowledges that many men are infected with many vices and even born with a proneness to them; but supposes withal that in some the natural good much overbalances the evil: the other declares that all men are conceived in sin and shapen in wickedness, that hence there is in every man a carnal mind which is enmity against God, which is not, cannot be subject to His law. . . . Hence we may secondly learn that all who deny this, call it original sin, or by any other title, are but heathens still in the fundamental point which differences heathenism from Christianity. They may, indeed, allow that men have many vices; that some are born with us; and that consequently we are not born altogether so wise or so virtuous as we should be; there being few that will roundly affirm we are born with as much propensity to good as to evil, and that every man is by nature as virtuous and wise as Adam was at his creation. But here is the *shibboleth*: Is man by nature filled with all manner of evil? Is he void of all good? Is he wholly false? Is his soul totally

[1] *Works*, vol. i. p. 176.

corrupted? Or, to come back to the text, is "every imagination of the thoughts of his heart evil continually"? Allow this, and you are so far a Christian. Deny it, and you are but a heathen still.'[1]

The greatest barrier in the way of a man's conversion is pride. As Whitefield says, 'It is the want of an humble mind, of a sense of their own depravity that makes men obstinately shut their eyes against the gospel. If they were pricked to the heart with a lively sense of their natural corruption, we should have no more scoffing at divine revelation.'

It was in accordance with their emphasis upon human depravity and helplessness that the Evangelicals made much of supernatural redemption. No one is able to save himself from sin and from the punishment which it entails. Only divine power can do it, and this is offered by Christ alone. The current interpretation of Christianity as a revelation, supplementing natural religion and bringing clearer light and stronger motives to virtue,[2] seemed utterly inadequate. Revelation alone is of no value. Even if a man knows his duty he cannot do it unless empowered thereto by God. Thus the doctrine of regeneration became of primary importance. To be born again, not of flesh and blood, but of the Spirit of God, this was indispensable to every man.

It is no accident, in view of the prominence they gave to the necessity of redemption, that the Evangelicals restored the doctrines of the deity and atoning work of Christ to the place of importance which they had widely lost. The German Pietists took these doctrines for granted, for scholastic theology, of course, accepted them without question. But by the rationalistic school, which made Christ's work chiefly or solely that of revelation, they had been generally denied or neglected, and it was inevitable that the Evangelicals should give them especial importance.

[1] *Works*, vol. v. p. 195. [2] See the next chapter.

They made so much of them, indeed, that vicarious atonement and the deity of Christ came to be regarded as peculiarly evangelical doctrines, and the churches that accept them, in distinction from the Unitarian bodies which reject both, are even to-day commonly known as evangelical churches. Thus at this point, as at many others, evangelicalism served to rehabilitate traditional doctrines common both to Catholicism and Protestantism.

I have spoken of the necessity of regeneration through the power of the Holy Spirit, but according to Wesley the continued presence of the Spirit is equally needed if the Christian man is to live as he ought. Even though born again, he cannot do God's will in his own strength. The true Christian life is supernatural from beginning to end. 'The author of faith and salvation is God alone. It is he that works in us both to will and to do. He is the sole giver of every good gift, and the sole author of every good work.'[1]

Consistently with this idea of the miraculous character of the Christian life, Wesley thought of it not as the condition of salvation but as salvation itself. 'By salvation I mean,' he says, 'not barely according to the vulgar notion deliverance from hell or going to heaven, but a present deliverance from sin, a restoration of the soul to its primitive health, its original purity; a recovery of the divine nature, the renewal of our souls after the image of God in righteousness and true holiness, in justice, mercy, and truth.'[2] In thus recognising salvation as a present reality, Wesley was true to Luther, but his interpretation of its nature was usually different. His interest, like Spener's, was chiefly ethical, and he was more concerned in escape from sin and the attainment of holiness than in escape from divine wrath and the attainment of peace with God. It thus became possible for him to assert a

[1] 'A Farther Appeal to Men of Reason and Religion,' *Works*, vol. viii. p. 220.   [2] *Ibid.* p. 219.

present salvation only by accepting the pietistic doctrine of Christian perfection. He taught that Christian perfection was attainable instantaneously by the believer in this life. By it he meant the uninterrupted reign of love in the heart.[1] But even this did not save him from inconsistency, and he frequently taught, in the common fashion of the day, that this life is a probation for the life to come, when alone salvation begun here will be complete.[2] And yet he was careful always to maintain intact the Reformation doctrine of salvation by faith alone. Nothing could be more fully in accord with Luther's own teaching than such a passage as the following : 'Justifying faith implies, not only a divine $\ell\lambda\epsilon\gamma\chi$os that God was in Christ " reconciling the world to himself," but a sure trust and confidence that Christ died for my sins, that He loved me and gave Himself for me. And the moment a penitent sinner believes this God pardons and absolves him. And as soon as his pardon or justification is witnessed to him by the Holy Ghost, he is saved. He loves God and all mankind. He has the mind that was in Christ, and the power to walk as He also walked.'[3]

It was in accordance with their recognition of the miraculous nature of the Christian life that the Evangelicals drew the sharpest possible contrast between the truly religious and the merely moral man. They denounced all man-made righteousness as filthy rags. He who trusted to his own virtue, who lived honestly and uprightly and purely, but did not depend for salvation upon Christ alone, was the most dangerous of men. For the abandoned sinner there was hope—he might be brought to

---

[1] Wesley gave many definitions of Christian perfection in his *Plain Account of Christian Perfection*. One of them is as follows: 'Question— What is Christian perfection? Answer—The loving God with all our heart, mind, soul, and strength. This implies, that no wrong temper, none contrary to love, remains in the soul; and that all the thoughts, words, and actions are governed by pure love' (*Works*, vol. viii. p. 27).

[2] Cf. *e g.* his 'Thoughts on Salvation by Faith,' *Works*, vol. x. p. 238 *sq.*

[3] *Works*, vol. viii. p. 219.

a sense of his corruptness and helplessness, and of his need of divine grace; but the righteous man who prided himself on his rectitude and moral strength was far from the kingdom. Humility is the first step toward the Christian life. To repudiate one's own goodness, and to abandon oneself completely to the mercy of Christ, is difficult for the righteous man, but it is absolutely necessary for him as well as for the worst of criminals. Christianity is for the sick, not for the well, and only the man who realises his diseased condition can profit by it.

Of a piece with all this was the interpretation of the Christian life as other-worldly. Like the German Pietists, the Evangelicals were ascetic in their tendency. Their ideal was to live with heart set constantly upon the future, and natural human interest in the present world was condemned as irreligious. 'Friendship with the world,' Wesley says, 'is spiritual adultery.' The Evangelicals were not as consistent and thoroughgoing as their mediæval prototypes; they did not advocate retirement from the world and seclusion in a monastery. But they denounced many of the ordinary pursuits and pleasures of society, commonly looked upon as indifferent matters, and insisted that they ought to be eschewed by the Christian. Card-playing, dancing, gaming, horse-racing, theatre-going, elaborate dressing, and frivolity of all kinds came in for most vigorous condemnation. To be a Christian very commonly meant above all to turn one's back upon such employments. Thus there grew up an externality of religion and an artificiality of practice even more complete than anything witnessed in mediæval Catholicism.

The same interest in the unworldly character of the Christian life led Wesley to advocate breaking with one's worldly acquaintances upon becoming a Christian.[1] Evil

[1] Cf. *e.g.* his sermon entitled 'In what sense we are to leave the world,' *Works*, vol. vii. p. 5 *sq.*, especially p. 12.

is contagious, and such acquaintances are bound to have a bad influence and keep the convert from living the new and higher life. Apparently he forgot the good that the Christian might do his worldly companion in thinking of the evil he would suffer from him. At the same time he did not overlook responsibility for the welfare of one's fellows. Indeed, he made love and service of others an important part of Christian virtue. And following him the evangelical party gave itself to humanitarian and social labour on a large scale, and with great effectiveness. They were not alone in this, to be sure; they were at one with the spirit of the century. But it meant much for the future that not rationalists and deists and unbelievers alone were fired with a new enthusiasm for humanity, but that the great representatives of a revived Christianity shared the same spirit.

Reference has been made to Wesley's insistence upon the presence and power of the Holy Spirit, both at the beginning and throughout the Christian life. It was inevitable in view of this that feeling should come to play a large part in evangelical piety. If a man is truly regenerate, he ought to retain the memory of the experience through which he passed at the time of his conversion, and he ought to be vividly conscious of the Spirit's control in all his activities. His should be the joy, the comfort, the inspiration of the realisation of the divine presence. If such emotions are lacking, if his heart is cold, and his life governed by the mere dictates of reason, he may well doubt whether he is indeed regenerate, for the influence of the Spirit cannot do otherwise than lift him out of himself and above himself in a new devotion and enthusiasm. The religious man, according to the Evangelicals, is not one who does his duty recognising it as God's will, as the rationalist said, but one who has had a vivid religious experience and enjoys continually a consciousness of the divine. The situation is the same as in pietism in general, and the contrast with rationalism is as great as with scholasticism. Both in England and in Germany the change of emphasis was prophetic of a revolution to follow with the dawning of the nineteenth century.

The presence of the Holy Spirit, according to Wesley, had intellectual as well as practical and emotional effects. It meant, not simply new feelings and a new power to do right, but also the ability to know and understand religious truth. 'Every good gift is from God, and is given to man by the Holy Ghost. By nature there is in us no good thing. And there can be none; but so far as it is wrought in us by that good Spirit. Have we any true knowledge of what is good? This is not the result of our natural understanding. The natural man discerneth not the things of the Spirit of God; so that we can never discern them until God reveals them unto us by His Spirit.'[1]

Consistently with this notion of present-day revelation Wesley taught that the Christian possesses an organ of spiritual knowledge by which he is enabled to apprehend the truth shown him by the Spirit. This organ is faith. It is a faculty of direct vision by which spiritual realities are perceived as immediately as physical realities by the bodily senses. 'Faith is that divine evidence whereby the spiritual man discerneth God and the things of God. It is with respect to the spiritual world what sense is to the natural. It is the spiritual sensation of every soul that is born of God.'[2] 'And seeing our ideas are not innate, but must all originally come from our senses,[3] it is certainly necessary that you have senses capable of discerning objects of this kind. Not only those which are called natural senses, which in this respect profit nothing, as being altogether incapable of discerning objects of a

[1] *Works*, vol. viii. p. 264.
[2] 'An Earnest Appeal to Men of Reason and Religion,' *Works*, vol. viii. p. 188.
[3] It is interesting to see the use to which Wesley here puts Locke's dictum.

spiritual kind, but spiritual senses, exercised to discern spiritual good and evil. It is necessary that you have the hearing ear, and the seeing eye, emphatically so-called ; that you have a new class of senses opened in your soul, not depending on organs of flesh and blood, to be the evidence of things not seen, as your bodily senses are of visible things ; to be the avenues to the invisible world, to discern spiritual objects, and to furnish you with ideas of what the outward " eye hath not seen, neither the ear heard." And till you have these internal senses, till the eyes of your understanding are opened, you can have no proper apprehension of divine things, no just idea of them. Nor consequently till then can you either judge truly, or reason justly concerning them ; seeing your reason has no ground whereon to stand, no materials to work upon.' [1] The contrast between this idea of faith and the current idea of Wesley's day is very striking. To one who has such a spiritual sense as this all proof of divine things is superfluous. One's faith does not rest upon argument, but upon direct vision, and the whole rational apologetic [2] becomes at a single stroke unnecessary and abortive. It is true that Wesley was not consistent at this point. He left the old scheme standing, and even appealed to it on occasion, to the confusion of the situation and the detriment of his own principles. But this fact, while it had very unfortunate consequences, should not blind us to the real significance of the evangelical position. Here, too, there was the prophecy of a new age.

The evangelical emphasis on the immediate presence of the Holy Spirit suggests a very different idea of God from that held by the rational school of Wesley's day. According to that school, God was transcendent, and no one could come into direct contact or immediate communion with Him. At the same time, it will not do to say that Wesley and the Evangelicals taught the immanence

[1] *Works*, vol. viii. p. 195.   [2] See the next chapter.

of God in any strict sense. They emphasised the immediate presence of the Spirit in the hearts and lives of believers, but to nature and humanity in general they denied divinity in the most emphatic terms. Only one possessed of saving faith enjoys the divine indwelling. The idea of a present Spirit might mean a step, but it was only a step, in the direction of the modern doctrine of divine immanence, and its significance should not be exaggerated. As a matter of fact, the strongest opponents of that doctrine in more recent days have been convinced and thoroughgoing Evangelicals.

It would seem as if their emphasis upon the Spirit, revealing divine truth as well as imparting moral power, would have led the Evangelicals to give up all notion of an external authority in religion, but their distrust of man was so great, and their hostility to the rationalism of the age so controlling that they took exactly the opposite course. The authority of the Bible was made more of by them than for a long time before. In opposition to the current recognition of the sufficiency of human reason, they delighted to belittle it, and to denounce its claims as presumptuous and irreligious. But they appealed in opposition to it, not to the Spirit in the hearts of all believers, as the Quakers did, but to the written and infallible word. It is due to evangelical influence, and not to scholasticism or the Protestantism of the Reformation period that the authority of the Scriptures has meant so much to English and American Christians of modern times. In German pietism the Bible was employed chiefly as a devotional book. But in evangelicalism its significance as a divine revelation, authenticating the orthodox faith over against deism and scepticism, became especially prominent. Interpreted evangelically, it was made a doctrinal and moral authority of the most binding character. To venture to criticise its statements, to question its authority, to raise doubts as to the authenticity of any part, to set one's own judgment above it, to treat it as in any way ill-adapted to present conditions, all this was intolerable to a genuine Evangelical. Reverence for it was carried so far that magical value was attached to the volume itself. To have it upon one's person was a safeguard, to open it at random in times of indecision, and to be guided by the words that first met the eye, was the course of a true believer. It is interesting to notice in this connection Wesley's attitude toward the modern view of the universe. He refused to accept the Copernican astronomy on the ground that it contradicted Scripture. He believed in witchcraft on Biblical authority, and interpreted natural calamities, such as the Lisbon earthquake, as direct visitations of God. In fact, in his supernaturalism and in his recognition of an external authority to which all conclusions about the physical universe should be made to conform, he was a genuine mediævalist, although his life fell wholly within the eighteenth century, the century of enlightenment. It is not meant to imply that evangelicalism is necessarily one with Wesley in these matters, that it involves the rejection of the conclusions of modern science and the retention of the mediæval world-view. But Wesley's attitude was significant nevertheless. It was simply an extreme expression of the common evangelical belief touching the authority of the Scriptures and of the common evangelical distrust of the powers of the natural man.

Evangelical emphasis upon the corruptness and inability of man was more in line with historic Calvinism than historic Arminianism. And yet, curiously enough, Wesley himself was an Arminian. This was because he was brought up in high church circles where Arminian views had long been popular; and William Law, whose influence was so dominant in the early part of his career, represented the same type of thought. The Arminianism of the high church party, which Wesley inherited, was not the fruit of liberalism or rationalism. It was due in part to hostility to Puritanism, which was emphatically Calvinistic, in part to paramount interest in the church and sacraments as means of grace. The significance of both seemed better conserved by a doctrine which left some share to man in working out his own salvation. This kind of Arminianism was in reality as conservative and as much out of line with rationalistic tendencies as Calvinism itself. Neither the one nor the other recognised any merit in the natural man, or any power to save himself without divine aid. It is therefore not surprising that when the practical revival interest laid hold on Wesley it should express itself in Arminian form. As a matter of fact it always proved impossible for him to put himself at the Calvinistic point of view, and to appreciate the moral incentive of the doctrine of absolute divine sovereignty. It seemed to him that Calvinism must deprive a man of the needed stimulus, and promote indifference and sloth. Thus Wesley's Arminianism was not an inconsistency as it is often represented. Nevertheless his strong emphasis upon the Fall and resulting depravity was more akin to historic Calvinism than to a system which arose in opposition to it, and which in its inception felt, though ever so slightly, the influence of the modern interest in the ability and worth of man. Under these circumstances, it is not surprising that the Calvinist Whitefield regarded Wesley's Arminian views as extremely dangerous, and that the two men fell into open and bitter controversy. But it is an interesting commentary upon the gospel's indifference to philosophy and theology that men representing, however crudely and inconsistently, two radically diverse types of thought should both accomplish so tremendous practical results. Ever since the time of Wesley and Whitefield there has been both Arminian and Calvinistic evangelicalism, but the underlying interest of the two types has been essentially the same, and their differences superficial and unimportant, in spite of the large prominence that has been given them.

The effects of evangelicalism on English religious life and thought are easy to constitute, complicated though they are. It put an end to the barren rationalism of the eighteenth century; it substituted immediate experience for ratiocination, direct knowledge for indirect, in the religious sphere, and so circumvented the sceptics whom the apologists were impotent to overcome; it brought the feelings once more into repute, and aided the nineteenth-century reaction against the narrow intellectualism of the eighteenth; it gave a new meaning and an independent value to religion; it promoted individualism and emancipation from the bondage of ecclesiasticism; and, above all, it vitalised and revived religion throughout the length and breadth of the land. On the other hand, it brought back much of the old system, including many of its most obnoxious features which rationalism had relegated to oblivion, as it supposed, for ever. It turned its face deliberately toward the past instead of toward the future in its interpretation of man and his need. It sharpened the issue between Christianity and the modern age, and promoted the notion that the faith of the fathers had no message for their children. Becoming identified in the minds of many with Christianity, its narrowness and mediævalism, its emotionalism and lack of intellectuality, its crass supernaturalism and Biblical literalism, its want of sympathy with art and science and secular culture in general, turned them permanently against religion. In spite of the great work accomplished by evangelicalism, the result in many quarters was disaster.

III. *The New England Theology*

Closely related to English evangelicalism, though of independent origin, was the New England theology of the

Edwardean School. Like evangelicalism, it was a reaction not only against religious indifference, but also against rationalism and unbelief. It is true that there is very little direct evidence of theological radicalism in the American literature of the early eighteenth century, but the attitude of Jonathan Edwards shows that there was more of it than now appears. There can be no doubt that in his active polemic against English liberals such as the Arminian Taylor, he was really striving to refute like views among his countrymen. On the other hand, the fact that he is silent about the writings of the Deists, and nowhere enters into discussion with them, though he lived while the deistic controversy was at its height, makes it plain that their influence was not as yet widely felt by his countrymen, and that there was no occasion for alarm on their account.

The incipient liberalism of the day, which took the form of a more or less distinct Arminianism, was in line with the modern spirit, and was out of sympathy with the traditional estimate of man and the traditional emphasis upon his depravity and helplessness. It was this feature of it which was most dangerous in Edwards' eyes, and in meeting it he set forth the opposite principle in the extremest possible form. New England was traditionally Calvinistic, and Calvinism offered the greatest contrast to the growing liberalism of the day. In it Edwards found the best means of opposing the new tendencies, and transformed the somewhat mild type of it prevalent in his day into the most rigid and uncompromising system the world has seen. His Calvinism was the least scholastic and the most profound, both philosophically and religiously, to be found in any school. His practical interest throughout was to humble man, to convince him of his total depravity and absolute bondage to sin, and so startle him out of his easy indifference and complacent self-confidence. The doctrine of unconditional predestination was but a corollary. It was not the greatness of God, but the nothingness of man that he was primarily interested to enforce, and all his theology was dominated by this aim. He was a great philosophical thinker, and he might have made important contributions to metaphysics had he continued the speculations recorded in his early *Notes on the Mind*; but he preferred to give himself to religious work, and all his writings, profound and abstruse as many of them are, were produced with the practical purpose of illustrating and enforcing the truth of man's complete dependence upon God.

As a result of his preaching, the revival in Northampton out of which the Great Awakening grew, had already begun before Whitefield appeared upon the scene, and even before the evangelical revival started in England, but its kinship with the contemporary English movement is shown by the ease with which Whitefield found himself at home in it.[1] If later there was division and estrangement, it was due, not to any essential difference of principle, but to the sensationalism of the English evangelist's methods and the censoriousness of his temper. It is true that the preaching of the English Evangelicals, including Whitefield, was commonly different from that of Edwards. While they laid the stress upon the love of God, he chiefly emphasised His wrath. But he aimed to secure the same results by driving man to despair, which they achieved by encouraging him to hope. Upon the fundamental importance of the doctrine of original sin, and upon the resulting depravity of man, and his utter inability to save himself, they were all agreed. They were at one also in emphasising the supernatural and cataclysmic character of conversion, in drawing the sharpest possible contrast between the regenerate and unregenerate, in insisting

---

[1] On the revival see Edwards's *Narrative of Surprising Conversions, Distinguishing Marks of a Work of the Spirit of God, Thoughts on the Revival*, and his masterly *Treatise on the Religious Affections.*

upon the other-worldliness of the Christian life, in giving love a supreme place in Christian virtue, in recognising a new spiritual sense or taste received in regeneration, and in bowing loyally to the absolute authority of the Scriptures. Thus we have in Edwardeanism a parallel to English evangelicalism in spite of the many and radical divergences; and it is no accident that in America, since the eighteenth century, evangelicalism has spread, not simply within the Wesleyan communions, which were the direct fruit of English Methodism, but also in those churches whose antecedents are Edwardean or akin thereto.

But Edwards was much more than an Evangelical, and much more, too, than a Calvinist, though it is his Calvinism which is chiefly remembered. He was one of the most profound theologians the world has seen, and he possessed philosophical gifts of a high order. It would carry us too far afield, and would be inconsistent with the plan of this volume to discuss his teaching in detail, but certain features of it are of sufficient interest to demand attention even though their influence on the development of Protestant thought has been slight. Not to dwell upon his *Notes on the Mind*, in which a thoroughgoing idealism similar to but not identical with Berkeley's found expression,[1] reference may be made particularly to his famous treatise on the will, and to his even more remarkable dissertations on *The End for which God created the World* and on the *Nature of True Virtue*. The treatise on the will,[2] the most celebrated of all his works, was written with a polemic purpose—to destroy the very foundations upon which Arminianism rested—and the argument employed was even more largely theological

---

[1] Edwards's idealism was essentially a form of mystical pantheism, and whether he owed the suggestion of it to Berkeley or to some one else, at any rate it gained a peculiar colour from his own religious temperament and experience.

[2] *A Careful and Strict Inquiry into the Prevailing Notions of the Freedom of the Will*, published in 1754.

than philosophical. At the same time the work displays extraordinary subtlety and dialectical skill, and a fearlessness in following the logic of one's position seldom equalled before or since. It maintains a complete necessitarianism. Men are free in so far as they possess the power of doing as they choose, but their choices are absolutely determined. This is not due to divine enactment, or to the fall of Adam bringing man into bondage; it lies in the very nature of the will itself, which is always controlled by motives, whether in man or God. Adam from the moment of his creation was in the same case as all his posterity in this respect, though the motives that controlled him were different in his primitive state of innocence and in his later state of sin. Edwards's independence of theological tradition, and his consistency in the application of his principles appear particularly in this departure from the common Calvinistic view.

The work is an argument, not a scientific treatise. Its chief historic significance consists in its exposure of the theological weakness of the current Arminianism of the day, and such originality as it possesses lies only in the persistence and pertinacity with which the subject is pursued into all its ramifications.

Of a very different character and philosophically more profound and important are the dissertations on *The End for which God created the World*, and on the *Nature of True Virtue*, both of which were written in 1755, but not published until after Edwards's death.

In the former there reappears the mystic pantheism of his youthful *Notes on the Mind*, of which few traces are to be found in his sermons and polemic writings of intervening years. Infinite being has a natural tendency to diffuse itself, and in this is to be seen the end of creation. 'Thus it appears reasonable to suppose, that it was what God had respect to as an ultimate end of His creating the world, to communicate of His own infinite fullness of good;

or rather it was His last end, that there might be a glorious and abundant emanation of His infinite fullness of good *ad extra*, or without Himself; and the disposition to communicate Himself, or diffuse his own *Fullness*, which we must conceive of as being originally in God as a perfection of His nature was what moved Him to create the world. But here, as much as possible to avoid confusion, I observe that there is some impropriety in saying that a disposition in God to communicate Himself *to the creature* moved Him to create the world. For though the diffusive disposition in the nature of God, that moved Him to create the world, doubtless inclines Him to communicate Himself to the creature, when the creature exists; yet this cannot be all: because an inclination in God to communicate Himself to an object, seems to presuppose the existence of the object, at least in idea. But the diffusive disposition that excited God to give creatures existence, was rather a communicative disposition in general, or a disposition in the fullness of the divinity to flow out and diffuse itself. Thus the disposition there is in the root and stock of a tree to diffuse and send forth its sap and life, is doubtless the reason of the communication of its sap and life to its buds, leaves, and fruits, after these exist. But a disposition to communicate of its life and sap to its fruits, is not so properly the cause of its producing those fruits, as its disposition to communicate itself, or diffuse its sap and life in general. Therefore, to speak more strictly according to truth, we may suppose, *that a disposition in God, as an original property of His nature, to an emanation of His own infinite fullness, was what excited Him to create the world; and so that the emanation itself was aimed at by Him as a last end of the creation.*'[1]

The universe is not a creation out of nothing, but an emanation from God. It has real existence only in so far

---

[1] Worcester edition of Edwards's *Works*, vol. ii. p. 206 *sq*. The italics are his.

as it partakes of God. God is interested in it, not for its own sake, but because He is Himself infused in it. His last end in creation is Himself. He loves Himself supremely, for He is supreme excellence and alone worthy to be the object of such love. The world exists for God's glory, and the happiness and well-being of the creature are only of subordinate and secondary concern. Independently of God the creature has no significance. But possessing as he does somewhat of the divine nature he shares in the blessedness of God, and is advantaged by the promotion of the divine glory. A considerable part of the work is taken up with a discussion of the meaning of the glory of God, which all Calvinists agreed was the end of creation, and it is found to consist in the diffusion of His fullness, and not simply in the exhibition of His attributes, as had commonly been said.

The general contention of Edwards's dissertation is stated with abundant emphasis and clearness, but the argument is beset with a fundamental difficulty which his theological and practical interest made it impossible for him to surmount. The result is ambiguity and confusion. His position is essentially pantheistic. The universe is conceived as an emanation from God, possessing reality only as it partakes of the divine nature, and yet the necessities of practical religion require him to give some measure at least of independent existence to human souls. He does not succeed in extricating himself from this difficulty. Indeed, while he evidently feels it, he does not grapple with it at all. As a consequence the essay is very unsatisfactory as a discussion of God's relation to the world, but it is profound and suggestive and strikingly unlike traditional Calvinistic treatments of the subject from Calvin himself down. That Deity was viewed under the aspect of infinite being rather than almighty will carried the whole matter into another sphere. It was inevitable that inconsistencies should emerge. They were similar to those which beset Augustine, who also felt as Edwards did the diverse influence of Neo-Platonic metaphysics and practical Christianity. The essay, both in its controlling contention and in its radical inconsistency, is one of the most significant and prophetic in the whole range of modern theological literature.

Equally profound and suggestive, and of more immediate influence was the parallel dissertation on the *Nature of True Virtue*. Edwards's general attitude and his philosophical assumptions are the same in both dissertations, and the two are very closely related in spite of the difference of theme. In genuine Neo-Platonic fashion he regards being itself as a good, and he goes on to draw the conclusion that excellence is proportioned to the degree of existence. The more of existence any being has, other things being equal, the more excellent it is. The infinite Being God is immeasurably more excellent than all creatures, for He possesses an infinitely greater amount of existence than they, and is infinitely farther from nonentity. Virtue, in accordance with the common opinion of his day, Edwards defines as benevolence. Consent to, good-will toward, or pleasure in being—this is what benevolence means, and it is in this that virtue consists. It is not in the benevolent attitude or emotion as such, nor in the acts to which it leads that Edwards finds virtue, but in the due proportion between benevolence and its object. To love a being more than he deserves violates harmony as truly as to love him less than he deserves, and lack of harmony means lack of virtue. Universal being is a system, and each part of it is excellent only in so far as it is in harmony with the whole. Virtue is to be defined as consent to, or harmony with, or love for Being in general, that is intelligent Being. But Being in general Edwards identifies with God, the infinite by whose communication or diffusion of Himself all that is exists. True virtue, therefore, consists in love for the infinite Being God. Benevolence toward Being in general means benevolence toward God, that is supreme delight in His happiness and the controlling desire to promote His glory. Toward all other beings virtue involves benevolence in the degree to which they possess existence, or, in other words, in the degree to which they partake of God. To love any creature—whether oneself or another—independently of God, or in greater degree than its scale of being warrants is wrong—wrong in God as well as in man. The evil of self-love is due, not to its selfishness, but to the fact that it accords to a creature a disproportionate amount of affection. Undue affection for another is as bad as undue affection for oneself; only in subordination to love for God, or Being in general, is love for a creature justified. God's holiness consists in a supreme regard for Himself. That it is self-love does not make it less holy, for it is love rightly bestowed, and in love so bestowed virtue consists and in nothing else. God is to be supremely loved, both by Himself and by the creature. Men are to be loved only in subordination to Him and as partaking of Him. And hence love for the non-elect, who in reality do not share at all in the divine nature, has no justification. ' The *first* object of a virtuous benevolence is *Being, simply* considered; and if Being, simply considered, be its object, then Being *in general* is its object; and what it has an ultimate propensity to, is the *highest good* of Being in general. And it will seek the good of every *individual* being unless it be conceived as not consistent with the highest good of being in general. In which case the good of a particular being, or some beings, may be given up for the sake of the highest good of Being in general. And particularly, if there be any being irreclaimably opposite, and an enemy to Being in general, then consent and adherence to Being in general will induce the truly virtuous heart to forsake that enemy and to oppose it.' [1]

Love, if it is to be virtuous, must be proportioned, not

[1] *Works*, vol. ii. p. 264.

to the need, but to the excellence of the object loved. Holy love is love for a holy object, not love which would make the unholy holy. Far from the gospel of Christ, with its emphasis upon love for the unlovely and unworthy, as this teaching is, religion is yet given a place of fundamental importance that has seldom been accorded to it. Never, in fact, have religion and ethics been more completely fused.

Edwards's identification of God at once with being in general, and with the personal God of the Hebrew and Christian revelation, introduces into the dissertation on Virtue an inconsistency similar to that which beset the dissertation on *God's End in Creation*. It is an ancient inconsistency, troubling theology ever since the time of Clement of Alexandria, but it becomes more acute than ever in such a metaphysical discussion as Edwards's. The influence of tradition and the interests of practical religion prevented him here too, as at so many other places, from following loyally the leading of his speculative genius.

The development of thought within the Edwardean school cannot be traced here. Edwards was the only genius of the school, and the theologising of his disciples had for the most part but local and passing interest. His theory of virtue, although it was not the subject most discussed, proved the most fruitful of all his ideas. It found consistent, even if paradoxical utterance, in the 'willingness to be damned for the glory of God,' upon which Samuel Hopkins, his greatest disciple, laid emphasis. The attitude thus expressed was ridiculed by many, including even Edwardeans, but they thereby only betrayed their lack of appreciation of the profound religiousness and sublime disinterestedness of Edwards's teaching. He was a rare and lofty spirit among the sons of men, so enamoured of the divine from the time he penned his youthful *Notes on the Mind*, to the closing years of his life, when he wrote his dissertations on *God's End in*

Creation and the *Nature of True Virtue*, that all else—earth and self and fellow-men—seemed but 'as the light dust in the balance (which is taken no notice of by him that weighs), and as nothing and vanity.'

We have been carried far afield from evangelicalism in this consideration of Edwards's theological and philosophical work, but he remained an Evangelical to the end, and his piety, suffused and transfigured though it was by his loftier genius, was in essence that of Spener and Wesley, and all true Pietists.

CHAPTER X

RATIONALISM

THE Protestant Reformation was mediæval, not modern, in its spirit and interest, and the Protestant scholasticism of the seventeenth century, which has been briefly reviewed, was a legitimate outcome of it. Bondage to an external law of faith and practice was for a long time as complete in Protestantism as in Catholicism, and the one was as conservative in the field of religious thought as the other. The immediate effect of the modern spirit, when it began to make its influence felt in Christianity, was as destructive of the new Protestantism as of the old Catholicism. This is seen clearly enough in Socinianism, and still more clearly in the rationalism of the eighteenth century, where the modern spirit first found large expression within the religious sphere. The rationalism of the period was of all sorts and degrees, but in every phase of it there was the tendency to reject or modify the mediæval estimate of man. Greater intellectual sufficiency, and commonly greater moral ability were attributed to him than traditional theology was willing to grant. Often the deviation from orthodox doctrine was slight, often very great, but in every case the modern spirit was influential, and those doctrines which were based on the theory of the depravity and helplessness of man received least emphasis or were repudiated altogether. It cannot be too strongly emphasised that rationalism was at bottom as much of a break with Protestantism as with Catholicism. Its principles were not Protestant, but involved the rejection of Protestant and Catholic principles alike. Against modern views of every kind, Protestantism set itself as uncompromisingly as Catholicism. That rationalism ultimately made its home in Protestantism rather than in the older communion, was not because the former was in principle more tolerant of divergent views, but because the divisions within the Protestant ranks made greater tolerance a necessity. The break with the old ecclesiastical institution and the rise of new churches independent of it and of each other facilitated the gradual growth of a freedom in religious thought which could not have come had all Christendom remained under a single ecclesiastical control; but the break itself, and not any particular principles leading to it, made the new liberty possible. In the conflict of authorities there was room for new ideas to grow and flourish.

In a previous chapter, the rationalistic tendency of Socinianism was spoken of. Its rationalism was of a very mild sort, and went hand in hand with a thoroughgoing supernaturalism. But the combination involved an unstable equilibrium which could not last. It is not due to Socinianism alone nor even chiefly that rationalism of a more consistent type made its way within the Protestant churches, and ultimately acquired a preponderating influence. The general spirit of the modern age was responsible for the phenomenon. Socinianism represented simply an early and very limited exhibition of tendencies which later became prominent and worked themselves out in a much more extreme form.

Socinian influence may be directly traced to some degree in Holland, where rationalistic tendencies were widespread in the early seventeenth century, and whence they made their way to England to find there a development which, in course of time, made English thought dominant throughout Northern Europe. Holland was the home of free thought in the seventeenth century. Thither came Descartes, and there he laid the foundations of modern philosophical rationalism; here Spinoza constructed the greatest of all rational systems; here Pierre Bayle published his famous dictionary, and here the Arminians nearly a century earlier rose in revolt against the dominant Calvinism of the day.

In Arminianism we have an interesting parallel to Socinianism which throws welcome light upon the controlling interest of the earlier movement. The Arminians rejected its principles, and yet their attack upon Calvinism was due to a similar interest. Indeed, it is in their case even more manifest than in the case of the Socinians. Though in other respects entirely orthodox, Arminius and his fellow Remonstrants felt the irrationality of the traditional doctrine of total depravity and the injustice of the Calvinistic dogma of unconditional election, and attacked them both. The emphasis which they laid upon the justice of God is instructive, for it means a regard for the dignity and rights of man not felt by the genuine mediævalists of the Reformation. To Calvin as to Zwingli, man is a creature who has no rights over against God. The Creator may do as He pleases with His own. But the spirit of the modern age, with its new estimate of man, was out of sympathy with such a doctrine. Man is not a mere cipher whose fate is of no importance; he is a rational being who may demand consideration and fair treatment from God. To the Arminians, the unconditional election which stood in the forefront of the Calvinistic system, seemed utterly indefensible, and against it their attack was levelled. To be sure, the attack was a mild one and lacked the effectiveness of a thoroughgoing application of a great controlling principle. Instead of asserting in unqualified terms the natural ability of man, and rejecting the whole system based upon his inability, the Arminians accepted the dogma of the Fall and the consequent need of divine grace, and criticised only the assertion that predestination is unconditional and independent of all human merit. The conflict was not between the avowed and consistent representatives of two opposite principles. All it meant was that the consistent application of one principle was subjected to criticism by those who had felt the influence of another, without at all understanding the latter's significance or being in the least prepared to follow it to its logical conclusion. The Calvinists had all the advantage of clearness and consistency on their side, and it was only natural that they should win the victory. But, as with Socinianism, so with Arminianism, there was more in the movement than appeared upon the surface. The Arminians of that day, as of later days, might not go beyond the half-way position of Arminius himself, and might retain the traditional system in all its main points unchanged, but there was in the movement the promise of a greater break to come, the prophecy of an application of the modern principle in a way to overthrow the old completely.

I. *In England*

In England, rationalistic tendencies began to make themselves felt in the seventeenth century, appearing in all sorts of forms and in various degrees. There was not an orderly progression from more moderate to more extreme views, for the deism of Lord Herbert of Cherbury and the materialism of Hobbes antedated considerably the milder supernatural rationalism of such men as Locke, Tillotson, and Clarke. But this is not surprising. The tendency was the same in all of them, but as is commonly the case, it found much more consistent and extreme expression in some than in others.

During the greater part of the century, controversy ran high, and the whole country was torn with religious dissension. A natural consequence was the gradual growth of a desire to find some common platform upon which all religious men could stand together regardless of their theological and ecclesiastical differences. Among the most important of the attempts in this direction was that of Lord Herbert. In his famous work, *De Veritate*, published in 1624, he set up common consent as the principal test of truth, and applying the criterion in the religious sphere, distinguished a natural religion shared by wise men of all ages and races, from the various positive faiths which had added many unessential tenets, obscuring the great and vital truths, and introducing religious dissension where there should have been universal harmony. Among other notable writings contributing to the growth of religious tolerance was Chillingworth's *Religion of Protestants, A Sure Way to Salvation* (1637), in which the Scriptures were made an all-sufficient guide, and differences among Christians in matters not defined by the Bible were minimised. The main purpose of Chillingworth's book was not to promote toleration, but to defend Protestantism. But the book contained many strong expressions in favour of liberty for all that accepted the Bible, and its influence made in that direction. Other books promoting the same tendency were Milton's famous *Areopagitica* (1644), which entered an eloquent plea for toleration of all minor differences of opinion, and his tract, *Of True Religion, Heresy, Schism, Toleration, and what best Means may be used against the Growth of Popery* (1673), an endeavour to unite all Protestants against the Roman Catholics on the basis of the Bible; Jeremy Taylor's *Liberty of Prophesying* (1647), which made the Apostles' Creed the all-sufficient standard, and maintained that all accepting it should be recognised as Christians; Locke's *Letters on Toleration* (1689), an elaborate and thoroughgoing discussion of the whole question of state toleration, in which the principle was laid down that the government should not interfere in religious matters, and should prohibit only avowed atheism and overt acts inimical to the civil life of the community; finally, Anthony Collins's *Discourse of Free Thinking* (1713), championing unlimited and unconditional liberty for all kinds of religious or irreligious opinion on the theory that his own individual reason is the supreme guide of every man, and that he should not be prevented from following it, in whatever direction it might lead, but on the contrary, should be encouraged to do so. The position taken by Collins was that of the Deists in general, of whom he was one. A fundamental tenet with all of them was complete religious freedom for men of all opinions and of all sects.

The writings referred to, and they are but a few of a large class of similar works, show a steadily growing breadth of toleration. After the Revolution of 1688, a reaction against the religious strife of the past hundred years made itself widely felt, and the necessity of at least some measure of toleration was generally admitted. Commercial and industrial interests, which had suffered greatly during the troublous years of the seventeenth century, began now to force themselves to the front, and peace and quiet came to be recognised as the supreme need of the country. In 1689, upon the accession of William and Mary, the famous Act of Toleration was passed by Parliament, ensuring religious liberty to all Protestants except Unitarians. Roman Catholic and anti-Trinitarian dissent remained still under the ban. Toleration of the former seemed to involve too great a danger to the State, and toleration of the latter was demanded by too small a group to make it seem worth while. Thenceforth though the English Establishment remained unimpaired, and though some sort of religious profession and attendance upon some form of religious worship were required, Protestant trinitarian dissent was legal in England, and every kind of non-conformity was practically, though not theoretically tolerated.

The rigid press licensing act of 1662 was repealed in 1695, and the embargo upon the publication of radical and heterodox opinions in religion was thus removed, but the laws against blasphemy were renewed in 1698, and thereafter process could be instituted against any one issuing works of too offensive a character. Under this act an occasional writer was fined and imprisoned, but in the main it was possible by the exercise of a little care to give utterance to any kind of religious radicalism one might wish. Voltaire, who was in England in the twenties, marvelled at the degree of liberty enjoyed by the most diverse parties, and hailed England as the haven of all men of advanced religious views.

Many causes besides those already indicated were uniting during this period to promote rationalism and to extend its influence among the thinking classes of England as well as of the Continent. In the philosophical sphere, the work of Descartes and his school, of Spinoza, Hobbes, and Locke, in the scientific world the discoveries and the theories of Bruno, Copernicus, Galileo, Kepler, Gassendi, Bacon, Newton, and others, combined to promote the credit of human reason and to undermine the authority of traditional systems and opinions. The scepticism and materialism of Hobbes called into being the Platonism, or rather the Neo-Platonism of the Cambridge school, with their emphasis upon reason as a faculty by which we may enjoy a direct vision of spiritual realities hidden from the senses and inaccessible by the ordinary processes of discursive reason.[1] The beauty and spirituality of the writings of some members of this school gave them a considerable following, and promoted, not only a spirit of

[1] On the Cambridge Platonists see Tulloch's *Rational Theology in England in the Seventeenth Century*, vol. ii. Prominent among them were Benjamin Whichcote, Henry More, Ralph Cudworth (author of the famous *Intellectual System of the Universe*), and John Smith.

tolerance, but also confidence in the use of human reason in the religious sphere, but their enthusiasm and mysticism were too foreign to the external and practical temper of the age to find wide acceptance, and their influence was largely exhausted in the general effects just referred to.

A few quotations from a discourse by John Smith on *The Excellency and Nobleness of True Religion* will sufficiently illustrate the general temper and attitude of the group. 'All perfections and excellencies are to be measured by their approach to and participation of the First Perfection,' and 'Religion is the greatest participation of God' (p. 369). 'A good man, one that is actuated by religion, lives in converse with his own reason; he lives at the height of his own being' (p. 376). 'A good man, one that is informed by true religion, lives above himself and is raised to an intimate converse with the Divinity. He moves in a larger sphere than his own being and cannot be content to enjoy himself except he may enjoy God too, and himself in God. This we shall consider two ways. First in the self-denial of good men; they are content and ready to deny themselves for God. I mean not that they should deny their own reason as some would have it, for that were to deny a beam of divine light and so to deny God, instead of denying ourselves for Him' (p. 378). 'The first property and effect of true religion whereby it expresses its own nobleness is this that it widens and enlarges all the faculties of the soul, and begets a true ingenuity, liberty, and amplitude, the most free and generous spirit, in the mind of good men' (p. 382). 'I doubt we are too nice logicians sometimes in distinguishing between the glory of God and our own salvation. We cannot in a true sense seek our own salvation more than the glory of God, which triumphs most and discovers itself most effectually in the salvation of souls; for, indeed, this salvation is nothing else but a true participation of the divine nature. Heaven is not a thing without us, nor is happiness anything distinct from a true conjunction of the mind with God in a secret feeling of His goodness and reciprocation of affection to Him wherein the divine glory most unfolds itself' (p. 399). 'The sixth property or effect wherein religion discovers its own excellency is this—that it spiritualises material things, and so carries up the souls of good men from earthly things to things divine, from this sensible world to the intellectual.' 'But how to find God here and feelingly to converse with Him, and being affected with the sense of the divine glory shining out upon creation how to pass out of the sensible world into the intellectual, is not so effectually taught by that philosophy which professed it most as by true religion: that which knits and unites God and the soul together can best teach it how to ascend and descend upon those golden links that unite, as it were, the world to God. That divine wisdom that contrived and beautified this glorious structure can best explain her own art and carry up the soul back again in these reflected beams to Him who is the fountain of them' (p. 419).

The spirituality of these men and their emphasis upon immediate apprehension of God and divine things were out of line with the tendencies of the period in which they lived, and their influence was but circumscribed and temporary. They were at one with the spirit of the age in recognising the dignity and power of human reason, but their interpretation of it was quite unlike that of their contemporaries, and was almost universally rejected.

On the other hand, the growing rationalism of the day found consistent expression in a number of writers of the late seventeenth and early eighteenth centuries, prominent among whom was the ecclesiastic and preacher, John Tillotson, Archbishop of Canterbury.[1] Archbishop Tillotson,

[1] Tillotson's *Works*, composed principally of sermons, have been frequently published. I have used the edition in twelve volumes published in London in 1857.

RATIONALISM

the most famous preacher of his day, was a foe of mysticism and religious enthusiasm in every form and a sturdy champion of the use of reason in religion. By reason he meant a faculty very unlike the Cambridge Platonists' faculty of direct vision. Of spiritual intuition or the immediate apprehension of supersensuous realities, he would hear nothing. When he insisted upon the use of reason in religion, he meant that religion is an affair that offers itself for acceptance like a philosophical system, a political principle, or a financial investment. He thought of it, not as something instinctive, which needs justification no more than hunger and thirst, or pleasure and pain, but as a system of rational propositions given from without and to be tested as any other propositions are tested, and to be established by rational evidence. Religion, according to Tillotson, is not an end in itself, worthful on its own account, independently of its effects; its only value lies in the fact that it provides divine sanctions for morality. These are given in natural religion which teaches that there is a God, that He demands virtuous living on the part of man, and that He will reward the righteous and punish the wicked.[1] But natural religion is not enough. Its sanctions have proved ineffective, and it has therefore been supplemented by revelation. The function of the latter is not to destroy or correct natural religion, but simply to make it clearer and more effective. 'Natural religion,' Tillotson says, 'is the foundation of all revealed religion, and revelation is designed simply to establish its duties.'[2] It is true that certain requirements are added by revelation, particularly that we should recognise Christ as the Son of God, worship God in His name, and receive the sacraments, but these are enjoined with the same purpose of promoting virtue.[3] The sacraments impress us with the heinousness of sin, and the figure of Christ supplies both example and inspiration.

[1] *Works*, vol. ii. p. 336 ff.   [2] *Ibid.* vol. ii. p. 333.   [3] Cf. *Ibid.* vol. iii. p. 463.

Revelation imparts no new faculties, nor does it appeal to any other faculty than reason, to which natural religion also appeals. The use of the term faith does not set either natural or revealed religion apart from other purely human affairs. Faith is simply a persuasion of the mind concerning the truth of any proposition or 'a persuasion of the mind concerning any thing.'[1] It is thus solely intellectual and is only a stronger form of opinion. We may have faith in the truths of natural religion, in the truths of revealed religion, or in the fact of revelation. In any case, faith is simply the conviction, based upon rational grounds, that certain things are true.[2] Faith thus leads to virtue, for the religious truths offered for our acceptance are all of them given with the promotion of virtue in view. This is particularly true of the future life with its rewards and punishments, belief in which Tillotson regards as 'the great motive and argument to a holy life.'[3] If we accept this and other truths given in religion we are convinced of the advantages of righteous living; if we reject them, no motive for such living remains.

According to Tillotson, as already said, revelation supplements natural religion. But what are the grounds for believing in revelation? How do we know that there has been such a thing and that any alleged revelation is true? This raises the whole question of Christian evidences, and to its discussion Tillotson devotes many sermons. He maintains that two things must be shown if an alleged revelation is to be accepted as genuine—that it does not contradict the principles of natural religion, and that there are positive reasons for supposing it a revelation stronger than those that can be brought against it. In defence of Christianity he urges its complete harmony with natural religion, the reasonableness of its precepts and their fitness to the nature of man, and finally, prophecy and miracle. Upon Christ's fulfilment of Old Testament

[1] *Works*, vol. xi. p. 203.　　[2] *Ibid.* vol. xi. p. 431 ff.　　[3] *Ibid.* vol. v. p. 99.

prophecy he lays considerable stress, but even more upon his miracles, which constitute, he says, the principal and only adequate proof of Christianity. In his sermon on 'The Miracles wrought in Confirmation of Christianity,'[1] after declaring that 'miracles are a divine testimony given to a person or doctrine,' he asks 'What a miracle is?' and 'In what circumstances and with what limitations miracles are a sufficient testimony to the truth and divinity of any doctrine?' In reply to the former question, he says, 'The shortest and plainest description of it I can give is this: that it is a supernatural effect, and wonderful to sense. So that there are two things necessary to a miracle: that it be a supernatural effect, and that it be evident and wonderful to sense. By a supernatural effect I mean such an effect as either in itself and in its own nature, or in the manner and circumstances of it, exceeds any natural power, that we know of, to produce it.' 'There is another condition also required to a miracle, that it be an effect evident and wonderful to sense; for if we do not see it, it is to us as if it were not, and can be no testimony or proof of any thing because itself stands in need of another miracle to give testimony to it, and to prove that it was wrought.' Transubstantiation, therefore, according to Tillotson, even if it were a fact, would not be a miracle, for a miracle is not merely a wonderful or supernatural event, but a sign wrought for purposes of proof. If the so-called miracles of Jesus, for instance, were merely works of mercy done for the good of the sufferer, and were not signs intended to substantiate the fact of a divine revelation, they were not miracles at all. This conception of miracle it is necessary to keep in mind if we would understand the development that followed.

In reply to his second question as to the circumstances and limitations under which miracles may be a sufficient testimony to the truth or divinity of any doctrine, Tillot-

[1] *Works*, vol. iii. p. 493 ff.

son says, 'Now there are two things must concur to give the mind of man full satisfaction that any religion is from God. First, if the person that declares this religion give testimony of his divine authority, that is, that he is sent and commissioned by God for that purpose. And secondly, if the religion which he declares contain nothing in it that is plainly repugnant to the nature of God.' And again, 'For though a doctrine be never so reasonable in itself, this is no certain argument that it is from God if no testimony from heaven be given to it; because it may be the result and issue of human reason and discourse; and though a doctrine be attested by miracles, yet the matter of it may be so unreasonable and absurd, so unworthy of God, and so contrary to the natural notions which man has of him, that no miracles can be sufficient to give confirmation to it; and therefore in some cases the Scripture forbids men to hearken to a prophet though he work a miracle. . . . From whence it is plain that a miracle is not sufficient to establish the worship of a false God. The sum of what I have said is this: that we do not found our belief of Christianity upon any one argument taken by itself; but upon the whole evidence which we are able to produce for it, in which there is nothing wanting that is proper and reasonable to prove any religion to be from God. But yet miracles are the principal external proof and confirmation of the divinity of a doctrine. I told you before that some doctrines are so absurd that a miracle is not a sufficient proof of them: but if a doctrine be such as is noways unworthy of God, nor contrary to those notions which we have of Him, miracles are the highest testimony that can be given to it, and have always been owned by mankind for an evidence of inspiration.'[1]

The external and formal conception of the divine is

[1] Compare also the sermon on 'The Trial of the Spirits,' *Works*, vol. ii. p. 29 *sq*. This contains Tillotson's famous argument against transubstantiation to which Hume refers in his *Essay on Miracles*.

noticeable throughout Tillotson's discussion. Even after a thing is proved good and true, there is needed the evidence of a miracle to show that it comes from God. No spiritual or moral effects warrant the assumption of divine activity. It can be guaranteed only by physical phenomena. The supreme and convincing proof of Christianity lies, not in its character or influence, but in the external miracles which attended its inception, and were wrought in confirmation of it. It would be unjust to Tillotson to leave the impression that he was interested only in Christian evidences and devoted all his sermons to proving the divine origin of Christianity in the way that has been indicated. A glance at the titles of his many published discourses shows that he had much else upon his heart, and that he covered a wide range of religious and ethical subjects. But it is the side of his thought that has been presented which has chief historical importance, and which alone needs notice here. He set the fashion for nearly all Christian thinkers that came after him for a number of generations. Emphasis was more and more laid upon the rational evidences for Christianity, upon its harmony with natural religion, and the miracles wrought in its support, making up its appeal to the cool and deliberate reason of the man of common sense, while the inner experience of the presence of the divine, the immediate vision of spiritual realities, was condemned as unwholesome enthusiasm and unfounded superstition.

The combination in Tillotson of the rationalist and the supernaturalist was typical of his age. Nothing is to be accepted that does not approve itself to the native human reason. The old dictum *credo quia incredibile* is the worst of heresies. The natural man is not a blind being who must believe whatever is told him, and must submit his judgment implicitly to the alleged authority of God. Even miracles should not lead him to stultify his reason and accept what seems to him irrational. And yet with so controlling an emphasis on the reason was associated faith in the supernatural. Miracles are entirely reasonable and become in certain circumstances the complete and sufficient proof of divine revelation.

With Tillotson agreed his younger contemporary, the philosopher, John Locke, whose discussion of the whole subject is so careful and acute, and presents so clearly the controlling principles of the entire rationalistic movement, that it may be well to dwell upon him for a little. In accordance with his general epistemological principles, Locke denies that we have any innate idea of God,[1] but maintains that by rational demonstration we may reach the certainty that God exists.[2] There is, therefore, such a thing as natural religion, that is, a religion which we may arrive at by the use of our unaided reason. As Locke employs it in this connection, reason is not intuitive, but discursive. 'The greatest part of our knowledge,' he says, 'depends upon deductions and intermediate ideas ; and in those cases where we are feign to substitute assent instead of knowledge, and take propositions for true, without being certain they are so, we have need to find out, examine, and compare the grounds of their probability. In both these cases, the faculty which finds out the means and rightly applies them to discover certainty in the one case and probability in the other, is that which we call reason.'[3] It is by this kind of reason that we reach our knowledge of God and of religious truth in general ; not by intuition or direct vision, but by the ordinary processes of rational demonstration.

In speaking of the use of reason in religion, Locke takes up the familiar phrases 'above,' 'contrary to,' and 'according to' reason, and says, 'By what has been before said of reason we may be able to make some guess at the distinction of things into those that are according to,

[1] *Essay on the Human Understanding*, bk. I. chap. iv.
[2] *Ibid.* bk. IV. chap. x.   [3] *Ibid.* § 2.

above, and contrary to reason. According to reason are such propositions whose truth we can discover by examining and tracing those ideas we have from sensation and reflection; and by natural deduction find to be true or probable. Above reason are such propositions whose truth or probability we cannot by reason derive from those principles. Contrary to reason are such propositions as are inconsistent with, or irreconcilable to our clear and distinct ideas. Thus the existence of one God is according to reason; the existence of more than one God contrary to reason; the resurrection of the dead above reason.'[1]

Divine revelation may give man a knowledge of things which are also discoverable by natural reason, that is, it may give him things that are according to reason, but 'In all things of this kind, there is little need or use of revelation, God having furnished us with natural and surer means to arrive at a knowledge of them. For whatsoever truth we come to a clearer discovery of from the knowledge and contemplation of our own ideas, will always be certainer to us than those which are conveyed to us by traditional revelation.' And again revelation may give us things that are above reason, 'there being many things wherein we have very imperfect notions or none at all; and other things of whose past, present, or future existence by the natural use of our faculties we can have no knowledge at all; these, as being beyond the discovery of our natural faculties and above reason, are, when revealed, the proper matter of faith. Thus that part of the angels rebelled against God, and thereby lost their first happy state; and that the dead shall rise and live again: these and the like being beyond the discovery of reason, are purely matters of faith with which reason has directly nothing to do.'

The category 'above reason' was more narrowly de-

[1] *Essay on the Human Understanding*, bk. IV. chap. xvii. § 23.

fined by a young Irish disciple of Locke, John Toland, in his interesting little book entitled *Christianity not Mysterious* (1696). According to Toland, when it is said that revelation gives us things above reason, it does not mean things mysterious or incomprehensible or difficult to understand, but simply perfectly rational matters that we should not otherwise have heard of, or events that have not fallen under our observation, and can therefore be known only on the testimony of others. In this sense, revelation may enlarge our knowledge, giving us an acquaintance with unfamiliar events or truths, but above reason as transcending our comprehension, or as too profound or mysterious for the natural man to penetrate, revealed facts cannot be. There are, therefore, strictly speaking, only two categories : according to, and contrary to reason, but reasonable facts and truths may be discovered by us for ourselves or may be made known to us by the testimony of others, and this testimony may be given by revelation. Although he was later known as a Deist, Toland did not deny the reality of revelation in this book, nor did he ostensibly go beyond the position taken by Locke, but he defined it more carefully and guarded it against misunderstanding, and in so doing, really advanced further than Locke and most Christians of the day were willing to go in the direction of rationalising all Christian truth. He performed a real service in calling attention to the irrational character of the category above reason as it was commonly understood, showing that it was often a hiding place for all sorts of beliefs in reality contrary to reason.

Toland's position was taken also, if possible with even greater clearness and emphasis, by Anthony Collins in a book entitled *Essay concerning the use of Reason in Propositions, the Evidence whereof depends on Human Testimony* (1707).

But to return to Locke himself. While he claims that

revelation may give us things according to reason or above reason, nothing contrary to reason can be admitted on its authority. 'For since no evidence of our faculties by which we receive such revelations can exceed, if equal, the certainty of our intuitive knowledge, we can never receive for a truth any thing that is directly contrary to our clear and distinct knowledge; for instance, the ideas of one body and one place do so clearly agree, and the mind has so evident a perception of their agreement, that we can never assent to a proposition that affirms the same body to be in two distant places at once, however it should pretend to the authority of a divine revelation: since the evidence—first that we deceive not ourselves in ascribing it to God, second, that we understand it right—can never be so great as the evidence of our own intuitive knowledge whereby we discern it impossible for the same body to be in two places at once. And, therefore, no proposition can be received for divine revelation or obtain the assent due to all such if it be contradictory to our clear intuitive knowledge.'[1] 'Whatever God hath revealed is certainly true, no doubt can be made of it. This is the proper object of faith: but whether it be a divine revelation or no, reason must judge; which can never permit the mind to reject a greater evidence to embrace what is less evident, nor allow it to entertain probability in opposition to knowledge and certainty. There can be no evidence that any traditional revelation is of divine origin, in the words we receive it and in the sense we understand it, so clear and so certain as that of the principles of reason; and therefore nothing that is contrary to and inconsistent with the clear and self-evident dictates of reason has a right to be urged or assented to as a matter of faith wherein reason has nothing to do.'[2]

'In all that is of divine revelation there is need of no

[1] *Essay on the Human Understanding*, bk. IV. chap. xviii. § 5.
[2] *Ibid.* § 10.

other proof but that it is an inspiration from God ; for He can neither deceive nor be deceived. But how shall it be known that any proposition in our minds is a truth infused by God ; a truth that is revealed to us by Him which He declares to us, and therefore we ought to believe ? Here it is that enthusiasm fails of the evidence it pretends to. For men thus possessed boast of a light whereby they say they are enlightened and brought into the knowledge of this or that truth. But if they know it to be a truth, they must know it to be so either by its own self-evidence to natural reason, or by the rational proofs that make it out to be so. If they see and know it to be a truth either of these two ways, they in vain suppose it to be a revelation. For they know it to be true by the same way that any other man naturally may know that it is so without the help of revelation. . . . If they say they know it to be true because it is a revelation from God, the reason is good ; but then it will be demanded how they know it to be a revelation from God ? If they say by the light it brings with it, which shines bright in their minds, and they cannot resist, I beseech them to consider whether this be any more than what we have taken notice of already, namely, that it is a revelation because they strongly believe it to be true. . . . For rational grounds from proofs that it is a truth, they must acknowledge to have none ; for then it is not perceived as a revelation, but upon the ordinary grounds that other truths are received ; and if they believe it to be true because it is a revelation, and have no other reason for its being a revelation, but because they are fully persuaded without any other reason that it is true, they believe it to be a revelation only because they strongly believe it to be a revelation ; which is a very unsafe ground to proceed on either in our tenets or actions.'[1]
' Thus we see the holy men of old who had revelations from God had something else besides that internal light of assur-

[1] *Essay on the Human Understanding*, bk. IV. chap. xviii. § 11.

ance in their own mind to testify to them that it was from God. They were not left to their own persuasions alone that those persuasions were from God, but had outward signs to convince them of the author of those revelations. And when they were to convince others they had a power given them to justify the truth of their commission from heaven, and by visible signs to assert the divine authority of a message they were sent with.'[1]

Evidently Locke's position is identical with Tillotson's. Nothing can be received as a divine revelation if it contradicts reason, and nothing is to be received as such except on external evidence, that is, the evidence of miracles which alone can prove a revelation to be from God. In his brief *Discourse of Miracles* (published posthumously in 1706), Locke discussed the nature of a miracle and the testimony which it gives. A miracle, he says, is ' a sensible operation, which being above the comprehension of the spectator and in his opinion contrary to the established course of nature, is taken by him to be divine.'[2] Its purpose is solely to give credentials to a person as God's messenger, and so to confirm the divine origin of the revelation brought by him. 'Divine revelation receives testimony from no other miracles but such as are wrought to witness his mission from God who delivers the revelation. All other miracles that are done in the world, how many or great soever, revelation is not concerned in.' And even the greatest miracles cannot prove a revelation to be from God which is out of accord with our natural knowledge of God, or, in other words, contrary to reason.

In his little book entitled *The Reasonableness of Christianity* (1695), Locke applied the general principles laid down in the fourth book of his *Essay on the Human Understanding*, to the Christian system, and undertook

[1] *Essay on the Human Understanding*, bk. IV. chap. xviii. § 15.
[2] *Discourse of Miracles*, p. 217.

to show that it is both rational and adequately attested. He recognised that there was much in traditional Christianity contrary to sound reason, and he therefore examined the Scriptures in considerable detail to discover the essence of Christianity as taught by Christ and His apostles. He found that they set forth only two conditions of salvation: the belief that Jesus is the Messiah, and a righteous life. 'These two, faith and repentance, that is, believing Jesus to be the Messiah, and a good life, are the indispensable conditions of the new covenant to be performed by all those who would obtain eternal life.'[1] To one who believes in Jesus as the Messiah, and tries to live as he should, his faith will be graciously reckoned for righteousness and allowed to make up for the imperfections in his conduct.[2] All this, according to Locke, is eminently rational. Viewed in this way, as Christ Himself and His apostles understood it, Christianity contains nothing inconsistent with reason, and moreover, it is positively attested by miracles.[3] Thus it fully meets the requirements of a true revelation.

In the same book Locke raises the general question why there should be a revelation. If natural religion is true and good, why is it not enough? It is evident that the greater the emphasis laid upon the truth and obligation of the religion of nature, the more pressing such a question as this becomes. Locke discusses it at some length, and concludes that a revelation was necessary because men had widely lost the knowledge of one God in spite of the fact that natural reason was sufficient to lead them to it; that they were more or less in the dark touching their moral duties, the light of reason being inadequate to give them clear information; that divine worship required simplifying and purifying; and that encouragement to virtue

---

[1] *The Reasonableness of Christianity*, p. 202. I quote from the second edition published in 1696.
[2] *Ibid.* pp. 243, 250.
[3] *Ibid.* pp. 259 ff., 280 ff.

was needed such as an assurance of future rewards and punishments was fitted to give.[1]

Closely related to Tillotson and Locke in his view of natural and revealed religion, was Samuel Clarke, the most famous theologian, and after Locke's death, the most famous philosopher of his day in England. He belonged to an entirely different philosophical school, standing for innate ideas and *a priori* reasoning over against the empiricism of the older philosopher, but his agreement in the matter of natural and revealed religion is all the more significant. In his second series of Boyle Lectures, given in 1705, and entitled ' A Discourse concerning the Unchangeable Obligations of Natural Religion, and the Truth and Certainty of the Christian Revelation,' he maintained that natural religion is based on the necessary distinction between good and evil, that our moral obligations express the will of God, that they must necessarily be attended with rewards and punishments, and that since such rewards and punishments are not equitably distributed in our present state of existence, there must be another life beyond the grave. Thus natural religion gives us a belief in God, in virtue as His will, and in a future life. But owing to the corrupt state and condition of mankind, very few are able to discover these things clearly for themselves, and hence there is needed divine revelation.

' There was plainly wanting a divine revelation to recover mankind out of their universal corruption and degeneracy, and without such a revelation it was not possible that the world should ever be effectually reformed. For if (as has been before particularly shown) the gross and stupid ignorance, the innumerable prejudices and vain opinions, the strong passions and appetites of sense, and the many vicious customs and habits, which the generality of mankind continually labour under, make it undeniably too difficult a work for men of all capacities

[1] *The Reasonableness of Christianity*, p. 257 ff.

to discover every one for himself, by the bare light of nature, all the particular branches of their duty; but most men, in the present state of things, have manifestly need of much teaching, and particular instruction: if those who were best able to discover the truth and instruct others therein, namely the wisest and best of the philosophers, were themselves unavoidably altogether ignorant of some doctrines, and very doubtful and uncertain of others, absolutely necessary to the bringing about that great end, the reformation of mankind: if those truths which they were themselves very certain of, they were not yet able to prove and explain clearly enough, to vulgar understandings: if even those things which they proved sufficiently, and explained with all clearness, they had not yet authority enough to enforce and inculcate upon men's minds with so strong an impression, as to influence and govern the general practice of the world, nor pretended to afford men any supernatural assistance, which yet was very necessary to so great a work: and if, after all, in the discovery of such matters as are the great motives of religion, men are apt to be more easily worked upon, and more strongly affected, by good testimony, than by the strictest abstract arguments; so that, upon the whole, 'tis plain the philosophers were never by any means well qualified to reform mankind with any considerable success; then there was evidently wanting some particular revelation, which might supply all these defects. There was plainly a necessity of some particular revelation, to discover in what manner, and with what kind of external service, God might acceptably be worshipped. There was a necessity of some particular revelation, to discover what expiation God would accept for sin, by which the authority, honour, and dignity of His laws might be effectually vindicated. There was a necessity of some particular revelation, to give men full assurance of the truth of those great motives of religion, the rewards and punishments of a future state, which, notwithstanding the strongest arguments of reason, men could not yet forbear doubting of. In fine, there was a necessity of some particular divine revelation, to make the whole doctrine of religion clear and obvious to all capacities, to add weight and authority to the plainest precepts, and to furnish men with extraordinary assistances to enable them to overcome the corruptions of their nature. And without the assistance of such a revelation, 'tis manifest it was not possible that the world could ever be effectually reformed' (Prop. vii. § 1).

Thus, in the opinion of Clarke, as well as of Tillotson and Locke, natural religion is good and true so far as it goes, but it does not go far enough, and hence needs to be supplemented by revelation which must not in any way contradict it, but must be consistent with it in all its parts.[1]

Christianity according to Clarke is the only alleged revelation in which there is any pretence of reason, and therefore its claims alone need examination. In proof of the fact that it is of divine origin, he asserts that the practical duties inculcated by Christ are agreeable to our natural notions of God, and conduce to human happiness and well-being; that the motives taught by Christ, particularly future rewards and punishments, are suitable to divine wisdom and fit the expectations of men; that the manner and circumstances in which the doctrine was promulgated were consonant with sound reason; that all

[1] In this connection it is worth while mentioning a striking book by William Wollaston, *The Religion of Nature Delineated*, published in 1722. The book contains no attack upon revelation. Indeed toward the close the author expressly disclaims any such intent, and declares 'That, therefore, which has been so much insisted on by me, and is as it were the burden of my song, is so far from undermining true revealed religion, that it rather paves the way for its reception' (fifth edition of 1735, p. 211). At the same time, whether this caveat was sincerely meant or not, the effect of the book was certainly to make revelation seem less necessary, for it was devoted to showing the completeness and adequacy of natural religion under which every man has ability and light, fully commensurate to his responsibility, and hence all he really needs. Wollaston's contribution to the subject of ethics, novel and interesting as it was, cannot be considered here.

the doctrines of Christianity are rational, that is, though not necessarily discoverable by the unaided intellect, when once revealed they are seen to be in harmony with its principles; that all of them have a tendency to reform men's lives; and finally, that Christianity is attested by the miracles of Christ,[1] by His fulfilment of prophecy, and by the witness of His apostles (Propositions 9 to 14). All this evidence is so conclusive according to Clarke, that no one can fail to recognise Christianity as a divine revelation unless enslaved by his lusts. The cause of unbelief is not want of better evidence, but wickedness and vice (Proposition 15).

All these men, as we have seen, made the twofold demand upon religion that it should be rational and that it should promote virtue. No religion, however well attested by supernatural evidence, can possibly claim acceptance from right-minded men, unless its teachings accord with sound reason, and tend to establish righteousness. Indeed, sound reason recognises virtue as the principal aim of religion, and hence no faith can claim to be rational unless it make for righteous living. The effect of this upon Christianity was to reduce the traditional system to relatively small compass, or at least to distinguish certain elements of it as alone essential. What this led to in Tillotson and Locke, we have already seen. They both accepted, apparently without much question, the

---

[1] Clarke's definition of a miracle is worth quoting: 'And now from these few, clear and undeniable Propositions, it evidently follows: First, that the true definition of a miracle, in the theological sense of the word, is this, that it is a work effected in a manner unusual, or different from the common and regular method of Providence, by the interposition either of God himself or of some intelligent agent superior to man; for the proof or evidence of some particular doctrine, or in attestation to the authority of some particular person. And if a miracle so worked be not opposed by some plainly superior power, nor be brought to attest a doctrine either contradictory in itself or vicious in its consequences (a doctrine of which kind no miracles in the world can be sufficient to prove), then the doctrine so attested must necessarily be looked upon as divine, and the worker of the miracle entertained as having infallibly a commission from God' (*Boyle Lecture*, p. 384 *sq.*).

greater part of traditional Protestantism, but they were clear that its essential features were few, and that the failure to recognise this was responsible for much of the scepticism and irreligion of the day. In 1690 there was published by Arthur Bury, Rector of Exeter College, Oxford, a notable tract entitled *The Naked Gospel*, which is very significant in this connection. Nothing in Christianity, Bury claims, is to be regarded as necessary unless it is explicitly set forth in the Bible as a condition of salvation. Faith in Christ, which alone is so required, means not accepting this or that doctrine about His person and work—His pre-existence, His deity, His incarnation, His atonement—but trusting Him as one's guide in the practical conduct of life. To give faith a value in and of itself is to obscure the gospel and make it ineffective and misleading. This the Catholics have done in demanding the acceptance of so many things which have no bearing upon virtue, and therefore lead a man away from the real duties of life. In opposition to them, as to many Protestants, it is necessary to assert the simple and naked gospel of Jesus.

In this little work we have an illustration of an attitude very widespread in the author's day. In it is to be found the explanation of the deistic controversy which made so much stir in the later years of the seventeenth and during the first half of the eighteenth century. That controversy had to do rather with practical than with speculative questions, with moral than with intellectual difficulties. This needs to be realised at the start or the whole deistic movement will be misunderstood. Like most of their contemporaries, the Deists were interested in religion primarily as a means to virtue,[1] and they agreed with Tillotson, Locke, and Clarke that the principles of virtue

---

[1] Shaftesbury was in part an exception to this, giving religion an independent value of its own, like aesthetics. But he was in many ways prophetic of a new age, and his influence was felt chiefly in the classicist movement of the end of the eighteenth century and particularly by Herder.

are rooted in the nature of man. The fundamental question, therefore, between them and their opponents was whether the positive duties required by traditional Christianity, based as they were upon revelation only, and not grounded in the reason of things, were to be regarded as divinely commanded, and hence necessary to salvation and godly living. Most Christians asserted that they were, but the Deists denied it on the twofold ground that the general assumption that God might be expected to enjoin positive duties by revelation, and the claim of Christianity to be such a revelation, were alike unfounded. It is important to examine these two lines of argument in some detail.

The former was set forth by Lord Herbert in his *De Veritate*, and particularly in his *De Religione Gentilium*.[1] According to him, God's perfection demands a way of salvation open and common to all. This cannot originate in a particular revelation which in the very nature of the case is not shared by everybody. It must be implanted in the natural reason of man, and be equally accessible in all ages and places. Herbert finds a way of salvation actually known by the wise and sagacious among all peoples. Its tenets are five: that there is one supreme God, that He ought to be worshipped, that virtue is the principal part of worship, that we ought to repent of our sins, and that there are rewards and punishments, both now and hereafter. Wherever men have used their reason they have discovered these great truths, which constitute the sum of natural religion. To it the various positive faiths have added all sorts of things on the basis of alleged revelations. The rites and ceremonies, and the other additions found in these religions, are commonly due to the machinations of priests, and they serve in every case only to weaken and obscure the common and fundamental truths.

In a volume entitled *The Oracles of Reason*, published in

[1] Published posthumously in 1663; English translation, 1705.

1693 by Charles Blount and others, the tenets of natural religion are summarised as follows: that there is one infinite, eternal God, Creator of all things, that He governs the world by His providence, that it is our duty to worship and obey Him, that worship consists in prayer and praise, that our obedience comprises the rules of right reason whose practice is moral virtue, that we are to expect rewards and punishments hereafter, and that when we err from the path of our duty, we ought to repent and trust in God's mercy for pardon (p. 197).

In this work, Blount asserts that religion consists wholly in morality, which means the imitation of God's perfections, and not obedience to positive precepts of any kind. God is not to be worshipped by an image, by sacrifice, or by a mediator, but 'by an inviolable adherence in all our lives to all the things which are just by nature, by an imitation of God in all His imitable perfections, especially His goodness, and believing magnificently of it' (p. 88).

The most complete and elaborate presentation of this line of argument is found in the famous work entitled *Christianity as Old as the Creation*, published in 1730 by Matthew Tindal, Fellow of All Souls College, Oxford. The evil of demanding, in the name of religion, beliefs and practices in themselves morally indifferent, is the chief burden of this book. In it, Tindal maintains, on *a priori* grounds, drawn from the justice, goodness, and infinite perfection of God, that natural religion has always existed as a perfect thing, and that therefore revelation can add nothing to it (chap. vi.). All additions must be, not only unnecessary, but false. God's great end in the creation and government of the world is not His own glory or advantage—for He is in want of nothing—but the good of His creatures; and hence He demands nothing of them which does not contribute to their perfection and happiness. The end of religion is morality—to render man as perfect as possible in all moral duties (p. 39). True religion consists 'in a constant disposition of mind to do all the good we can, and thereby render ourselves acceptable to God in answering the end of our creation' (p. 18). The only difference between morality and religion is that the former is 'acting according to the reason of things considered in themselves,' while the latter is 'acting according to the same reason of things considered as the will of God' (p. 272). That things merely positive should be made ingredients of religion is inconsistent with the good of mankind as well as with the honour of God, for the more the mind of man 'is taken up with the observation of things which are not of a moral nature, the less it will be able to attend to those that are' (p. 125). To imagine that indifferent matters are commanded equally with matters of morality is to open the door to superstition, cruelty, and all sorts of evil.[1]

In this connection Tindal quotes from Tillotson a passage to the same effect (p. 153), but his conclusion is more thoroughgoing than the archbishop's, for he claims that everything is superstitious which is not of a moral nature, and therefore rejects all positive enactments whatsoever, while Tillotson, as was seen, recognised the obligation of certain Christian duties of a morally indifferent character. Tindal also maintains, in disagreement with Clarke, and with Tillotson and Locke as well, that miracles can be no proof of the divine origin of a doctrine; the only proof is the nature of the doctrine itself. 'Every doctrine that carries any degree, much more the highest

[1] 'As long as men believe the good of society is the supreme law, they will think it their duty to be governed by that law; and believing God requires nothing of them but what is for the good of mankind, will place the whole of their religion in benevolent actions, and to the utmost of their abilities copy after the divine original; but if they are made to believe there are things which have no relation to this good, necessary to salvation, they must suppose it their duty to use such means as will most effectually serve this purpose, and that God, in requiring the end, requires all those means as will best secure and propagate it. And 'tis to this principle we owe the most cruel persecutions, inquisitions, crusades, and massacres' (p. 134).

degree, of goodness and perfection in it, has the character of divinity impressed upon it'; and 'duties neither need nor can receive any stronger proof from miracles than what they have already from the evidence of right reason'[1] (p. 342 ff.).

The supreme duty of man is to live in such a way as to promote the public good. Benevolence is the highest attribute, both in God and man, and to live in accordance with its dictates is to fulfil the will of God. 'To imagine He can command anything inconsistent with this universal benevolence is highly to dishonour Him; 'tis to destroy His impartial goodness, and make His power and wisdom degenerate into cruelty and craft' (p. 63). 'And, indeed, power and knowledge in themselves can't engage our love; if they could we should love the devil in proportion to His power and knowledge. 'Tis goodness alone which can beget confidence, love, and veneration; and there's none of those questions, whether relating to God or man, but what may be easily determined by considering which side of the question carries with it the greatest goodness; since the same light of nature which shows us there is such a good being, shows us also what such goodness expects' (p. 66). This needs no revelation to prove it true. Reason itself leads necessarily to the recognition of universal love and kindness as the highest duty of man, in whose practice consists his perfection (cf. pp. 66, 372).

Tindal's book constituted a very telling argument against the common Christian assumption of the day, that God demands something more from man than the practice of virtue, and that true religion involves and salvation depends upon the performance of duties in themselves morally indifferent.

But the Deists did not content themselves with the

[1] The same position is taken by Dr. Thomas Morgan in his *Moral Philosopher* (1737), p. 85 ff.

general line of argument described. They also attacked directly the claim of Christianity to be a divine revelation, some turning their attention to the Christian evidences, others to the content of the Christian system.

It has been seen that the principal evidences of Christianity, relied upon by the apologists of the day to prove its divine origin, were prophecy and miracle. In 1722 there was published a curious book by William Whiston, who had been for a few years Newton's successor as Professor of Mathematics at Cambridge, but had lost his professorship because of heretical views. The book was entitled *An Essay toward Restoring the True Text of the Old Testament, and for Vindicating the Citations made Thence in the New Testament*. In this work Whiston maintained that the fulfilment of Old Testament prophecy constituted the principal proof of Jesus' Messiahship, and of the divine origin of Christianity, but he recognised in certain cases a lack of correspondence between prophecy and alleged fulfilment. He attempted to remedy the difficulty by restoring the true text of the Old Testament, which he claimed had been intentionally corrupted by the Jews. Whiston's work was made the occasion of an acute and telling criticism upon the evidence from prophecy by Anthony Collins. In 1724 he published *A Discourse on the Grounds and Reasons of the Christian Religion*, in which he maintained that the fulfilment of prophecy is not only the most important, but the only proof of the divine origin of Christianity. If the evidence from prophecy be invalidated, Christianity falls to the ground. Its one essential fact is the Messiahship of Jesus, and this only prophecy can prove. Miracles have no relation to the matter, except in so far as they, too, may have been foretold (cf. p. 37). Collins then declared that the lack of correspondence between prophecy and fulfilment which Whiston had noticed in some cases is true of every case, when the prophecies are literally interpreted, and as such a corruption of the original text, as Whiston assumed, does not adequately account for the differences, he proposed to meet the difficulty by interpreting the prophecies allegorically (p. 39 ff.). The book amounted to a very severe attack upon the evidence from prophecy, for the allegorical method could not be taken seriously, and was not meant to be ; and in a second book, published in 1727, entitled *The Scheme of Literal Prophecy Considered*, it was practically abandoned, and the assault made direct and explicit. The seriousness of the attack was widely recognised, and many replies were published. More than thirty of them are mentioned by Collins himself in the second work just referred to. Some of the replies admitted his contention that prophecy is the principal proof of Christianity, and endeavoured to show its literal fulfilment by Jesus, but others practically gave up the proof from prophecy and staked everything on miracles. The result of the controversy was decidedly to weaken the force of the prophetic argument and to lead to a more exclusive emphasis upon the evidence of miracle.

But this evidence was not allowed to go unchallenged. In 1727 a former Cambridge Fellow, Thomas Woolston, who had anticipated Collins in using the allegorical method of interpreting the Scriptures,[1] and had seconded him in his attack upon the evidence from prophecy,[2] came out with the first of a series of tracts in which a similar method was applied to the miracles of Christ. Woolston's ostensible purpose was to recall Christians to a dependence upon prophecy, the only adequate argument for Christianity. He maintained that the miracles recorded in the gospels were quite without value as signs or testimonies to Christ's

[1] In a work entitled *The old Apology for the Truth of the Christian Religion against the Jews and Gentiles Revived* (1705), written while he was still a Fellow of Sidney-Sussex College, Cambridge.
[2] In a racy and satirical book entitled *The Moderator between an Infidel and an Apostate* (1725), in which Collins was denounced and ostensibly opposed as an enemy of the faith, but was really supported in his attack upon the evidence from prophecy.

divine mission.[1] Taken literally, indeed, they were often not miraculous at all, and were in most cases foolish, trivial, contradictory, absurd, unworthy of a divinely commissioned teacher, and characteristic rather of a sorcerer and wizard (pp. 15, 66 ff.). They have value only when they are interpreted allegorically, as the Fathers interpreted them, and are understood as representations of Christ's spiritual influence and operations in the life of mankind, as they were meant to be.[2] Thus, for instance, the reported casting of devils out of the Gadarenes, and sending them into a herd of swine, is interpreted to mean the release of mankind from their sins by Jesus and the entrance of evil spirits into heretics (First Discourse); while the alleged resurrection of Christ is only a parable setting forth the liberation of Christianity from the bondage of the Jewish letter, and its emergence into the freedom of the Spirit (Sixth Discourse).

Moreover, Woolston maintained that the power to work physical miracles, even if it were granted that Jesus possessed it, would be no proof that He was eminent for piety, virtue, or wisdom, and hence a messenger from God (First Discourse, p. 12). Even the apologists of the day recognise that miracles have been performed by all sorts of persons, often under demoniacal instead of divine influence. There is, therefore, no evidential value whatever in such miracles, even if their reality be assumed.

Woolston's tracts, of which half a dozen appeared between 1727 and 1729, were coarse and scurrilous, containing in some cases shocking language concerning the

[1] 'I will show that the miracles of healing all manner of bodily diseases which Jesus was justly famed for are none of the proper miracles of the Messiah, neither are they so much as a good proof of His divine authority to found a religion' (p. 4; sixth edition of 1729).
[2] 'That the literal history of many of the miracles of Jesus as recorded by the Evangelists, does imply absurdities, improbabilities, and incredibilities; consequently they either in whole or in part were never wrought as they are commonly believed nowadays, but are only related as prophetical and parabolical narratives of what would be mysteriously and more wonderfully done by Him' (p. 4).

works and teaching, and even the character of the Jesus of the gospels, but at the same time they were often very ingenious, acute, and witty, and it is not surprising that they had a tremendous circulation. In spite of their profane character, they exposed in a very effective manner the artificial nature of the current apologetic and the futility of using the miracles of Christ for evidential purposes.

Woolston's attack upon the miracles called out many replies, notable among which was Bishop Sherlocke's *Trial of the Witnesses* (1729) in defence of the resurrection of Christ. He and others were abundantly successful in showing the groundlessness of Woolston's accusation of deliberate conspiracy to deceive on the part of Jesus and His disciples, but whatever measure of success may have attended their defence of the fact of the resurrection, it is clear enough from all the replies to Woolston that the miracles could no longer be appealed to with the same confidence in their convincing power.

A still severer blow at the apologetic value of miracles was struck by David Hume in his celebrated *Essay on Miracles*, published in 1748. In order to understand the significance of this essay it is necessary to remember that the term miracle was employed by the apologists of the day, not to denote any wonderful or unique or otherwise unheard-of event, but a sign wrought for the purpose of proving the authority of a divine messenger. What Hume was chiefly interested to show was not the impossibility of a miracle understood in this or any other sense, nor, as is commonly supposed, the impossibility of proving a miracle, understood as a unique and otherwise unknown event, but the impossibility of proving such an event in a way to give it evidential value. In other words, he was interested to show the impossibility of proving a miracle in the strict apologetic sense of that word as a supernatural sign wrought to establish the authority of a divine messenger. Most of the replies to Hume, made in his own day and since, have entirely misapprehended the real point of his essay. He invited misinterpretation by employing the word miracle in different senses, and also by stating the real point of his essay only toward the close, after he had devoted the greater part of it to discrediting human testimony to unusual events. The impression was thus left that he maintained that it is inherently impossible to prove such events. But this is not the case, as is abundantly shown by the closing sentence of the following passage, which occurs toward the end of the essay: 'Upon the whole then it appears that no testimony for any kind of miracle has ever amounted to a probability, much less to a proof; and that, even supposing it amounted to a proof, it would be opposed by another proof derived from the very nature of the fact which it would endeavour to establish. It is experience only which gives authority to human testimony; and it is the same experience which assures us of the laws of nature. When, therefore, these two kinds of experience are contrary we have nothing to do but subtract the one from the other, and embrace an opinion either on one side or the other with that assurance which arises from the remainder. But, according to the principle here explained, this subtraction with regard to all popular religions amounts to an entire annihilation, and therefore we may establish it as a maxim that no human testimony can have such force as to prove a miracle, and make it a just foundation for any such system of religion. I beg the limitations here made may be remarked when I say that a miracle can never be proved so as to be the foundation of a system of religion. For I own that otherwise there may possibly be miracles or violations of the usual course of nature of such a kind as to admit of proof from human testimony; though, perhaps, it will be impossible to find any such in all the records of history.'

Critics of Hume are quite right in saying that it is not necessarily impossible to prove a miracle, that is, they are right if a miracle be understood simply as an otherwise unheard-of event inexplicable in the light of our present knowledge. But Hume was really concerned primarily to destroy the apologetic value of miracles, and for that purpose his argument was valid, and has never been successfully refuted. That it cannot be historically proved that any particular event was wrought by a supernatural power with the purpose of testifying to a person's divine commission is a commonplace among historians to-day. For such proof assumes a complete knowledge of all possible natural forces which may have operated to produce the event, a knowledge to which no one now thinks of pretending. While Hume's essay then tended to throw discredit upon all reports of wonderful and unusual events, it did not show them to be unprovable, but it did destroy the apologetic value which had been ascribed to them. Against the apologetic position of the day Hume's argument was really final. Miracles had been regarded, not simply as a proof, but the supreme proof of Christianity. This they could no longer be where his essay was understood.

Hume's attack, though its real significance was not recognised, and though the general impression in Christian circles was that his argument had been successfully refuted by the many who replied to it,[1] really proved very effective, and contributed to a marked shifting of emphasis in Christian apologetics. On the one hand, apologists now found it important to show that miracles were themselves supported by an antecedent probability in their favour drawn from the necessity and nature of divine revelation. Of this Paley's *Evidences of Christianity*,

[1] Among the many replies that appeared in Hume's own day the most important were Bishop Douglas's *Criterion* (1752); Dr. Adams's *Essay on Mr. Hume's Essay on Miracles* (1752); and Dr. Campbell's *Dissertation on Miracles* (1762).

which appeared almost at the close of the eighteenth century (1794), offered a classical illustration. At the beginning of the work, he says, 'In what way can a revelation be made but by miracles? In none which we are able to conceive. Consequently in whatever degree it is probable, or not very improbable, that a revelation should be communicated to mankind at all; in the same degree is it probable or not very improbable that miracles should be wrought. Therefore when miracles are related to have been wrought in the promulgating of a revelation manifestly wanted, and if true of inestimable value, the improbability which arises from the miraculous nature of the things related is not greater than the original improbability that such a revelation should be imparted by God.' Thus miracles, while still used to support Christianity, required themselves to be supported by other evidence drawn from the general need of a revelation, and from the fitness of Christianity to meet that need. And so their place in Christian apologetic, even where they were still retained, was altered under the influence of Hume's attack.

On the other hand, apologists felt themselves driven to seek other and stronger evidence for the divine origin of Christianity, and to cease staking everything upon miracle. In 1776 appeared a very significant book by Soame Jenyns, entitled *A View of the Internal Evidences of the Christian Religion*, in which prophecy and miracle were minimised, and Christianity was proved from its character alone. Jenyns says at the beginning of his work, 'The miracles recorded in the New Testament to have been performed by Christ and His apostles were certainly convincing proofs of their divine commission to those who saw them; and as they were seen by such numbers, and are as well attested as other historical facts; and above all, as they were wrought on so great and so wonderful an occasion they must still be admitted as evidence of no inconsiderable force; but I think they must now depend for much of their credibility on the truth of that religion whose credibility they were first intended to support. To prove, therefore, the truth of the Christian religion, we should begin by showing the internal marks of divinity which are stamped upon it: because on this the credibility of the prophecies and miracles in a great measure depends: for if we have once reason to be convinced that this religion is derived from a supernatural origin, prophecies and miracles will become so far from being incredible, that it will be highly probable that a supernatural revelation should be foretold and enforced by supernatural means.' Thus Christianity supported the miracles and the prophecies instead of being supported by them, and the method of Christian apologetic had undergone a radical change, the effects of which were felt throughout the nineteenth century. In view of this fact it is clear that the common statement, that in the controversies of the eighteenth century the Christian apologists won a complete victory, is far from true, at least so far as the question of the evidences is concerned. They were actually forced to take their stand upon a new platform altogether.

Meanwhile the attack upon Christianity took the form of a criticism, not only of its evidence, but also of its contents, particularly the Bible and traditional theology. That the Christian revelation was given so late in the history of the world, and was brought to the knowledge of so small a portion of the human race; that it narrowed the conditions of salvation set up by natural religion, requiring things in themselves morally indifferent, and thus closing the door to many virtuous and noble men of all ages and nations; that the Old Testament is full of inconsistencies, inaccuracies, bad ethics, and bad theology; that even the New Testament is beset in less degree with the same difficulties; that the history of Christianity and the traditional theology of the Church contain much that is contradicted by sound reason and morality—all this was emphasised over and over again. One of the most restrained and yet effective presentations of this kind of argument is found in the thirteenth and longest chapter of Tindal's *Christianity as Old as the Creation*. In it he criticises both Old and New Testament in considerable detail, and even passes some strictures on the preaching of Jesus Himself, on the ground that, as reported in the gospels, it is often extravagant, impracticable, and opposed to common sense, and can therefore, in many cases, not be taken literally (p. 310 ff.). Tindal maintains, in agreement with all the Deists, that the only safe guide in morality and religion is the natural reason. This must be applied also to the interpretation of the Bible, and only those things in it are to be taken for divine scripture, which tend to the honour of God and the good of man. 'As in the Old Testament there are several things, either commanded or approved, which would be criminal in us to observe, because we can't reconcile our doing this with the reason of things, so in the New Testament its precepts are for the most part delivered, either so hyperbolically that they would lead men astray were they governed by the usual meaning of the words; or else expressed in so loose, general, and undetermined a manner that men are as much left to be governed by the reason of things as if there were no such precepts: And the Scripture not distinguishing between those precepts which are occasional and those which are not, we have no way to distinguish them but from the nature of things, which will point out to us those rules which eternally oblige, whether delivered in Scripture or not' (p. 322).

It has generally been taken for granted, upon the basis of such attacks as these, and in view of the reputation which they enjoyed among their contemporaries, that the Deists opposed Christianity altogether, and regarded it as wholly evil and vicious. This, however, is a great mistake. Many of them may have thought of it thus, but some of the most notable of them took quite a different attitude. The title of Tindal's principal work shows what that attitude was—*Christianity as Old as the Creation*—that is genuine Christianity is identical with the religion of nature, and so is a true, not a false religion. Almost at the beginning of his work Tindal states his purpose in the following words: ' And, therefore, I shall attempt to show you, That Men, if they sincerely endeavour to discover the will of God, will perceive, that there's a *law of nature* or *reason*; which is so called, as being a Law, which is common, or natural, to all rational Creatures; and that this Law, like its Author, is absolutely perfect, eternal, and unchangeable; and that the design of the Gospel was not to add to, or take from this Law; but to free Men from that load of Superstition, which had been mixed with it: so that True Christianity is not a Religion of yesterday, but what God, at the beginning, dictated, and still continues to dictate to Christians, as well as others. If I am so happy as to succeed in this attempt, I hope, not only fully to satisfy your doubts, but greatly to advance the honour of *external* Revelation; by showing the perfect agreement between *that* and *internal* Revelation; and by so doing, destroy one of the most successful attempts that has been made on Religion, by setting the Laws of God at variance. But first, I must premise, That in supposing an external Revelation, I take it for granted, that there's sufficient evidence of a Person being sent from God to publish it; nay, I further own, that this divine Person by living up to what he taught, has set us a noble Example; and that as he was highly exalted for so doing, so we, if we use our best endeavours, may expect a suitable reward. This, and everything of the same nature, I freely own, which is not inconsistent with the Law of God being the same, whether internally, or externally revealed ' (p. 7 ff.).

And again, on p. 347, he says : ' It can't be imputed to any defect in the Light of Nature, that the Pagan World ran into idolatry, but to their being entirely governed by Priests, who pretended communication with their Gods, and to have thence their Revelations, which they imposed on the credulous as divine Oracles : Whereas the business of the Christian dispensation was to destroy all those traditional Revelations, and restore, free from all Idolatry, the true primitive, and natural Religion, implanted in Mankind from the Creation.'

Traditional Christianity is far removed from the true religion of nature, but genuine Christianity, that of Christ Himself, is identical with it. The important thing, therefore, is to distinguish true from false Christianity, and to accept the former and reject the latter. ' If this be true, have I not shown some resolution,' Tindal asks, ' in daring to attack the darling weaknesses, and follies of false Christians ; in proving that true Christianity is so far from being indefensible, that it carries its own evidences with it ; or in other words, all its Doctrines plainly speak themselves to be the will of an infinitely wise, and good God ; as being *most friendly to society, most helpful to government, and most beneficial to every individual* ; or, in one word, free from all Priestcraft ' (p. 388). To those who shared his position in this matter, Tindal gave the name of Christian Deists (p. 337), showing clearly enough that he was actuated, not by hostility to Christianity as such, but to the notion that it involved doctrines and duties not founded in the reason and nature of things.

Tindal's contrast between true and false Christianity was drawn still more emphatically by Thomas Chubb, in a work entitled *The True Gospel of Jesus Christ Asserted* [1] (1738). In this work it is maintained that Jesus' aim was

---

[1] Chubb was a tradesman without university education, but with considerable acuteness and skill as a controversialist. He wrote extensively upon religious subjects.

to save men's souls, that is, 'to prepare men for and to insure them the favour of God and their happiness in another world, and to prevent them from bringing great and lasting misery upon themselves' (p. 1). To this end He proposed for their acceptance certain truths which were fitted to affect their lives, and these truths constitute the gospel. 'The important truths which Christ has thus recommended to public consideration may be summed up in the following particulars. First, He requires and recommends the conforming our minds and lives to that eternal and unalterable rule of action, which is found in the reason of things (which rule is summarily contained in the written word of God), and this He lays down as the only ground of divine acceptance, and as that which will entitle men to the favour of God and the happiness of another world; and consequently this will prevent them from being greatly and lastingly miserable. Secondly, if men have lived in a violation of this righteous law, by which they have rendered themselves highly displeasing to God, and worthy of His resentment; then Christ requires and recommends repentance and reformation of their evil ways as the only and the sure ground of the divine mercy and forgiveness. And thirdly, in order to make those truths have the greater impression on the minds and lives of men, He declares and assures them that God has appointed a day in which He will judge the world in righteousness, and that He will then either acquit or condemn, reward or punish them, according as they have or have not conformed their minds and lives to that rule of righteousness before mentioned, and according as they have or have not repented and amended their evil ways. This is the true gospel of Jesus Christ, and this is the way and method which Christ has taken to save men's souls' (p. 18 ff.). 'I would also desire my reader to observe that our Lord Christ did not propose or point out to men any new way to God's favour and eternal life, but on the contrary, He recommended that good old way which always was, and always will be, the true way to life eternal; viz. the keeping the commandments, or the loving God and our neighbour, which is the same thing, and is the sum and substance of the moral law. This plain pathway to heaven lay neglected, and for the most part unfrequented; men, both Jews and Gentiles, having forsaken the fountain of living water that is the true way to life eternal; and hewn for themselves cisterns, broken cisterns, that can hold no water; that is, they had found out new and false ways of recommending themselves to God's favour. And this rendered our Saviour's undertaking and ministry so much the more needful' (p. 30). The tract is devoted largely to the establishment of this thesis, and to the exhibition of the contrast between traditional Christianity and the gospel of Jesus, with the practical aim of enforcing the obligation of virtuous living.[1]

The same general position appears clearly set forth in Dr. Thomas Morgan's *Moral Philosopher* (1737). Morgan was a physician, who had been at one time a dissenting clergyman. He called himself a Christian Deist, and understood Christianity to be 'a revival of the religion of nature; in which the several duties and obligations of moral truth and righteousness are more clearly stated and explained, enforced by stronger motives, and encouraged with the promises of more effectual aids and assistances by Jesus Christ, the great Christian prophet, than ever has been done before by any other prophet, moralist, or law-giver in religion' (p. 392).

To claim that such men as Tindal, Chubb, and Morgan were opposed to Christianity, and were trying to destroy it, is to misrepresent them altogether. They did not deny

---

[1] A similar assertion of the identity of true Christianity with the religion of nature, and a similar emphasis of the contrast between the teaching of Jesus and the tenets of traditional Christianity are found frequently in Lord Bolingbroke's *Works*, for instance, vol. v. pp. 204 ff., 589 ff. (Mallet's edition of 1793).

that Jesus was a divine messenger, or that Christianity is a true religion. They denied only that the additions to the religion of nature, the many positive precepts which mark traditional Christianity, were of divine origin. They were doing exactly what Locke and Tillotson and Bury and many others had long been doing, attempting to distinguish the essential and the non-essential in Christianity, with the design of promoting true morality and religion, and doing away with the superstitions of the traditional Christian system which so commonly interfered with both.

The tremendous interest of most of the Deists in the public good, and their hostility to selfishness and self-seeking, are very noticeable. In our own day similar attempts to distinguish between the true and the false in Christianity with the like purpose of promoting the good of humanity, or as it is commonly said, of establishing the kingdom of God in the world, are made by men who are within the Christian Church, and regard themselves as genuine Christians. This should throw light upon the situation in the eighteenth century, and lead us to speak at least of some of the Deists as defenders rather than opponents of Christianity. As a matter of fact, the difference between them and the avowed apologists was far less than has commonly been supposed. There was a vital kinship between them, more significant than any differences. They were upon opposite sides in the religious controversy, not so much because of any great disagreement in religious beliefs and in ethical ideals, as because of a difference of attitude toward the ecclesiastical establishment and the ecclesiastical authorities. A common note running through all the deistic writings was hostility to, or impatience with, both. The bigotry and intolerance of organised Christianity were denounced as severely as its superstitions and misplaced emphases. Many of the apologists recognised clearly, and admitted frankly, the evils arising from priestcraft and sacerdotalism, and tried earnestly to broaden the religious platform and to promote the spirit of toleration, but organised Christianity meant too much to them to be rejected on account of its existing evils, and they put up with them and stood by the institution as the Deists were unwilling to do.

The writings of Tindal, Chubb, and Morgan, particularly Tindal's *Christianity as Old as the Creation*, called forth many replies, in which positions similar to those of Tillotson, Locke, and Clarke were reasserted more or less consistently. Of all these the best and clearest was by John Conybeare, Rector of Exeter College, Oxford, entitled *A Defense of Revealed Religion against the Exceptions of a Late Writer in his Book Intituled Christianity as Old as the Creation, etc.* (1732). The book contains a strong and effective argument against Tindal's *a priori* conception of religion as a perfect thing always and everywhere the same, but in general it is nothing more than a restatement of the old position against which Tindal protested. Natural religion is true and good so far as it goes, but it does not go far enough. Men need more light than can be gained from it, and so revelation has come to supplement it, and adds to the requirements of the natural law positive doctrines and precepts, morally indifferent in themselves, but binding upon all to whom a knowledge of the revelation is brought. By their acceptance and by their practice, virtue, the ultimate end of all true religion, is forwarded, not hindered. The authority of the Christian revelation, in which these requirements are taught, is supported by prophecy, by miracles, and by the testimony of the primitive records. It is evident that for Conybeare, —and there were many others like him—the rationalistic platform still stood intact.

Upon some men, on the other hand, the Deists' exaltation of natural religion, and their assertion of its universality and perfection, had the effect of producing a reaction against the whole notion of natural religion, and of leading to a denial of its claims. The result was that deism was followed by scepticism, and the doubt thrown by the Deists upon Christianity was now thrown by others upon natural religion itself, that is, upon all religion. This sceptical attitude was promoted, or at any rate foreshadowed, among others particularly by four writers, two of them Christian apologists, and two of them sceptics. They wrote from very different points of view, the first two with the aim of defending Christianity, but the tendency of all their works was to break down rational religion in general, and so to promote scepticism.

The first of them was William Law, the famous non-juror and mystic, who published in 1731 a reply to Tindal with the title *The Case of Reason or Natural Religion fairly and fully stated in Answer to a Book entitled Christianity as Old as the Creation*. In this book Law rejected completely the common assumption of both Deists and apologists that a revelation claiming to be divine must approve itself to the reason of man. God's character and will are unfathomable, and we are quite unable to judge what is right or wrong, true or untrue, antecedently to divine revelation. Nothing is good or evil in itself, only the will of God makes it so, and consequently only by revelation can we know what is right and what is wrong. 'A revelation is to be received as coming from God, not because of its internal excellence, or because we judge it to be worthy of God; but because God has declared it to be His in as plain and undeniable a manner as He has declared creation and providence to be His. For though no revelation can come from God but what is truly worthy of Him and full of every internal excellence; yet what is truly worthy of God to be revealed cannot possibly be known by us, but by revelation from Himself. And as we can only know what is worthy of God in creation by knowing what He has created; so we can in no other way possibly know what is worthy of God to be revealed but by a revelation' (p. 101).

But how can we know whether an alleged revelation be divine or not? Only by the external proofs of prophecy and miracle. 'The credibility, therefore, of any external divine revelation with regard to human reason, rests wholly upon such external evidence, as is a sufficient proof of the divine operation or interposition. . . . I appeal, therefore, to the miracles and prophecies on which Christianity is founded, as a sufficient proof that it is a divine revelation' (p. 107). 'It seems, therefore, to be a needless and too great a concession which some learned divines make in this matter, when they grant that we must first examine the doctrines revealed by miracles, and see whether they contain anything in them absurd or unworthy of God, before we can receive the miracles as divine. For where there can be nothing doubted, nor any more required, to make the miracles sufficiently plain and evident, there can be no doubt about the truth and goodness of the doctrine which they attest. Miracles in such a state as this are the last resort; they determine for themselves and cannot be tried by anything further' (p. 109). 'A course of plain undeniable miracles attesting the truth of a revelation is the highest and utmost evidence of its coming from God, and not to be tried by our judgments about the reasonableness or necessity of its doctrines' (p. 110).

This is, of course, the completest possible repudiation of the position of Tillotson, Locke, and all the other rational theologians of the day, apologists as well as Deists. In the presence of omnipotence manifested by the performance of miracles, man must be dumb and submit without question. To pass judgment upon the teaching so accredited, to examine it in order to see whether it is rational and good, is to set oneself above God and commit the worst of all sins. 'If sin had its beginning from pride, and hell be the effect of it; if devils are what they are through spiritual pride and self-conceit; then we have great reason to believe that the claiming this authority to our reason in opposition to the revealed wisdom of God is not a frailty of flesh and blood, but that same spiritual pride which turned angels into apostate spirits ' (p. 60).

It is interesting to notice that in his effort to defend revelation, Law anticipated Butler's famous argument that natural religion and the natural course of events in general are beset with as many difficulties, and are enshrouded in as impenetrable mysteries as Christianity itself, and therefore if these difficulties and mysteries do not prevent our believing in divine creation and providence, they should not hinder our faith in revealed religion (cf. pp. 66, 103 ff.). Such a line of argument was, of course, fraught with danger, suggesting, as it could hardly help doing, the abandonment both of Deism and of Christianity. Law's criticism of Tindal's exaggerated estimate of human reason, and of his *a priori* construction of natural religion, acute and forceful as it was, could only have the effect of undermining the common religious platform of the day, and driving men, either to find an altogether new basis of religious faith, or to content themselves with thoroughgoing scepticism.

Of similar import was Butler's famous *Analogy of Religion, Natural and Revealed, to the Constitution and Course of Nature*, which appeared in 1736. Butler's work, as indicated by the title, consisted of two parts, the first dealing with natural, and the second with revealed religion, and the two parts had very different readers in view. In the first the existence of God and the creation of the world by Him are assumed without argument, and it is then maintained that there are grounds for supposing that His government of the world is moral, and that there will be a future life in which virtue and vice will be respectively rewarded and punished. Butler does not claim that there is adequate proof for this conclusion, but only that the objections commonly brought against it are invalid, and that the likelihood of its being true is sufficient to justify the prudent man in proceeding as if it were. No harm will result if he should be mistaken in the assumption, while on the other hand, if he act as if it were not true, he may suffer serious consequences in another life (Part I., conclusion). The general tone of the argument is not at all uplifting. The appeal to prudential considerations has a degrading sound and contrasts unpleasantly with the loftier and more disinterested motives urged, for instance, by Shaftesbury and Tindal. It must, however, be recognised that it was addressed only to a particular class of persons, and those not the deistic or sceptical writers of the day—with such the argument could have little force—but to the frivolous and immoral who took for granted, when they thought of it at all, that there is a God, but did not seriously consider the practical consequences of such a belief. The argument, in fact, is to be judged as a practical moral sermon addressed to the careless and indifferent rather than as an apology addressed to the serious thinkers of the day.[1]

The second part of the work bears a very different character. It is difficult to believe that the two were conceived originally as parts of one whole. The second has a direct bearing upon the deistic controversy, and was called forth by it, while the first faces a different situation altogether. One might be tempted to think that the second part was planned first, and that the use of a similar method to meet frivolity, immorality and irreligion was an afterthought. It is the second part, at any rate, which alone has historic significance in the development of religious thought in England. It had its place in the great

---

[1] Compare the remark in part II. chap. viii.: 'The design of this treatise is not to vindicate the character of God, but to show the obligations of men; it is not to justify His providence, but to show what belongs to us to do.'

controversy of the day, and apologetic as its intention was, it constituted a step in the evolution of deism into scepticism. The general position of the author is negative. The power of human reason to judge conclusively in religious matters is denied. Man does not know the whole course of nature, and so cannot tell what God must do in any given circumstances, or what qualities must mark a divine revelation. Seeming irrationality is no argument against a revelation, for even natural religion is not free from it. The only ground for rejecting it would be its immoral tendencies, and even here it might contain things which, taken by themselves and apart from the whole scheme of divine government, would offend our moral sense. 'Upon supposition that God exercises a moral government over the world, the analogy of His natural government suggests and makes it credible that His moral government must be a scheme quite beyond our comprehension, and this affords a general answer to all objections against the justice and goodness of it' (Part I. chap. vii.). 'And, therefore, though objections against the evidence of Christianity are most seriously to be considered, yet objections against Christianity itself are, in a great measure, frivolous; almost all objections against it, excepting those which are alleged against the particular proofs of its coming from God. I express myself with caution, lest I should be mistaken to vilify reason; which is, indeed, the only faculty we have wherewith to judge concerning anything, even revelation itself, or be misunderstood to assert, that a supposed revelation cannot be proved false from internal characters. For it may contain clear immoralities, or contradictions, and either of these would prove it false. Nor will I take upon me to affirm that nothing else can possibly render any supposed revelation incredible. Yet still the observation above is, I think, true beyond doubt, that objections against Christianity, as distinguished from objections against its evidence, are frivolous' (Part II.

chap. iii.). 'And now what is the just consequence from all these things? Not that reason is no judge of what is offered to us as being of divine revelation. For this would be to infer that we are unable to judge of anything, because we are unable to judge of all things. Reason can, and it ought to, judge, not only of the meaning, but also of the morality and the evidence of revelation. First, it is the province of reason to judge of the morality of the Scripture; *i.e.* not whether it contains things different from what we should have expected from a wise, just, and good Being; for objections from hence have been now obviated: but whether it contains things plainly contradictory to wisdom, justice, or goodness; to what the light of nature teaches us of God. And I know nothing of this sort objected against Scripture, excepting such objections as are formed upon suppositions, which would equally conclude that the constitution of nature is contradictory to wisdom, justice, or goodness, which most certainly it is not. Indeed there are some particular precepts in Scripture given to particular persons, requiring action which would be immoral and vicious were it not for such precepts. But it is easy to see that all these are of such a kind, as that the precept changes the whole nature of the case and of the action, and both constitutes and shows that not to be unjust or immoral which, prior to the precept, must have appeared and really have been so; which may well be, since none of these precepts are contrary to immutable morality. If it were commanded to cultivate the principles, and act from the spirit of treachery, ingratitude, cruelty, the command would not alter the nature of the case or of the action in any of these instances. But it is quite otherwise in precepts which require only the doing an external action; for instance, taking away the property or life of any. For men have no right to either life or property, but what arises solely from the grant of God: when this grant is revoked, they cease to have any right at all in either ; and when this revocation is made known, as surely it is possible it may be, it must cease to be unjust to deprive them of either. And though a course of external acts, which without command would be immoral, must make an immoral habit, yet a few detached commands have no such natural tendency. I thought proper to say thus much of the few Scripture precepts, which require, not vicious actions, but actions which would have been vicious, had it not been for such precepts ; because they are sometimes weakly urged as immoral, and great weight is laid upon objections drawn from them ' (*ibid.*).

Thus Butler did not go as far as Law in this matter, and reject altogether the competency of reason in religious matters, but he reduced it to narrow limits and denounced the common rationalistic dependence on it as unjustified.

The contention of Butler was a very effective rejoinder to the thesis of Tindal, that natural religion is a complete and perfect thing, and therefore nothing can be added to it by revelation. As against this *a priori* conclusion Butler's argument has a very scientific and modern sound, but it is a dangerous weapon cutting both ways at once. It may actually remove one's difficulties concerning Christianity, as Butler intended it should, or it may lead to the conviction that both Christianity and natural religion are equally irrational, and thus turn Deists into sceptics. Against this result Butler's positive argument for Christianity from prophecy and miracle, which he called the direct and fundamental proofs of the Christian religion, was not a sufficient safeguard. Here, too, his position was negative rather than positive. The ordinary presumption urged against miracles is not sufficient to render them incredible. They are recounted in the same way that the rest of the Old and New Testament history is, and the burden of proof is upon him who would reject them. Such a treatment of the matter was hardly enough to give them strong evidential value.

In connection with his discussion of the improbability of miracles, Butler betrayed a singular lack of logical insight, hardly in keeping with his usual sagacity. '*First* of all, there is a very strong presumption against common speculative truths, and against the most ordinary facts before the proof of them, which yet is overcome by almost any proof. There is a presumption of millions to one against the story of Cæsar, or of any other man. For suppose a number of common facts so and so circumstanced, of which one had no kind of proof, should happen to come into one's thoughts, every one would, without any possible doubt, conclude them to be false. And the like may be said of a single common fact; and from hence it appears, that the question of importance, as to the matter before us, is concerning the degree of the peculiar presumption supposed against miracles; not whether there be any peculiar presumption at all against them. For if there be the presumption of millions to one against the most common facts, what can a small presumption additional to this amount to, though it be peculiar? It cannot be estimated, and is as nothing' (Part II. chap. ii. § 3).

The confusion shown here between what Mill called improbability before the fact and improbability after the fact is so gross as to do little credit to the author of the *Analogy*. It is not unlike the confusion of thought which led him over and over again to take the answering of objections to a proposition for a positive argument in its favour. This, in spite of his frequent protestations, and the exceeding modesty of his claims, Butler was in reality continually doing.

The Analogy, as a whole, shows great penetration and keenness, and is filled with profound observations and striking aphorisms. The reader is conscious throughout of being in contact with a mind of uncommonly fine fibre. But as an apology, either for natural or revealed religion, it is extraordinarily weak, and the line followed in it has been pursued by no important apologist since. This is not because the work was so effectively done as not to need repeating, but because it was too dangerous in its results. The actual effect of the book upon Butler's contemporaries we do not know, for, singularly enough, though in the nineteenth century it was reckoned among the greatest of all apologetic writings, and was widely used for apologetic purposes, both in England and America, we hear almost nothing of it in Butler's own day. The ambiguous character of the argument was evidently realised. It was calculated to meet admirably a particular situation, but it met it in such a way as to imperil the larger issue, and so was ill-adapted for general and permanent use. That it later gained such a vogue was due to the fact that the English-speaking religious world had travelled far from the platform of the early eighteenth century, and had lost all appreciation of what the work really involved. With such effectiveness as it may have had in the immediate situation which called it forth vanished also its noxious quality for the average mind, and it remained an interesting and stimulating piece of dialectic, fitted to whet the logical faculty of students, and as such it maintained until very recently its place and its value in the curriculum of many a college.

It would be unjust to Butler to judge him by the *Analogy* alone. Of far greater historical importance were his sermons on human nature, in which he made a real contribution to the subject of ethics. His analysis of the moral nature of man and his discussion of moral motives are very suggestive, and of great significance. But all this belongs to another field, and must not be further pursued here.

Of similar effect to Butler's *Analogy*, so far at least as concerned the rationalistic platform of the day, was a striking and acute little book by Henry Dodwell, the younger, entitled *Christianity not founded on Argument*, *and the True Principle of Gospel Evidence Assigned,* which was published in 1742. In the form of a letter addressed to a student at Oxford, it struck a severe blow at the very heart of the rational theology of the day, both orthodox and deistic. Dodwell maintains that religious faith has no relation to reason. To try to support it on rational grounds is to promote scepticism. The foundation of religion is acquiescence and belief; the foundation of philosophy is doubt; and to try to found religious truth on argument is to invite scepticism and irreligion. 'Religion will not admit of the least alliance with reason'[1] (p. 81). We must deny our reason 'to give our faith scope' (p. 84). The Roman Catholic principle of infallibility, absurd as it is, is much to be preferred to the folly of allowing all men to judge for themselves, and yet expecting them to believe the same things (p. 92 ff.). Religion demands immediate and unquestioning faith, faith in the unseen, not in the seen, in the unproved, not in what has been demonstrated. The only power to bring us to religious faith is the Holy Spirit (p. 56). The miracles of Christ and His apostles were not meant as arguments; they were simply acts of benevolence, and have no evidential value. Only the continued miracle of a living divine witness in our own breasts can be the basis of Christian faith (p. 60). 'My son, trust thou in the Lord with all thine heart, and lean not unto thine own understanding' is the quotation with which the book closes. Like the books of Law and Butler, it represented an abandonment of the rationalistic platform, but it was even more consistent and thoroughgoing than they. It insisted upon the rejection, not only of rational proof, but also of the external evidence of prophecy and miracle, and based everything upon the inner illumination of the Holy Spirit.

Unlike Law and Butler, Dodwell wrote with a sceptical purpose, but his book was calculated to produce a similar

[1] I quote from the second edition of 1743.

effect, either to drive men into complete scepticism, or to lead them to find some other basis for faith than human reason and testimony. In other words, it was calculated in either case to break down the common rational platform of the day.[1]

The sceptical tendency found its clearest and completest expression in three writings by David Hume, his *Essay on Providence and a Future State* (1748), his *Dialogues Concerning Natural Religion* (written in 1751, but not published until after his death in 1779), and his *Natural History of Religion* (1757). All of these were directed, not against Christianity particularly, but against natural religion in general as understood in that day, and were therefore sceptical, not deistic in their purpose.

In the brief essay on *Providence and a Future State*, Hume contends that from given effects we can argue only a cause sufficient to produce them. Having observed that the present world is imperfect, we have no right to assume an infinite creator, and then conclude that being perfect He will yet produce a perfect world. Having observed that in this life rewards and punishments are not distributed in exact accordance with human deserts, we have no right to conclude that there must be a future life in which they will be so distributed. 'That the divinity may possibly be endowed with attributes which we have never seen exerted; may be governed by principles of action, which we cannot discover to be satisfied: all this will freely be allowed. But still this is mere possibility and hypothesis. We never can have reason to infer any attributes, or any principles of action in him, but so far as we know them to have been exerted and satisfied. "Are there any marks

[1] In replies to Dodwell's book by Philip Doddridge (*Three Letters Theological*, 1742) and John Leland (*Remarks on a Late Pamphlet Entitled Christianity not Founded on Argument*, 1744), while the rational proof of Christianity was still given the chief place, emphasis was put also upon the convincing force of the inner spiritual experience of the Christian, thus showing the influence of Dodwell's attack, and foreshadowing a position which later became general under the influence of evangelicalism.

of a distributive justice in the world?" If you answer in the affirmative, I conclude, that, since justice here exerts itself, it is satisfied. If you reply in the negative, I conclude, that you have then no reason to ascribe justice, in our sense of it, to the gods. If you hold a medium between affirmation and negation, by saying, that the justice of the gods, at present, exerts itself in part, but not in its full extent: I answer, that you have no reason to give it any particular extent, but only so far as you see it at present exert itself' [1] (p. 140).

In the *Dialogues on Natural Religion*, the ontological, cosmological, and teleological arguments for God's existence are successively attacked. The universe may be self-existent as well as its cause. We have no right to argue from the analogy of a finite cause to the cause of the universe, and assume a mind back of it, for the universe is a unique effect. Order may belong to matter as well as to mind, and hence order may be natural and self-caused. From a finite world we could argue at best only a finite cause. Assuming that the universe had an author, he may have been a bungler, or a god since dead, or a male and female god, or a multiplicity of gods. He may have been perfectly good or perfectly evil, or a mixture of good and evil, or morally quite indifferent—the last hypothesis being the most probable.

The work is obscure and involved, suggestive rather than systematic as a dialogue is apt to be, but it constituted an exceedingly effective attack upon the common rational arguments for the existence of God.

The third work was historical rather than polemic in form, but it was also destructive of the natural theology of Hume's day. The common deistic notion that natural

---

[1] It is interesting to notice the agreement at this point with the contention of Law and Butler, that we have no right to make *a priori* statements about God and His providence. We can judge only in the light of what he actually does. Throughout his argument it is probable that Hume had Butler particularly in mind.

religion is a perfect thing, existing everywhere alike, is shown to be entirely erroneous. Polytheism is more primitive than monotheism. The latter is a later and artificial development, and has proved worse for the world than polytheism, because of the intolerance always associated with it.

As an account of the development of religion, Hume's work was crude enough, but it was prophetic of a new method of dealing with religious questions, and as against the assumptions of Tindal and other eighteenth-century exponents of natural religion, both deistic and orthodox, it was conclusive.

It is often asserted that in the controversy of the eighteenth century in England the victory was won by the orthodox apologists over both Deists and sceptics. Nothing could be further from the truth. The victory was won, so far as there was any victory at all, over both the orthodox apologists and the Deists by the sceptics, of whom Hume was the greatest. They may not have promoted largely the vogue of scepticism in England, but they drove both apologists and Deists from their traditional position, and broke down the authority and credit of the rational school. That religious faith and devotion still survived and flourished was due, not to the apologists, but to altogether different influences, of which the great evangelical revival was the most important.

II. *In France*

The rationalism which found so clear an expression and underwent so interesting a development in England, voiced itself also in France, and that partly under English influence, though ultimately in still more radical forms. Of the rational supernaturalism of Tillotson, Locke, and others, there was very little in eighteenth-century France, but of deism there was a great deal. The position of

Voltaire is typical, and finds characteristic expression in the following passage from the conclusion of his work on Bolingbroke. 'Every man of sense, every good man, ought to hold the Christian sect in horror. The great name of theist, which is not sufficiently revered, is the only name one ought to take. The only gospel one ought to read is the great book of nature, written by the hand of God and sealed with his seal. The only religion that ought to be professed is the religion of worshipping God and being a good man. It is as impossible that this pure and eternal religion should produce evil, as it is that the Christian fanaticism should not produce it.'[1]

Voltaire did not draw the distinction drawn by Tindal, Chubb, and Morgan between the gospel of Jesus and the traditional Christian system. It was not a purified Christianity that he wished to substitute for the current system. On the contrary, he desired to get rid of Christianity altogether, both the thing and the name. 'The true religion brings peace, Jesus came to bring not peace, but a sword' (*ibid.*). These words sufficiently reveal his attitude toward Jesus Himself. In estimating his position in this matter and that of his countrymen, it must be remembered that Christianity was known in France only in the form of a bigoted, intolerant, and unenlightened Romanism. Of a liberal and more or less rationalistic Protestantism, such as existed in England, there was none at all.

Voltaire's hostility to Christianity did not, however, mean hostility to religion. 'But what!' he says in his *Dictionnaire Philosophique,* 'because we have chased away the Jesuits, is it necessary to chase away God? On the contrary, it is necessary to love Him the more' (art. *Dieu*). And again, 'Faith consists in believing what seems false. To believe in a wise creator, eternal, and

[1] I quote from the edition of Voltaire's *Works* published by Armand Aubrée, Paris, 1829.

supreme, is not faith, it is reason' (art. *Foi*). 'In the opinion that there is a God, there are difficulties; but in the contrary opinion there are absurdities' (*Traité de Métaphysique*, p. 22). Moreover, while in private life it is possible to do without a belief in God, it is not possible in public life. Immorality and anarchy are sure to follow if a nation's religious faith is destroyed. And yet it is better to have no God than a cruel and barbarous one; atheism is to be preferred to intolerance and bigotry (art. *Athée*).

Voltaire was thus a believer in God and in natural religion, but he was at the same time a bitter and uncompromising foe of superstition and illiberalism. He was also an ardent champion of humanitarianism, and he did much, both by word and deed, to awaken the conscience of France to the injustice and cruelty and indifference to others' welfare, which were so marked in the life of the age.[1]

One of the most beautiful expressions of Deism or natural religion to be found in all literature is the profession of faith of the Savoyard vicar, in the *Emile* of Voltaire's contemporary, Rousseau. The spirit of it is very different from that of Voltaire. There is no bitterness or sharp hostility to the existing Christian system, and the simple, inner, emotional, and even mystical character of religion is emphasised, so that we are no longer moving in the sphere of pure rationalism. But in general the construction of natural religion and the arguments urged to support it are the same as in the rational school of the day. 'My son, keep your spirit always in such a state as to desire that there be a God, and you will never doubt it. And then, whichever side you may take, believe that the true duties of religion are independent of the institutions of men; that a just heart is the true

---

[1] Compare *Dictionnaire Philosophique*, art. *Théisme*: 'What is a true theist? It is one who says to God I adore you and I serve you; it is one who says to the Turk, the Chinaman, the Indian, and the Russian I love you.'

temple of divinity ; that in every country and every sect to love God above all else, and one's neighbour as oneself, is the sum of the law ; that there is no religion which dispenses one from the duties of morality ; that there are no essentials but these ; that the worship of the heart is the first of these duties, and that without faith there is no true virtue '[1] (p. 339). 'I converse with Him ; I permeate all my faculties with His divine essence ; I wait upon His benefactions ; I bless Him for His gifts ; but I do not pray to Him. What should I demand of Him ? That He should change the course of events for me ; that He should perform miracles in my favour ? I, who ought above all to love the order established by His wisdom and maintained by His providence, should I desire that this order be disturbed for me ? No, this rash wish would merit punishment rather than praise. Nor do I ask of Him the power of doing right. Why should I ask of Him what He has bestowed upon me ? Has he not given me conscience to love the right, reason to know it, liberty to choose it ? If I do wrong I have no excuse ; I do it because I desire to. To ask him to change my will is to ask of Him what He asks of me ; is to wish that He would do my work, and that I might receive the reward. Not to be satisfied with my state is to wish that I were not a man ; is to wish something else than that which is ; is to wish disorder and evil. Source of justice and of truth ! God merciful and good ! In my confidence in Thee, the supreme wish of my heart is that Thy will be done ' (p. 297). 'Yes, if the life and the death of Socrates were those of a sage, the life and death of Jesus were those of a God. Shall we say that the gospel history was invented at will ? My friend, it is not thus that one invents ; and the deeds of Socrates, which no one doubts, are less well attested than those of Jesus Christ. . . . The gospel contains marks of truth so great,

[1] I have used the edition of the *Œuvres Choisies de Jean Jacques Rousseau*, published by Fleischer, Leipsic, 1817.

so striking, so perfectly inimitable, that the inventor of them would be more extraordinary than the hero. With it all, this same gospel is full of incredible and irrational things, which it is impossible for a man of sense either to conceive or admit. What shall one do in the midst of all these contradictions? Be always modest and circumspect, my child. Respect in silence that which you can neither reject nor comprehend, and humble yourself before the great Being, who alone knows the truth' (p. 331).

The religion of nature defended by Voltaire, and in a very different spirit by Rousseau, seemed to many of their contemporaries only another form of superstition and bigotry, and in the latter part of the century Deism was largely displaced by atheism. D'Holbach's *Système de la Nature* (1770) is the most complete and systematic expression of the general spirit.

III. *In Germany*

In Germany the rationalistic tendency was promoted particularly by the Leibnitz-Wolffian philosophy, which made clearness and reasonableness the sole marks of truth. That is possible which involves no contradiction, and that is actual for which there exists a clear and sufficient reason why it should be so, and not otherwise. Under this influence there developed toward the middle of the eighteenth century a rational supernaturalism similar to that of Locke and others in England, though the philosophy underlying it was very different. There was the same idea that natural religion is good as far as it goes, but needs supplementing by divine revelation, which may impart truths above reason, but not in any way out of accord therewith. In 1738 Shaftesbury's *Characteristics*, and in 1741 Tindal's *Christianity as Old as the Creation*, were put into German, and were followed by translations of many other English books, both radical and conservative. From that time on the influence of English rationalism, and particularly of English Deism was widely felt, and had the effect of promoting more extreme views in the German religious world.

One of the most important representatives of the genuine deistic position was Reimarus, a Hamburg philologist, who published apologies for natural religion against materialism and atheism,[1] and left in manuscript an attack upon Christianity,[2] fragments of which were published by Lessing in 1774 ff. under the title of *Wolfenbüttel Fragments*.[3] These contained a sharp criticism of the notion of revealed religion in general, and of the Old and New Testament in particular. Reimarus agreed with orthodox Christians that Christianity and the Bible stand or fall together. He therefore believed, as they did, that an attack upon the Bible was an attack on Christianity. Lessing, on the other hand, in editing the fragments, maintained, as Tindal, Chubb, and Morgan had done, that the two are to be distinguished. Christianity is older and other than the historic records that recount its origin, and the severest criticism of them does not affect it in the least. Its essence lies, not in book or dogma, but in character. It consists simply in love, and the man who loves his neighbour is the true Christian.[4] Historic Christianity, like all positive religions, is only a stage in the evolution of the highest spiritual religion—in the education of the race which God has been carrying on since the beginning of human life.[5] In the supreme and final religion, the essence of all true religion, which is one with Christianity itself, will exist freed from the temporary limitations and entanglements which have so generally prevented its understanding and hindered its influence.

[1] *Die Vornehmsten Wahrheiten der natürlichen Religion* (1754); *Die Vernunftlehre* (1756).
[2] *Apologie oder Schutzschrift für die Vernünftigen Verehrer Gottes.*
[3] Other fragments of this work were published in the *Zeitschrift für historische Theologie*, 1850-1852.
[4] Cf. *Testament des Johannes* and *Nathan der Weise.*
[5] See his *Erziehung des Menschengeschlechts.*

Like Rousseau, Lessing was much more than a mere rationalist. His conception of revelation as God's continuous education of the race is alone sufficient to prove this. He was prophetic of a new age which found in him one of its greatest forerunners. But this lies beyond the horizon of the present volume. It is only as an exponent of the type of rationalism which distinguished the essence of Christianity from its historic manifestation, and identified the former with ' the religion of all good men '—the true religion of nature—that we are concerned with him here.[1]

The classical expression was given to German rationalism of a non-supernatural type by the philosopher Kant, in his famous work on *Religion within the Bounds of Mere Reason*.[2] Religion is the recognition of one's duties as commands of God. Where we must know a thing to be the will of God before we regard it as our duty, we have revealed religion; where we know it as our duty before we recognise it as the will of God, we have natural religion. A religion made up only of tenets discoverable by human reason is self-vindicating, but if composed only of revealed truths it will disappear, if the tradition of its origin be lost. But even a revelation, if it is to gain any credence, must contain some rational tenets, and hence Kant considers Christianity under the two heads of natural and revealed religion. He finds that it is a perfect natural religion, because it inculcates the law of love to God, which means duty for duty's sake, and love for one's neighbour, which means disinterested service. And its precepts are enforced by the perfect example of Jesus. It needs no other support, neither prophecy nor miracle; it is rational and self-vindicating. As a revealed religion Christianity contains

---

[1] In addition to Lessing's notes on the *Wolfenbüttel Fragments*, see also *Eine Duplik*, *Axiomata*, and *anti-Goeze* which were called out by the controversy over the *Fragments*; also the unfinished *Das Christenthum der Vernunft* and *Entstehung der geoffenbarten Religion*; *Beweis des Geistes und der Kraft*; *Das Testament Johannis*; *Nathan der Weise*; and *Erziehung des Menschengeschlechts*.

[2] *Religion innerhalb der Grenzen der blossen Vernunft*, 1793.

positive precepts, which are legitimate only in so far as they make the duties of natural religion clearer, or enforce them more strongly. As an end in themselves they are wholly evil. The notion that we can do anything to please God, except to live rightly, is superstition. And to suppose that we can distinguish works of grace from works of nature is a delusion. All such supernaturalism lies beyond our ken. There are three common forms of superstition—the belief in miracles, in mysteries, and in means of grace. The genuine rationalism of all this is evident. It is simply a clear and forceful statement of a mild and lofty type of eighteenth-century Deism.

Kant, it is true, was much more than a rationalist. While the book that has been referred to was little else than a summary of positions already familiar, in other and more important writings, he transcended the rationalism of his day and opened a new era in religious as well as in philosophical thought. This side of his work and its influence upon those who came after him cannot be dealt with here. It belongs to a subsequent volume in the series. And the same is true of the many other attempts at religious and theological reconstruction which began in Kant's day, and have constituted an important feature of Protestant thought ever since.

While the rational supernaturalism of Tillotson and others like him was strong during the first half of the eighteenth century in orthodox Anglican circles, and among the clergy of the Establishment, its influence rapidly waned during the latter half of the century, and Deism remained throughout a proscribed and hated thing. In Germany, on the other hand, not only supernatural rationalism, but rationalism of a more or less deistic type, which minimised or even rejected altogether the supernatural, was strong in the pulpits and theological faculties at the end of the eighteenth, and well on into the nineteenth century. It was later in making its appearance within German theological circles, but it lasted longer, and in its extremer form got a much firmer hold upon German than upon English Christianity. In England evangelicalism followed rationalism and crowded it off the field. In Germany rationalism followed pietism, instead of being followed by it, and hence its development went on unchecked for a much longer time. It is no accident that German theology ever since the latter part of the eighteenth century has been much more rationalistic than English, although the rational tendency first found expression on a large scale in England, not in Germany.

IV. *In America*

In eighteenth-century America, Deism found but rare literary expression.[1] Much more important and influential was the rationalism of the early Unitarians, but they belonged for the most part to the nineteenth century, and can therefore be no more than referred to here. They were not primarily interested, as is often supposed, in the person of Christ, or the nature of the Godhead, but in the character of man. It was against the doctrines of total depravity and unconditional election, emphasised with so tremendous power by the New England school of theology, that they revolted. As Channing said: 'We consider the errors which relate to Christ's person as of little or no importance compared with the errors of those who teach that God brings us into life wholly depraved and wholly helpless, that he leaves multitudes without that aid which is indispensably necessary to their repentance, and then plunges them into everlasting burnings and unspeakable torture for not repenting.'[2]

They were thus, like the rationalists in general, in sympathy with the spirit of the modern age, and humanitarianism was a passion with them. They were devout supernaturalists, accepting as loyally as the Socinians

---

[1] For instance in Ethan Allen's *Reason the Only Oracle of Man*, 1784.
[2] In a letter to the Rev. Samuel C. Thacher, written in 1815; quoted in Channing's *Memoir*, vol. i. p. 387.

the inspiration of the Bible; but like the Socinians they had difficulties with the traditional doctrines of the atonement, the deity of Christ, and the Trinity, which were historically based upon the belief in human depravity. Their Christology, to be sure, was commonly Arian rather than Socinian, but in the main they stood very much upon Socinian ground, though their underlying interest in the dignity and worth of man, and their revolt against the traditional notion of human depravity, were even more apparent and more clearly avowed. This was not an accident. They faced one of the extremest forms of Calvinism the world has seen, the theology of the Edwardean school. In it human depravity and bondage were emphasised in the most uncompromising fashion, as was also the correlated doctrine of unconditional predestination. Humility was the one great Christian virtue. To realise one's lost condition, and to submit without protest or question to the decree of God, even though it meant eternal damnation—this was the first step toward salvation. In opposition to this extreme type of Calvinism, it was not unnatural that men of modern sympathies should lay emphasis upon the dignity and worth of man, and should put this conception in the forefront of their system. What was often only tacit in the rationalism of Europe was here given the most explicit utterance. American Unitarianism is thus very instructive to the student of modern religious thought. Its kinship with the rationalism of the eighteenth century in general is apparent, and the spirit which really controlled the whole movement here comes to clearer and more unequivocal expression than anywhere else.

Rationalism appeared, as we have seen, in many forms, sometimes more and sometimes less radical. But it is evident that the principle underlying the whole movement, whether in England, France, Germany, or America, was antagonistic to the traditional Christian system. Where the rationalistic tendency worked itself out in the most thoroughgoing way, the break with the past was most complete. That in many cases considerable parts of the old system were retained meant that the rationalistic principle was applied only in a half-hearted or inconsistent way. That a system founded on the notion of the blindness and helplessness of the natural man should be uncongenial to one who exalted the moral and intellectual power and independence of humanity, goes without saying. Two opposing principles were represented, the one by the traditional system, the other by the rationalism of the modern age. And to what the latter led when it found free and untrammelled expression was seen in Deism, scepticism, and atheism. The eighteenth century was not controllingly atheistic, or even deistic, but there was a strong tendency in that direction, and the more consistently the spirit of the century voiced itself, the more radical was the result. But it was inevitable that radicalism should breed reaction. That reaction came particularly in English evangelicalism, which has already been considered. At the close of the century the religious crisis was acute. Either a mediæval man and a Christian, or a modern man and a sceptic—this seemed the sole alternative as viewed by many of the clearest-headed thinkers of the day.[1] It is true that the great mass of rationalists were less consistent and clear-sighted, that they thought they could be modern, and yet retain, not all, but a considerable part of the traditional system. And it is true that multitudes of evangelicals combined with their evangelicalism features of systems radically opposed to it.

[1] It may not be out of place to remark here that one sees in this connection, with uncommon clearness, the vicious consequence of universalising an individual experience. Because one man feels his need of divine grace, therefore all men must need it; or because one man feels sufficient unto himself, therefore all men are. The history of theology is full of this kind of thing, and many of the most serious controversies and misunderstandings have resulted from it.

But these inconsistent positions should not blind us to the significance of the two opposing tendencies, and to the seriousness of the issue. Mediævalism or irreligion, this was the alternative offered by consistent Evangelicals, and accepted by consistent rationalists. It is the alternative still offered and accepted by many of both schools. But in the meantime, it has ceased to be the only alternative, for toward the close of the eighteenth century new influences began to be felt which have completely changed the religious situation. New conceptions of religion have emerged and have resulted in forms of Christianity congenial to the temper and discoveries of the modern age, so that it has become possible for a man to be fully in sympathy with the modern spirit and yet remain a Christian.

When Kant, the great innovator, began his epoch-making labours in philosophy and religion, pietism and rationalism were the two great forces disputing the field throughout the larger part of the Protestant world. In England, in Germany, and in America, the situation was much the same, though here the one, there the other, preponderated. The future was with neither of them. Rationalism, equally with pietism, failed to meet the developing religious needs of the modern world. Both contributed elements of permanent value, but both were proving more and more inadequate and unsatisfying to religious men of modern sympathies. That the effort should be made to transcend them was inevitable. The efforts were many. By Kant himself, by Herder, Jacobi, Hegel, Schleiermacher, Coleridge, and many others, reconstructions of one kind and another were attempted under various and often conflicting influences. All these attempts lie beyond the horizon of the present volume. If the situation at the time they began has been made clear, at least one of the aims of the volume has been realised.

BIBLIOGRAPHY

For the entire history of Protestant thought: J. A. Dorner, *Geschichte der protestantischen Theologie* (1867); Frank, *Geschichte der protestantischen Theologie* (1875); A. Dorner, *Grundriss der Dogmengeschichte* (1899); Fisher, *History of Christian Doctrine* (1896); Allen, *Continuity of Christian Thought* (1884); Troeltsch, *Protestantisches Christenthum und Kirche* (in the *Kultur der Gegenwart*, i. 4, 1906).

CHAPTER I

Harnack, *Lehrbuch der Dogmengeschichte*, vol. iii. (3rd ed. 1909, English translation, vols. v. *sq.*); Loofs, *Leitfaden zum Studium der Dogmengeschichte* (4th ed. 1906); Seeberg, *Lehrbuch der Dogmengeschichte*, vol. ii. (1898, English translation); Schwane, *Dogmengeschichte der mittleren Zeit* (1882); Ritschl, *Rechtfertigung und Versöhnung*, vol. i. (4th ed. 1903, English translation, 1872); K. Müller, *Kirchengeschichte*, vol. ii. (1897 *sq.*); Eicken, *Geschichte und System der mittelalterlichen Weltanschauung* (1887); Janssen, *Geschichte des deutschen Volkes seit dem Ausgang des Mittelalters*, vol. i. (1883); Michael, *Geschichte des deutschen Volkes seit dem 13ten Jahrhundert bis zum Ausgang des Mittelalters* (1897-1906); Berger, *Die Kulturaufgaben der Reformation* (1895). An excellent summary of conditions on the eve of the Reformation, with copious references to the sources and literature, is given by Lindsay, *History of the Reformation*, vol. i. book I. (1906).

CHAPTER II

The principal editions of Luther's works are the *Walch*, 1740 *sq.* in twenty-four volumes (wholly in German); the *Erlangen*, 1826 *sq.*, containing the German works in sixty-seven volumes, and the Latin in thirty-eight; and the *Weimar*, the new critical edition, in process of publication, 1883 *sq.* The best editions of his letters are by De Wette, 1825 *sq.*, in six volumes, and by Enders (supplement to the Erlangen edition) 1884 *sq.*, in process of publication. A number of Luther's works have been translated into English. Since 1903 a general translation has been in process of publication under the editorship of J. N. Lanker. The references to Luther's works in chapter ii. are to the Erlangen edition of the German works, unless otherwise stated.

On Luther's thought: *The Histories of Doctrine*, by A. Harnack, Loofs, and Seeberg; Ritschl, *Rechtfertigung und Versöhnung*, vol. i.; Tschackert, *Die Entstehung der lutherischen- und der reformirten Kirchenlehre* (1910); Koestlin, *Luthers Theologie in ihrer geschichtlichen Entwickelung und ihrem inneren Zusammenhange* (2nd ed. 1883, English translation, 1897); Theodosius Harnack, *Luthers Theologie mit besonderer Beziehung auf seine Versöhnungs- und Erlösungslehre* (1862 *sq.*); Hermann, *Der Verkehr des Christen mit Gott* (3rd ed. 1896, English translation, 1895); Thieme, *Die Sittliche Triebkraft des Glaubens; eine Untersuchung zur Luther's Theologie* (1895); Denifle, *Luther und Lutherthum in der ersten Entwickelung* (1904 *sq.*); Weiss, *Lutherpsychologie als Schlüssel zur Lutherlegende* (*Ergänzungsband zu Denifles Luther*, 1906).

CHAPTER III

Zwingli's works have been edited by Schuler and Schulthess, 1828 *sq.* in eight volumes. The references in chapter iii. are to this edition. A new edition in the *Corpus Reformatorum*, vol. 88 *sq.* is in process of publication (1905 *sq.*). An English translation of a few of his tracts is given in Jackson's *Selected Works of Huldreich Zwingli* (1901).

On his thought: Loofs, *Dogmengeschichte*; Seeberg, *Dogmengeschichte*; Tschackert, *Die Entstehung der lutherischen- und der reformirten Kirchenlehre*; Schweizer, *Die protestantischen Central-*

dogmen in ihrer Entwickelung innerhalb der reformirten Kirche, vol. i. (1854); Zeller, *Das theologische System Zwinglis* (1853); Siegwart, *Ulrich Zwingli: der Charakter seiner Theologie* (1855); A. Baur, *Zwinglis Theologie, ihr Werden und ihr System* (1885 *sq.*); Stähelin, *Huldreich Zwingli, sein Leben und Werken nach den Quellen dargestellt* (1895 *sq.*); Jackson, *Huldreich Zwingli* (Heroes of the Reformation Series, 1901).

CHAPTER IV

Melanchthon's works are published iu the *Corpus Reformatorum*, vols. i.-xxviii. (1834 *sq.*).

On his thought: Loofs, *Dogmengeschichte*; Seeberg, *Dogmengeschichte*; Galle, *Versuch einer Charakteristik Melanchthons als Theologen* (1840); Herrlinger, *Die Theologie Melanchthons in ihrer geschichtlichen Entwickelung* (1879); Hartfelder, *Philipp Melanchthon als Praeceptor Germaniae* (1889); Troeltsch, *Vernunft und Offenbarung bei Johann Gerhard und Melanchthon* (1891); Richard, *Philip Melanchthon* (Heroes of the Reformation Series, 1898).

CHAPTER V

Calvin's works are published in the *Corpus Reformatorum*, vols. xxix.-lxxxvii. (1863 *sq.*). A considerable part in English translation by the Calvin Translation Society in fifty-two volumes (1843 *sq.*). Letters in Herminyard, *Correspondance des Réformateurs dans les pays de langue française* (1878 *sq.*).

On Calvin's thought: Loofs, *Dogmengeschichte*; Seeberg, *Dogmengeschichte*; Ritschl, *Rechtfertigung und Versöhnung*, vol. i.; Tschackert, *Entstehung der lutherischen- und der reformirten Kirchenlehre*; Schweizer, *Die protestantischen Centraldogmen*; Kampschulte, *Johannes Calvin, seine Kirche und sein Staat in Genf* (1869 *sq.*); Doumergue, *Jean Calvin, les hommes et les choses de son temps* (1899 *sq.*); Lobstein, *Die Ethik Calvins* (1877); Scheibe, *Calvins Praedestinationslehre* (1897); Fairbairn, 'Calvin and the Reformed Church' (*Cambridge Modern History*, vol. ii., 1904); Walker, *John Calvin* (Heroes of the Reformation Series, 1906).

CHAPTER VI

I

Ritschl, *Geschichte des Pietismus*, vol. i. (1880) ; Keller, *Geschichte der Wiedertäufer* (1880) ; *Die Reformation und die ältern Reformparteien* (1885) ; Heath, *Anabaptism from its Rise at Zwickau to its Fall at Münster* (1895) ; Newman, *History of Anti-Pedobaptism* (1897) ; Belfort Bax, *Rise and Fall of the Anabaptists* (1903); Vedder, *Balthazar Hübmaier* (Heroes of the Reformation Series, 1905) ; Lindsay, *History of the Reformation*, vol. ii. book v. chap. ii. (1907), for bibliography of the numerous and widely scattered sources.

II

Bibliotheca Fratrum Polonorum (1656 *sq.*) ; Trechsel, *Die protestantischen Antitrinitarier vor Faustus Socinus* (1839 *sq.*) ; Fock, *Der Socinianismus nach seiner Stellung in der Gesammtentwickelung des christlichen Geistes*, etc. (1847) ; Ritschl, *Rechtfertigung und Versöhnung*, vol. i. ; Harnack, *Dogmengeschichte*, vol. iii. (English translation, vol. vii.).

CHAPTER VII

Writings of English Divines, published by the Parker Society: Dixon, *History of the Church of England from the Abolition of the Roman Jurisdiction* (1878 *sq.*) ; Gairdner, *The English Church in the Sixteenth Century* (1904) ; Frere, *The English Church in the Reigns of Elizabeth and James* (1904); Pollard, *Thomas Cranmer* (Heroes of the Reformation Series, 1904) ; Hardwick, *A History of the Articles of Religion* (3rd ed., 1876) ; Tomlinson, *The Prayer Book, Articles and Homilies* (1897) ; Makower, *Constitutional History of the Church of England* (1895) ; Neal, *History of the Puritans* (1754) ; Barclay, *Inner Life of the Religious Societies of the Commonwealth* (1876).

CHAPTER VIII

Tholuck, *Vorgeschichte des Rationalismus* (1853); Schweizer, *Die protestantischen Centraldogmen*; Gass, *Geschichte der protestantischen Dogmatik* (1854); Krauth, *The Conservative Reformation and its Theology* (1872); Schaff, *Creeds of Christendom*, vol i. (1877); O. Ritschl, *Dogmengeschichte des Protestantismus* (vol. i. 1908); Tschackert, *Entstehung der lutherischen- und der reformirten Kirchenlehre*.

CHAPTER IX

Tholuck, *Das kirchliche Leben des 17ten Jahrhunderts* (1861 *sq.*); *Geschichte des Rationalismus*, part i. (1865); H. Schmid, *Geschichte des Pietismus* (1863); Ritschl, *Geschichte des Pietismus* (1880 *sq.*); Sachsse, *Ursprung und Wesen des Pietismus* (1884); Hübener, *Der Pietismus geschichtlich und dogmatisch beleuchtet* (1901); Grünberg, *Philipp Jakob Spener* (1893 *sq.*).

II

G. Smith, *History of Wesleyan Methodism* (1757 *sq.*); Stevens, *History of the Religious Movement of the Eighteenth Century, called Methodism* (1858 *sq.*); Abbey and Overton, *The English Church in the Eighteenth Century* (1878); Lecky, *History of England in the Eighteenth Century*, vol. ii. (1888); Tyerman, *Life and Times of the Reverend John Wesley* (1870 *sq.*); *The Oxford Methodists* (1873); Julia Wedgworth, *John Wesley and the Evangelical Reaction of the Eighteenth Century* (1870); Rigg, *The Churchmanship of John Wesley, etc.* (1879); *The Living Wesley* (1891); *A New History of Methodism*, edited by Townsend, Workman, and Eayrs (1909).

III

Allen, *Jonathan Edwards* (1889); Foster, *A Genetic History of the New England Theology* (1907); Riley, *History of American Philosophy, The Early Schools* (1907); Wendell, *A Literary History of America* (1900).

CHAPTER X

Noack, *Freidenker in der Religion* (1853 sq.); Draper, *History of the Intellectual Development of Europe* (1864); Lecky, *History of the Rise and Influence of the Spirit of Rationalism in Europe* (1865); Pfleiderer, *Geschichte der Religionsphilosophie* (1893); Pünjer, *Geschichte der christlichen Religionsphilosophie* (1880-83, English Translation, 1887); K. Fischer's and Höffding's *Histories of Modern Philosophy*; Hettner, *Litteraturgeschichte des 18ten Jahrhunderts* (1874 sq.); Robertson, *A Short History of Free Thought, Ancient and Modern* (second edition greatly enlarged, 1906).

I

Tulloch, *Rational Theology in England in the Seventeenth Century* (1872); Hunt, *Religious Thought in England in the Seventeenth Century* (1870); Leland, *A View of the Principal Deistical Writers that have appeared in England in the Last and Present Century* (1754 sq.); Lechler, *Geschichte des englischen Deismus* (1841); Mark Pattison, *Tendencies of Religious Thought in England, 1688-1750* (in *Essays and Reviews*, 1860); A. S. Farrar, *Critical History of Free Thought* (1862); Leslie Stephen, *History of English Thought in the Eighteenth Century* (1876); Carrau, *La Philosophie Religieuse en Angleterre* (1888); Benn, *The History of English Rationalism in the Nineteenth Century*, vol i. (1906).

II

Bartholmée, *Histoire des doctrines religieuses modernes* (1855); Damiron, *Mémoires pour servir à l'histoire de la philosophie au 18ème siècle* (1857 sq.); Lanfrey, *L'Eglise et les Philosophes au 18ème Siècle* (1857); Faguet, *Le 18ème Siècle* (1890); Picavet, *Les Idéologues* (1891); Texte, *Rousseau et les Origines du cosmopolitisme littéraire* (1895); Morley, *Voltaire* (1886); *Rousseau* (1878.)

III

Saintes, *Histoire critique du rationalisme en Allemagne* (1841);
B. Bauer, *Geschichte der Politik, Kultur und Aufklärung des* 18*ten Jahrhunderts* (1843 *sq.*); Hagenbach, *German Rationalism* (1865);
J. Schmidt, *Geschichte des geistigen Lebens in Deutschland,* 1687 bis 1781 (1862 *sq.*); Kohn, *Aufklärungsperiode* (1873); Kahnis, *Der innere Gang des deutschen Protestantismus* (1874); Oncken, *Zeitalter Friedrichs des Grossen* (1881).

IV

Ellis, *A Half Century of the Unitarian Controversy* (1858); Allen, *Our Liberal Movement in Theology* (1892); *A History of the Unitarians* (American Church History Series, 1894); Cooke, *Unitarianism in America* (1902); Foster, *Genetic History of the New England Theology* (1907).

INDEX

Arminianism vs. Calvinism, 176, 178, 179

Bible, authority of, 8, 12-13;
vs. word of God, 56-57;
Luther on, 55, 59-60;
Zwingli on, 62-3, 65, 80;
Melanchthon on, 80;
Calvin on, 88-89, 90, 94, 95;
Anabaptists on, 101, 106;
Socinians on, 116-117;
Puritans on, 126;
Anglicans on, 126-128;
Scholastics on, 146-147;
Reformed, 149;
English Evangelists on, 172-173;
Arminianism on, 173-174;
Rationalists, 216ff

Christian Liberty:
Luther's idea of, 30, 31, 78;
Zwingli's, 66, 67;
see Predestination
Christian life:
Calvin on, 89, 90;
Anabaptists on, 101-102, 103, 105;
Socinians on, 114-115
Christology:
Luther on, 49-50, 51;
Zwingli on, 87-88;
Calvin on, 87-88, 92;
Socinians on, 111-112;
Scholastics on, 148-149;
Reformed, 149;
in English Evangelism, 165-166, 169, 170, 171;
of the New England school, 252
Christianity, Rationalist interpretations of:
Whiston on, 216;
Sherlocke's defense of, 219;
Paley on, 221-222;
Tindal on, 225-226;
Chubb on, 226-227;
Morgan on, 228;
Reimarus on, 248;
Lessing on, 248-249;
Kant on, 249
Church:
Wycliff on, 17-19;
Luther's concept of, 42-43;
Calvin on, 93-94, 95;
Anabaptists on, 101-102, 103-104;
Socinian view of, 112;
Browne's theory of, 130, 132-133, 134, 135, 136, 138, 139-140
Church and State, relation of:
Calvin on, 96-97;
Zwingli on, 96;
Luther on, 59, 96;
Anabaptists on, 104-105;
Browne on, 130, 131, 137, 138

Controversies:
In Protestant Scholasticism, 143;
Deistic, Butler on, 234

Deists, 211-216, 224-225, 228-229, 239-231
divine grace:
medieval doctrine of, 2, 3;
means of, 7;
Luther's concept of, 27-28;
word of God as a means of, 40;
Zwingli's view of, 66;
Calvin on, 92-93
Doctrine of the Person of Christ, *see* Christology

INDEX

Edwardeanism compared with English Evangelism, 177-178

Formula Consensus, 153
Formula of Concord, 144, 145, 147, 148

humanism, 10-11, 119
  Erasmus as humanist, 11-12;
  Zwingli under influence of, 61, 62, 63, 65;
  Melanchthon as humanist, 71, 72, 75;
  Socinianism, influence on, 107, 109, 112

immediate imputation, 152

Lollardy, 119

Miracles:
  Tillotson on, 197-198, 199;
  Locke on, 205;
  Tindal on, 214-215, 224;
  Woolston on, 218-219;
  Hume on, 219-222;
  Jenyns on, 222-223;
  Law on, 232;
  Butler on, 237, 238

Original Sin, doctrine of:
  rejected by Socinians, 110;
  in English Evangelism, 164-165;
  see Predestination

Predestination:
  Zwingli on, 68-69, 82, 83;
  Calvin on, 82, 85-86, 87, 88;
  Luther on, 82;
  Bucer on, 83, 86
  Anabaptist view, 105;
  Socinian view, 109, 110;
  Melanchthon vs. Luther on, 143;
  Reformed doctrine on, 149

religion and Christianity:
  Voltaire on, 244-245;
religion, nature of:
  Butler on, 233-239;
  Dodwell on, 239-241;
  Hume on, 241-243
  Voltaire on, 244;
  Rousseau on, 245-247
religion, natural:
  Reimarus on, 248;
  Kant on, 249;
  and revealed religion, 207
revelation:
  Evangelicals on, 165;
  Tillotson on, 196-197;
  Locke on, 201, 202-205, 206-207;
  Toland on, 202;
  Clarke on, 207-209;
  Law on, 231-233;
  Butler on, 233-234;
  Reimarus on, 248;
  Lessing on, 249;
  Kant on, 249-250

Sacraments:
  Zwingli on, 66-67;
  Congregationalists on infant baptism, 135;
  Browne on infant baptism, 136;
  Bucer on Eucharistic doctrine, 82-83
Salvation, doctrine of:

Paul's, 25, 52;
Luther's, 25-26, 27, 28, 29, 30ff, 52, 55, 104;
Catholic, 26-27;
humanistic, 63;
Zwingli's, 63;

Calvin's, 85;
Anabaptists on, 105;
Spener on, 159-160;
in English Evangelism, 165, 166-167